About the author

Former teacher, social worker and lecturer, Jeremy Seabrook has worked as a writer and journalist for 25 years, both in the UK and India. He has written plays and features for the theatre, tv and radio. He has also written widely on development issues, especially migration and urbanisation in the South. The most recent of his 28 books include *The Myth of the Market* (Green Books), *Travels in the Skin Trade* (Pluto Press), *Notes from Another India* (Pluto Press), *Victims of Development* (Verso), *In the Cities of the South* (Verso), and a novel, *Colonies of the Heart* (GMP). In 1999, he published *Love in a Different Climate* (Verso), which is a study of men who have sex with men in South Asia, and the implications of this for the spread of the HIV virus. Jeremy Seabrook has worked closely with a number of non-governmental organisations in South Asia, including the Consumers' Association of Penang, Arban and Proshika in Bangladesh. He currently contributes to *New Internationalist*, *Race and Class*, *The Ecologist*, and he writes regularly for Third World Network in Malaysia.

Selected South Asia Titles from Zed Books

Itty Abraham
The Making of the Indian Atomic Bomb:
Science, Secrecy and the Postcolonial
State

Siddharth Dube
In the Land of Poverty:
Memoirs of an Indian Family,
1947–1997

Gustavo Esteva and Madhu Suri Prakash
Grassroots Post-Modernism:
Remaking the Soil of Cultures

Betsy Hartmann and James K. Boyce
A Quiet Violence:
View from a Bangladesh Village

Bertus Haverkort and Wim Hiemstra
Food for Thought:
Ancient Visions and New Experiments
of Rural People

John Hutnyk
The Rumour of Calcutta:
Tourism, Charity and the Poverty of
Representation

Christophe Jaffrelot (ed.)
Pakistan: Nationalism Without a Nation

Rounaq Jahan
Bangladesh: Promise and Performance

Smitu Kothari and Zia Mian (eds)
Out of the Nuclear Shadow

Joanna Liddle and Rama Joshi
Daughters of Independence:
Gender, Class and Caste in India

Ashis Nandy
The Secret Politics of Our Desires:
Innocence, Culpability and Indian
Popular Cinema

Govindan Parayil
Kerala:
The Development Experience

Kalima Rose
Where Women are Leaders:
The SEWA Movement in India

Vandana Shiva
Staying Alive:
Women, Ecology and Development

Sarah C. White
Arguing with the Crocodile:
Gender and Class in Bangladesh

For full details of these books and Zed's other titles, as well as our subject catalogues,
please write to:
The Marketing Department, Zed Books, 7 Cynthia Street, London N1 9JF, UK
or email Sales@zedbooks.demon.co.uk
Visit our website at: **http://www.zedbooks.demon.co.uk**

Jeremy Seabrook

Freedom Unfinished

Fundamentalism and Popular Resistance in Bangladesh Today

Zed Books
LONDON & NEW YORK

IN ASSOCIATION WITH

Proshika
DHAKA

Freedom Unfinished was first published in 2001 by
Zed Books Ltd, 7 Cynthia Street, London N1 9JF, UK and
Room 400, 175 Fifth Avenue, New York, NY 10010, USA

in association with Proshika, 1/1–GA Section 2, Mirpur 2,
Dhaka 1216, Bangladesh.

Distributed in the USA exclusively by Palgrave, a division of
St Martin's Press, LLC,175 Fifth Avenue, New York, NY 10010, USA.

Cover design by Andrew Corbett
Designed and set in 10.6/13 pt Sabon and Lydian display
by Long House, Cumbria, UK
Printed and bound in the United Kingdom
by Biddles Ltd, Guildford and King's Lynn

A catalogue record for this book
is available from the British Library

ISBN   Hb 1 85649 907 3
        Pb 1 85649 908 1

Library of Congress Cataloging-in-Publication Data
has been applied for

� Contents

Acknowledgements

I should like to acknowledge the help of many people in making this book. I am deeply indebted to all those I met on my travels through Bangladesh, the activists, members of Proshika and all those encountered casually, all of whom contributed to the creation of this portrait of contemporary Bangladesh. In particular I am grateful to Mahabub and his family in Moghbazar, Dhaka, Mr Khaled Hossein and his colleagues, the White House Hotel in Dhaka, to Ridoy and his family, to Kushi and Kamal Uddin and the staff at the Association for the Realisation of Basic Needs (ARBAN), to Iqbal and his family, and all the others who showed such warmth and hospitality.

I acknowledge the support of Md Idris of the Consumers' Association of Penang and P. Rajamoorthy of Third World Resurgence, where extracts of this book have appeared; of Peter Wilby and Cristina Odone at the *New Statesman* in London and the editors of *The Ecologist*; these magazines have also published articles based on some of the material here.

I am especially grateful to Dr Faruque Ahmed, for our discussions at Koitta. As the guiding spirit of Proshika, his contribution, both to the organisation and to the continuing liberation struggle in Bangladesh, has been unique. His analysis and insights form a considerable portion of the book, and his voice is heard throughout. I am indebted to Mr Syed Shamsul Haq for his friendship, support and guidance in Bangladesh, and especially to Mr Abdur Rob, without whose patience and friendship this book would not have been possible. Above all, I am thankful for the wisdom and courage of all those women and men in

Bangladesh committed to the defence of Bangali humanism and social justice against the forces of dominance and intolerance, whatever form they take in present-day Bangladesh. To them I offer this work in homage to the struggle for a liberation that is never wholly won and can never be taken for granted.

Jeremy Seabrook
Dhaka/London

❧ Glossary

almirah	cupboard
aman	rain-fed
Ameer	spiritual leader
amjam	variety of tree
ashato	fig tree
Ashina	month in the Bangali calendar
Ashraf	Muslim
Atraf	non-Muslim
badami	insect pest
balam	type of rice
banami	false
Bangla math	local alcohol made from fermented rice
benaroshee	fine silk
bhadralok	gentlefolk
bhavbad	fatalism
bhoot	spirit
bidi	local cigarette
bigha	a measure of area: 33 decimals; c. 1,350 square metres (c. ⅓ acre)
bodh	banyan tree
boisha	bamboo
bonerfol	jungle-flower
boro	dry season
burkha	all-enveloping garment worn by Muslim women
bustee	slum compound
chakri	'service'
Chamcha	servant
nastik	atheist
channa	peanuts
chappals	sandals
charka	spinning-wheel
charpai	string bed
chetai	woven bamboo
chor	spit of land
choto lok	working class
chulla	stove
dalal	traitor

dao	axe
decimal	a measure of area; c. 41 square metres (1/100 acre)
dekhi	rural foot-operated rice-mill
deshi	local, country
dhormo	religion
dothara	musical instrument made of wood and leather
ekthara	musical instrument
fatwa	authoritative ruling on a religious matter
Galam	type of rice
gamari	variety of tree
gamcha	a male garment
ganguli	ballad singers
garam pani	liquor made from fermented rice
ghasporim	insect pest
gobar	cow-dung
godown	warehouse
golpata	reed
gopi	milkmaid
gur	molasses
haddi	type of clothing
hari	open-air theatre
hartal	general strike
hat	weekly market
hilsha	national fish of Bangladesh
hujur	a spiritual
Insh'allah	God willing
jakat	charity
jari	open-air theatre
jatra	open-air theatre
jhum	slash-and-burn agriculture
jihad	holy war
jotdar	small landowner
kachuri panna	water-hyacinth
kafila	gum-tree
karai	type of tree
karam	a board game, often played on the sidewalk
karbani	sacrifice
kejur	date-palm
khadi	homespun cloth
khas	government-owned land
Koborok	variety of rice
kotla	freshwater fish
kurta	a garment
lakh	100,000 (written 1,00,000)
laru	mixture of coconut and gur
lathi	stick
lunghi	male garment
madrasa	Koranic school
majra	insect pest

mandir	Hindu temple
mastaan	strong-arm man
maulavadi	Muslim fundamentalist
maulvi	religious leader
maund	a measure of weight: about 40 kg
mela	festival
mistri	mechanic
montor	mantra
mowghanda	scent of the mango-tree flower
Muktibahini	liberation army
Muktijudda	the War of Liberation
namaz	prayers
neem	a tree with pesticidal properties
noshto	spoiled
paisak	green-leaf vegetable
pangash	freshwater fish
pantha	leftover rice diluted with water
paratha	flat bread
pardah, purdah	literally, 'curtain': seclusion of women
parishad	local government
paw khela	water game
pinon	type of clothing
poka	insect pest
poori	puffed rice
poothi	open-air theatre
pot	traditional type of song
puja	Hindu worship
rajanivanda	type of flower
rangan	shrub
Rauwolfia	type of herb
roti	flat bread
rui	freshwater fish
ryot	peasant
salwar kamiz	trouser suit
samiti	group
shamiana	tent
shapla	water-lily
sonar Bangla	golden Bengal
svadeshi	self-reliant
tabla	musical instrument, pair of hand-drums
talak	triple-hand-clap method of divorce
tetral	red edible paste
thana	district
til	sesame seed
tokai	waste
topee	Muslim headwear
udarshin	nonchalance

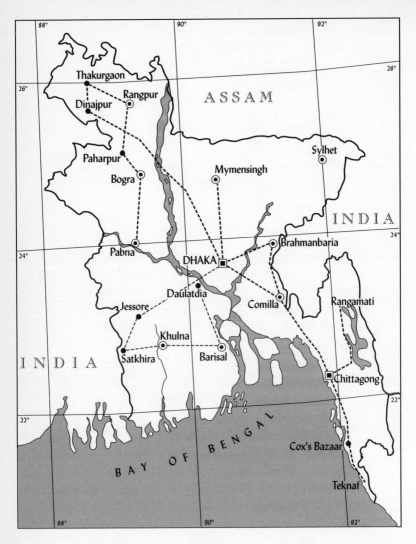

Bangladesh: journeys described in this book

1 Arrival

My guide in Bangladesh

This book describes a journey through Bangladesh between 1999 and 2000; a journey through the seasons and landscapes, through the social and moral sensibility, through the cultural and political struggles of the country.

My guide has been Proshika, one of the most significant non-governmental organisations in Bangladesh. Proshika grew directly out of the liberation war which created Bangladesh in 1971. Many of Proshika's founders and early recruits had themselves fought against Pakistan for an independent country. The new state was born in blood and hope: the massacre of Bengalis by the retreating Pakistanis was one of the great genocides of the century. The freedom fighters thought they were ridding East Bengal of alien occupiers for the second time in a generation. The new country was exhausted, its infrastructure ruined, drained by centuries of extractive occupation.

In this context, the expectations aroused by freedom were doomed to rapid disappointment. It was not simply that floods and famine soon overwhelmed the country, but within four years, Sheikh Mujib ur Rahman, together with most of his family, had been murdered. The country was soon in the hands of military dictatorship, which encouraged by stealth the return of what are euphemistically called 'the anti-liberation forces'. This means those sympathetic to Pakistan, who had fought against the independence movement, and who now are making such inroads into the country in the form of a fundamentalist Islamic revival.

religious stereotype

Proshika grew out of the disillusionment of the mid-1970s. It has maintained a vigorous, committed stand in favour of secularism and socialism, which were struck from the Constitution during the years of military rule. Its stand against fundamentalism, against social injustice, against elites, and in favour of minorities – Hindu, Christian and indigenous peoples – and especially in favour of the participation of women in the economy and society, brings it into sometimes violent conflict with other social forces, both within and outside Bangladesh.

How Bangladesh is perceived

At the travel agency where I booked a flight to Dhaka, I was careful to specify not Dakar in Senegal (a frequent misunderstanding). The woman wrote 'Dachau' and kept referring to Dachau in her conversation with the airlines. Tactfully, I said 'Not Dachau, Dhaka'. I reminded her that Dachau was the site of a Nazi concentration camp in Bavaria during the Second World War. What I didn't say was that Dhaka may be a labour camp, but it has not yet witnessed the level of atrocities seen in Dachau.

Perhaps she had been influenced by images of Bangladesh which reach the West. No wonder people associate the country with every imaginable disaster, when human actions seem to mimic the epic cruelties of nature. What can mere people do that is worse than the perpetual erosion of land, cyclones that destroy whole regions, floods which every year engulf about one-fifth of the land-mass, and which, in a really bad year like 1998, covered almost two-thirds of the country? How can social injustice be more damaging than the destruction wrought by tidal waves and storms, which catch up whole villages in their turbulent path and scatter them like matchwood?

Extremes of poverty, political corruption and violence, dependence upon international aid, child labour – infants breaking bricks, children exposed to the hazards of glass-making or chemicals in plastic and rubber factories, maidservants of 9 or 10 locked in the houses of their employers – above all, the issue of population, that sinister distortion of the country's greatest resource and only real hope – its people. Such impressions are rarely balanced by any sense of the courage and endurance of the poor, their inventiveness and creativity. The question to ask is not why the country is so poor, but rather by what

2

miracles of ingenuity and effort 120 million people survive on a mere 57,000 square miles.

The ravages of nature, political violence, corruption – all conceal the fact that Bangladesh is still in the grip of a continuing and indeed undeclared civil war, the unfinished business of its creation in 1971. Bangladesh was lost to Pakistan then; a loss which Pakistan and a powerful minority in Bangladesh never accepted. What was lost to Pakistan may still be regained for Islam, but not the traditional fluid and tolerant Islam of Bengal. ⮡ Post 1971 stereotype

Religion against fundamentalism

The present struggle is complicated by the fact that Bangladesh is now more than 90 per cent Muslim. At the time of Partition, in 1947, there was a significant exodus of Hindus, which was repeated after 1971. The fault-line within Bangladesh now strikes at the heart of the identity of the people, for it sets Bangali culture, language and tradition against the growth of Islamic fundamentalism. Not against Islam; for centuries, this division presented no problem, indeed, was not experienced as division at all. At issue is the global resurgence of a form of Islam not rooted in the soil of Bengal. ⮡ religious Islam stereotype

Bengali culture – pluralist, humanist, rooted, with its songs, dance, folklore, drama and literature – confronts the austere discipline of Islam, often within the same people. The confusion this creates is immobilising, and helps to explain the stagnation of Bangladesh, the slow pace of development, the survival of feudal values, the persistence of poverty. What some observers identify as fatalism and inertia are no such thing; they are symptoms of the uneasy stalemate that has produced a caricature of democracy and locked the country into its apparent beggar-role in the drama of globalisation.

the back to the cultural aspect

In this dispute, Proshika is far from neutral. It is committed both to the rich cultural heritage of Bengal and to the principles on which liberation was won, embodied in its first Constitution – secularism, socialism, nationalism and democracy. Proshika works for the economic and political emancipation of the poor, the equality and liberation of women, human rights and democratic participation; and against fundamentalism, exclusivism, communalism, privilege and the defence of feudalism.

The crucial difference is between religion and fundamentalism.

3

Secularism is not a denial of the intense spirituality of Bengal, but means respect for all the faiths of a pluralist Bengal – Islam, Hinduism, Buddhism, Christianity and animism. It is these values which direct and inspire the 'human development' at the heart of the work of Proshika. It is an intensely political project, but it belongs to no party.

The political strike

When I reached Dhaka, the city was paralysed by a *hartal* – a total stoppage of the country – called by the opposition Bangladesh National Party (BNP). The only vehicles on the streets were the cycle-rickshaws, which provide the poorest with a livelihood. In the absence of traffic, the rattle of wheels and ringing of bells made a curiously pre-industrial sound. Groups of youths, some little more than children, roamed the city, surrounding any car, bus or baby-taxi breaking the strike. Sometimes they turned out the occupants and set it on fire. The shops were shuttered. Those selling food and medicine were permitted to open, but many traded only between half-closed grilles. The metal workshops, with the hammering of metal, the boys welding among fountains of blue and yellow sparks, were silent.

The *hartal* was devised as a protest against the British colonial authorities. Curiously, it has become a 'democratic right' of the opposition in free Bangladesh. The BNP has called strikes on 60 or more occasions since the Awami League government was elected in 1996. While the BNP was in power, from 1991 to 1996, following the return to democracy after sixteen years of military rule, activists of the Awami League closed down the country 140 times.

With every shutdown, the garments industry, which now earns about three-quarters of the country's foreign exchange, loses millions of dollars. The livelihood of the poor ceases, and, since most depend on daily wages, on those days they do not eat. It seems perverse and incomprehensible.

The two main parties deny each other's right to rule. The distant reason for this may be found in the bitter but inconclusive struggles between religion and culture, or, to describe it in another way, between Bangladeshi identity (Muslim, nationalistic) and Bangali identity (secular and not excluding the Hindus of Bangladesh and West Bengal). India, from which Bangladesh was amputated at the time of Partition, remains, a brooding, dominating presence which shadows

religious stereotype

4

and (almost literally) encircles Bangladesh. The role of India in supplying support and refuge to Bangladeshi freedom fighters in 1971 was an irksome reminder of its power, and of its loathing of the Pakistani entity that it never fully accepted.

Bengal has been for so long occupied, dispossessed by invaders, ruled from elsewhere, that ancient habits of resistance to those in power persist. This may be a factor in the ruling parties' resentment and intolerance of one another.

The roots of Bangladesh

Soon after the Partition of India, the people of East Bengal, which had opted to become East Pakistan, realised they had exchanged one colonial regime for another. This presentiment was soon confirmed, when Pakistan tried to impose Urdu as the national language. There was powerful resistance from Bengali-speakers, and when five students were shot dead in Dhaka University by the police in February 1952 – an event that has become known as Ekushey February – the first martyrs were created. This was an early sign of the fragility of Pakistan.

The liberation war and the creation of Bangladesh in 1971 appeared to resolve the issue. Sheikh Mujibur Rahman was undisputed leader, and his Awami League came to power with overwhelming popular support. The dreams of the liberation of Bangladesh from its status as East Pakistan were soon destroyed by the miserable reality of destitution and impoverishment which it inherited after the *Muktijudda,* the war of independence. It says much of the psyche of Bengal that people truly expected to enter into the patrimony of *sonar Bangla* – the Golden Bengal of its poetry and literature, a mythic place of freedom and plenty – as soon as foreign domination was ended. Such was their faith, it seems the Bangladeshis believed in the power of imagination to transform their shattered, beautiful land.

Not only was the country in ruins, but it was immediately beset by the worst floods in memory; these were followed by famine. Bangladesh, unrecognised by the Western powers, was compelled to seek support from the Soviet bloc. In 1974, Sheikh Mujib, against his inclinations, declared a one-party state.

When Sheikh Mujib was murdered in a coup in 1975, the exhausted country did not respond with a display of anger. People did not take to the streets. A faction of the ruling party appeared to have seized power, but it was soon clear that the army was in control. Later in 1975 Zia ur-Rahman took over, an ambitious army officer who had been in the freedom movement, and who had actually announced over the radio the independence of Bangladesh on behalf of Sheikh Mujib in 1971. He created the Bangladeshi National Party, and deleted secularism and socialism (but not nationalism or democracy) from the Constitution.

The continuing impasse

It was during the period of disillusionment and despair that Proshika was born. The relief and rehabilitation after the war brought a good deal of foreign help to the country, and many idealistic young Bangladeshis were drawn to make a contribution to their stricken land; this impulse was given a further push by the dawning realisation that the values for which they thought the war had been fought were in danger of being lost. Army rule soon turned out to have little to do with freedom or poverty abatement, and the vanquished anti-liberation forces swiftly reappeared in public life.

Zia was assassinated in 1981, and a subsequent coup in 1982 brought General Ershad to power. Military rule remained until 1991. That year saw the election of Khaleda Zia, widow of Zia ur-Rahman and inheritor of his Bangladesh National Party. She, in turn, was defeated in 1996 by Sheikh Hasina, daughter of Sheikh Mujib and leader of the Awami League.

Personal emnity between the two women has helped to freeze the politics of Bangladesh. To say that they embody the opposing values of the low-intensity conflict that sets Bengali against Islamic culture would be to accord them too exalted a status. Their dynastic struggle makes of them symbols as much of what their opponents loathe as of what they positively represent. In any case, governments of both BNP and Awami League have been defined by corruption, rapacity, maladministration and neglect of the poor. As in many countries in the South, politics has become detached from ideology (one of the further consequences of the death of the Soviet Union), and taken the form of an increasingly bitter quarrel between factions of the elite over the spoils of power. This has both criminalised politics and politicised crime.

Both Khaleda Zia and Sheikh Hasina claim the right to rule, and deny each other's legitimacy, but their actual ideological positions are only a shadow-play of the forces they claim to represent. Neither opposes the free market, globalisation or the integration of Bangladesh into the world economy.

Whatever alliances are made between the mainstream parties, they have one thing in common. Those who aspire to power – like those who wield it – have no more intention of divesting themselves of privilege for the sake of their faith than they have for the sake of the poor. They are not going to forfeit the advantages associated with the lifestyle of ruling castes the world over. Their overriding objective is to retain control of the resources that permit them to travel to Calcutta for medical treatment if they have some slight indisposition, to the Gulf or Singapore for more serious conditions, and to Europe or the USA for major surgery. They are not contemplating renunciation of their bank accounts abroad, nor of the education of their children in Australia or the USA.

On the other side, the defenders of the Bengali tradition want to see religion subordinated to an inclusive Bengali identity. They invoke great literary figures – national poet Nazrul Islam, Rabindranath Tagore – social reformers such as Begum Rokeya, pioneers of women's education such as Sufia Kemal, as well as fighters in two liberation struggles, against the British and against the Pakistanis. They are threatened from many sides, by fundamentalism, by Western economic dominance with its business culture and pop culture, and by the power politics of India and the impact of Hindi movies upon the young.

Meanwhile the march of globalisation has caught up the life of Bangladesh in a choiceless world, about which its pople were never consulted and over which they have no control. During the past 15 years, 1.5 million people, more than three-quarters of them young women, have entered the garments industry. At eight o'clock in the morning, and again at ten o'clock at night, Dhaka, this male-dominated metropolis, becomes, briefly, a city of women, its dusty streets a procession of young women, their scarlet and gold, violet and lime-green sarees or *salwar kamiz* (trouser suits) dazzling in the morning sunlight, wilting with fatigue beneath the muted street-lamps at night. The women have come from all over the country, and it is by their excessive hours of labour that whole families survive on the few hundred taka they send home each month.

About US$1.5 billion comes each year in remittances from Bangla-

7

deshi workers abroad. It comes at a high cost, from labourers in the dying rubber plantations of Malaysia, from abused servants in the marble palaces of Jeddah and Kuwait, from the workers in the sweatshops of London's East End threatened by racism, from petrol-pump attendants in the USA, and from construction workers on sites all over South-East Asia.

Freedom unfinished

Outside forces are reshaping the lives of the people: money from the Gulf, zealotry from Pakistan and Afghanistan, economic prescriptions from the International Monetary Fund and World Bank, smuggled goods from India, which undermine local manufacture – cloth, sugar, fertiliser, even plastic goods and household vessels, and the ubiquitous Phensidyl, a cough syrup to the morphine content of which tens of thousands of young Bangladeshis are addicted.

The growth of fundamentalism is no longer checked by a Left which promised secularism and social justice, but which disintegrated with the death of socialism. In default of this, the struggle has been taken up by an alliance of Bengali cultural movements, human rights groups, people's social and cultural movements and those NGOs committed to the emancipation of the poor and the empowerment of women, Proshika prominent among them.

Almost three-quarters of the people remain in the countryside, where they live a life apart, in another, older Bangladesh. A poverty which looked no further than self-reliance has preserved Bengali rural culture. Poverty has also sheltered the people from the assault of Western consumerism and entertainment culture. Poverty has insulated them against the values of Bollywood and Hindi dominance. Poverty has also locked them in the prisons of archaic feudal beliefs, illiteracy, dependence upon moneylenders and merciless local elites.

This is now changing fast. People are taking sides as the struggle for the sensibility of Bengal becomes more open, a struggle which is itself part of a wider global conflict, which cuts across all countries and all continents. It is the war between rich and poor, that other civil war in which no one can remain neutral, since it affects all humanity.

Continuing resistance

When the military took over less than five years after Independence, overt political activity was impossible. But the concept of the non-governmental organisation was just emerging in Bangladesh, as a result of the rehabilitation efforts after the war. This presented an opportunity for radicals to reconnect with the silent and watchful poor, who form the great majority of the people of Bangladesh. It was from the coming together of a group of former freedom fighters and some young idealists from the Canadian University Service Organisation (CUSO) that the idea of Proshika arose.

'Development' at that time appeared to be a desirable and ideologically uncontentious objective. It was not politicised. It seemed to pose no threat to the existing order. Just how potentially radical it was became plain only later, as the forces that had been opposed to the liberation of Bangladesh made their presence more and more strongly felt.

This book is about the values formulated by Proshika and its allies; how they carried forward – surreptitiously at first, more openly later – the ideas of secularism and social justice, which were dropped by the ruling power in the years of repression. The purpose of the book is to set out, as clearly as possible, the lineaments of this struggle which has continued for thirty years, and which now confronts the people with what is perhaps its hardest choice of all, the destiny of a humanistic Bengali tradition – secular, open, celebratory – as it faces the threat of a sterner, narrower Bangladeshi nationalism, underpinned by the disciplines of a redefined, fundamentalist Islam.

The choice is *not* between Bengali culture and Islamic culture: the demands of religion have always co-existed with the Bengali sensibility, although the asperities of fundamentalism cannot. That this drama should be unfolding in a wider context of globalisation and in the shadow of an India increasingly under the sway of Hindu fundamentalism only adds further dimensions of uncertainty and confusion to the still unresolved struggle.

The roots of Proshika

DR FARUQUE:

In 1973, I had sat the Civil Service exam, and had to wait a year for the results. While waiting I found work with a non-government organisation called Canadian University Service Overseas, which was giving technical assistance to the government after liberation, providing appropriate technology.

My first project was to improve the traditional potter's wheel. They rotated the wheel by hand, which gave no scope for intricate design. I had an idea for a potter's wheel similar to the Western model, highly advanced but operated by foot not by electricity. The traditional furnace could reach a temperature of only 500 degrees, too low for permanent glazing that would stick to the object. There was a danger of lead poisoning – the glazing came off when hot food was placed on it. I wanted to raise the temperature of the furnace.

I took up the challenge in a potters' village at Savar, just outside Dhaka. I created a wheel operated by foot, and improved the traditional furnace so it did not dissipate heat. They could then make more complicated, ornamental objects. Potters still sell their wares outside the National Martyrs' Monument, using that technology.

Soon after came the floods and famine of 1974. I volunteered to work for Oxfam. I was sent to a remote area called Romari, near Rangpur. I had no idea how remote. Relief had been sent, but it was such a difficult place, they could not find anyone to organise fair distribution. The journey was dramatic. I got directions from Rangpur town. 'You take the train to Chilmari, and from there go to Romari.' I didn't ask how. I took the train at ten at night. The train was completely without lights. I reached Chilmari at two or three in the morning.

It was December. Very cold. I saw nothing. No station, nothing. The flickering light of a tea-shop. I asked, 'Can I rest in your shop?' The owner said, 'There.' About 20 bodies were sleeping. 'There is no space.' He said, 'Lie down and you'll find space.' Around five-thirty I woke up and asked, 'Can I get a rickshaw to Romari?' 'What are you talking about? You have to cross two rivers. They are not very deep now.' There was no road. He said, 'If you start walking now, you may reach by evening.'

It was about thirty kilometres. The rivers were knee-deep; I could wade through. I reached the Dak bungalow by five-thirty in the evening. The official said, 'Welcome, are you Japanese?' I thought he was joking. 'What do you mean?' A group of Japanese photographers had come by helicopter to take pictures of the scenes of distress. The area had so little connection with Bangladesh, he thought anyone from outside must be from Japan. He gave me food and a bed and I slept.

The bungalow was near the market. Every morning I saw eight or ten bodies dead in the market. They had come to ask for food and stayed and died there. But there was food in the market for those who could buy. It was well stocked. This was a terrible revelation: the famine was man-made. I knew little about how the rural power structure operated. There were two big landowners in the area, one supporting the Muslim League, the other the Awami League. They had a lot of land, their godowns were full. As soon as these people heard I had come, they invited me to meals. They wanted the food given by Oxfam to be distributed as wages to the poor who worked on their land. Then I understood. They had monopolised the food sent as relief. I didn't say no, because I wanted time to think of a strategy. I said I didn't have the authority, but I would write to Oxfam to get their agreement.

I made an alliance with some young people who were against the rural power-brokers. We organised people to go and demand food. We confronted them with hundreds of hungry people. They had allowed people to starve while their godowns were full. This made me realise that organisation was the most important thing to fight the structure of privilege, its power of life or death over people.

The famine was the beginning of what was to become Proshika. It taught me a fundamental lesson. Only by organising, understanding and overcoming these power relationships would the poor be able to change their lives. This is an animating principle of Proshika.

2 ❀ South

The journey south
The first of two cyclones that devastated Orissa in India late in 1999
sent its storms over Southern Bangladesh. The week I spent in Barisal
was a time of incessant rain. The earth liquefied, ponds overflowed,
lakes and pools drowned the land. The pale purple spindles of water
hyacinths were coming into flower. These plants were brought here
from the Mediterranean on a whim by Lady Hamilton. Within a
decade they had colonised Bengal, choking the waterways, killing
fish.

The journey out of Dhaka passed through choking fogs of dusty
pollution over the almost stationary traffic. A degraded, semi-
industrialised countryside marks the gravitational pull of the capital,
which is itself like the intensifying core of a cyclone, sucking resources
to its centre, uprooting villages, excavating paddy-fields.

The road towards the crossing at Aricha is a thread of small settlements, no longer villages, not quite towns. In their markets, plastic
goods have displaced older bamboo artefacts, just as tin has replaced
the houses' *chetai* (bamboo) and *golpatta* (reed) roofs, an urbanising
limbo which parallels the industrialising of agriculture. The tin is
new; corrugated roofs gleam in the sunlight. Tin is not cheaper than
clay or bamboo, but it lasts longer, and is secure against rain and
wind (not against cyclones, however, which scatter tin and turn it into
a dangerous projectile). Metal is no ornament to the countryside, but
it is seen as a symbol of industrial progress.

The Aricha ferry-crossing is besieged by a chaotic jumble of traffic from every epoch – pedestrians and pushers of ancient carts, bicycles, rickshaws, motor-cycles, trucks, buses and white Japanese limousines: the remote past lives close to the edge of tomorrow. The journey across the Padma takes fifty minutes. On the ferry, trucks loaded with jute, vegetables, bricks, cement, paddy; old snub-nosed Bedfords with highly painted bodywork; buses scraped by hundreds of near misses, dented and decrepit, vastly overloaded, with a pyramid of people and goods on the roof, a tableau of migratory restlessness; new buses, Hino or Mitsubishi, with tinted, curtained windows, bunches of plastic flowers and Koranic inscriptions above the cab; Pajeros and Toyotas, the white cars of the middle class; then the cyclists, the foot-passengers of migrant labourers returning from Dhaka, having sold their vegetables, paddy, dates, papaya or other home-grown produce.

The ferry is called Enayetpuri, after a 19th-century Muslim saint. Syed Shamsul Haq, the Bengali writer, is travelling with us. He says the Muslim saints no longer have a real function. In the past, they served as helpers of the poor, settling disputes, while some had medical or other social skills. 'They had a profound social utility, not only in such rituals as circumcision and marriage, but their knowledge of herbal medicines, and their wisdom led people to consult them on issues of land ownership or neighbours' quarrels.' Today, many have turned to politics, where their influence is less benign. Fundamentalism, according to Syed, is an attempt to reclaim a purpose they have lost.

The ferry is a huge rusting structure, with a powerful engine from 'West Germany'. A man of about 50 leans against the rail. Unsmiling, bitter, he was a freedom fighter in 1971. After the war, he was rewarded with a job as a driver with the Special Branch. After the assassination of Sheikh Mujib, he was dismissed, since the military replaced all government personnel. He is a truck driver, taking bricks to Dhaka. He says many freedom fighters were disabled; they still lack land and live in want. 'Sheikh Hasina should have rewarded those who remained loyal to her father. The government should help us.' He spits in contempt.

The evening is wide over the river; an orange spillage from a gash in the sky bleeds into the water; rafts of uprooted water-hyacinths rush past in the swift current; the thick silty water is the colour of strong coffee. The last vehicle on the ferry is an ambulance; two red ribbons tied to the headlights indicate that it is carrying a dead body. In the back, women keep the air moving with bamboo fans, leaning on the large wooden box which is taking the deceased back to the village for burial. The ambulance has priority and is first to leave the ferry.

We disembarked in the twilight at Daulatdia on the other side of the Padma in a disorder of vehicles. The area is crowded with small eating-houses: wooden benches and tables on platforms above the sandy margin of the river, bamboo stilts gouging the earth, gaps in the wooden floor showing the turbid marsh below. Hundreds of trucks and buses were parked, the drivers resting, sleeping, eating or making use of the sex workers who live in the brothel-town at Daulatdia. In the dying light, the metal glowed a fiery red in the township dedicated to sexual servicing of male travellers in this disturbed, migratory land.

The political strike

We passed through Faridpur, where, for ten days, a strike of truck-owners had disrupted all traffic to and from Barisal.

Trucks were stalled on both sides of the road, and lines of buses parked, leaving a narrow channel through which only cycle-rickshaws could pass. The dispute was between vehicle owners – one group from the Bangladesh National Party, the other from the Awami League. The political deadlock that had paralysed Dhaka was also being played out here. The stoppage, of course, was not being conducted on the ground by the owners, much less by their political protectors. Groups of young men, no older than 16 or 17, armed with bamboo staves stopped vehicles trying to pass through the blockade. Cars that failed to slow down were violently beaten with sticks. The youths' anger was frightening; faces tense, eyes blazing with rage: mercenaries of political parties, fury displaced from their own frustration and disappointment with their arduous – and often fruitless – education, into contrived wars manipulated by gang-lords and business mafia. These live symbiotically with the politicians, the hieratic figures of Hasina and Khaleda at their head. Their struggles have little to do with democracy, but are a form of modernised feudalism; a contemporary version of war-lords fighting over this poor, beautiful, violated land.

The watery south

Barisal is the site of one of the ancient kingdoms of Bengal. It was known as the Venice of Bengal because of its system of canals and waterways. Its beauty is nothing like that of Venice, with its paddy and its varieties of banana, its palms, mahogany and raintrees, its majestic *korai* and mangoes. Barisal was also the granary of Bengal, produced fragrant *balam* rice, and supplied the region with coconut. It yielded rich harvests of fish, but many have been killed by pesticides. In World-Bank-backed flood protection projects, water stagnated behind dams. Chemical run-off in the water wiped out many strains of fish.

The Green Revolution, promoted by Ayub Khan in the 1960s, also ruined the production of *balam* rice. As costs of producing high-yielding varieties rose, many people gave up their land. Increasing yields lowered the price farmers received in the market, and they became poorer. Many went into debt, mortgaged and lost their land. Here, the landless find work in Barisal town as rickshaw-drivers and labourers.

This southern part of the country remained hard to reach because of its water-expanses, sinuous rivers and flooding ponds. It is full of *chors,* spits of land which emerge from the water when floods subside. Because of its inaccessibility, Barisal retains dense forest cover.

Barisal also produced Sher-e-Bangla (Lion of Bengal), Fazlul Haq, who founded the peasant Krishak Proja Party. Although he came from an educated Muslim zamindar family, he fought for peasants and sharecroppers against moneylenders and zamindars (for a discussion of the *zamindari* system, see pages 98–9). He wanted to abolish the system and to give land rights to the peasants. After the 1935 India Act, his party became the largest in the Bengal Assembly, defeating even the Muslim League. He won on a platform calling for cancellation of all debts from moneylenders, and cuts in perks and salaries of government servants, issues that still have resonance today. He did not have a majority, but was invited by the Governor of Bengal to form a minority administration. He couldn't make a coalition with Congress, because, like the Muslim League, its most influential members were zamindars and moneylenders. His government fell apart, and as the Muslim League grew, Fazlul Haq's group lost ground. In 1940, he moved the Muslim League Lahore Resolution.

This earned him the name Sher-e-Bangla. His last triumph came in 1954, when he became Chief Minister of East Pakistan. He continued to inspire new generations of progressive people in Barisal till the 1960s.

Land is crucial in Bangladesh. Eighty per cent of farmholdings are less than 2.5 acres, and almost two-thirds of the people are landless – twice the number at Independence. Although agriculture employs 63 per cent of the people, it accounts for only 30 per cent of GDP.

A *provincial town*

We stayed in Barisal town, an overblown country town of four or five hundred thousand people. It is a melancholy place, a first refuge for migrants from the countryside. The rickshaw – a delicate object, with its folding canopy, silver metalwork and painted panels – is a symbol of great violence: each one represents lost land, a dowry, a debt, river erosion, inputs that became too expensive, falsified deeds, cheating by the rich. The rickshaw is a symbol of measureless pain and loss. The bodies of the drivers shine with sweat, the ribcage is so close to the skin you can almost see the beating – and perhaps broken – heart.

Perhaps the gloom came from incessant rain, olive-coloured puddles, the constant drip of water, as though the whole town were melting; elegant zamindars' villas from the Raj mildewed by monsoons, the ragged brickwork of ruinous Pakistani houses, new concrete already leprous with dark fungus. Everything is tepid and damp: lichen makes the gravestones of even the recently dead disappear into distant memory. Bead curtains of rain fall in front of shops, where orange-and-white boxes of drugs made in Karachi or Mumbai by Roche or Ciba-Geigy are stored behind dusty glass, walls covered with clocks showing contradictory times, wedding jewellery nestling in crimson velvet. The street vendors sit beneath crumpled black umbrellas – round piles of apples from India, oranges from Australia washed by rain – while shoe-menders work over broken heels and plastic straps, their hair and faces silvered with water. Men hold their *lunghis* between thumb and forefinger, graceful as mannequins, trying to avoid the mud. A few boys, hair sleek with water, stand in front of the grille of a cinema-hall, staring at lurid paintings of violet-coloured villains and plump pink heroines. In a shop, which is also an improvised cafe, young boys are drinking

Lipton's tea against a backdrop of Coca Cola, Pringles, Cadbury's, Lux and Lifebuoy – the highest luxury the town affords.

Barisal exudes the languor and yearning of small towns the world over. Its daughters have left for the garment sweatshops of Dhaka, its sons for university, its workers for Saudi Arabia, its women to serve in luxurious homes in Abu Dhabi or Riyadh. The greatest energy is at the bus stand and river terminal, where comings and goings create constant excitement – boats carrying jute, paddy or bamboo, passengers for Khulna, the landless leaving for an elsewhere which may provide a livelihood the homeplace no longer can.

It speaks of a spare insufficiency; once a place of wealth, now a makeshift city, a service town with no industry and not much service either. It is a refugee camp for those evicted from agriculture, lives shaped by the seasons of transplanting and harvesting now learning the more brutal seasons of money. Barisal, a jumble of iron, cement, stone, rust and mildew, a place marked by too many departures, where no one comes, unless to take something away, something more from the injured people, to rob them of more energy, land or labour.

Yet the activities of survival animate the town with a furious energy. The resourcefulness of people amid the ruin of their resources is a powerful paradox. Hope and stoicism, a resolute cheerfulness and endurance create a sensibility quite foreign to the troubled inertia of the people of the rich world: there, everything seems to have been settled; here, in spite of conspicuous suffering, the last word has not been spoken. There, the verb 'to struggle' has been struck from the vocabulary of daily life; here, it informs every aspect of living.

The political is cultural

The struggle against fundamentalism does not always appear overtly political. Invoking religion, fundamentalists make of it a pseudo-spiritual and moral crusade. This creates obstacles for those who resist the political implications of what appears as a religious movement. But since fundamentalists object to Bengali culture, a main arena of resistance is cultural. Proshika works with organisations all over the country celebrating Bengali music, literature, drama and song. Proshika has also set up its own cultural groups, and supports musical, dramatic and literary movements which share its commitment.

We visited the Area Development Centre at Baburganj, outside

Barisal town. Mr Azahar belongs to the cultural group, which performs traditional songs and stories and dramas about daily life. 'We make plays about our affections and sorrows, about oppression and hope. We use theatre to help people understand why they are poor. Culture celebrates being Bengali, but it is also an instrument of change.'

Azahar has four children between 8 and 15. He has no land but his homestead, and cultivates four bighas as a sharecropper. The land-owner takes 50 per cent of the crop, and pays for all seeds and fertiliser. If there is a natural disaster, Azahar may get nothing. The landlord lives outside: he is a 'service-holder', with a government job. Sharecropping gives four months' food security. The rest of the year, food is bought in the market. Azahar, whose father was in the British Army, became a sharecropper when his land was eroded by the river.

With his share of a collective loan from Proshika, Azahar leased land to grow paddy. This provides another 5 or 6 month's food security. The best measure for judging poverty in rural Bangladesh is the number of months of sufficiency and scarcity. This describes more accurately than money the degree and intensity of poverty. The primary group has received training and technical help as well as social education. 'This has been one of the most important experiences in my life. As well as a skilled cultivator, I am now a leader in my village. I was elected to the school, mosque and bazaar committees. The bazaar committee is important, because it keeps the peace between traders, makes sure the poor have access and the market is not monopolised by the rich.'

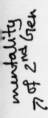

Azahar says he is 'first Bangali, then Muslim'. This version of identity is significant in Bangladesh. Giving priority to Bengali identity suggests commitment to a pluralist, non-communalist society. Those who say they are Muslim first give comfort to fundamentalism. Many primary groups – in which Hindu, Christian, Buddhist or animist minorities are represented – have come to appreciate the tolerance of Bangali inclusiveness. Azahar says, 'My forefathers were Bangalis. I took birth as a Bangali, then I became a Muslim. My language was Bangali, the folk-songs and dramas of my village were Bangali.

'The moneylenders, the rich, the religious tried to talk us out of organising. They said Proshika would cheat us, seize our land, make us Christians. But we know who has been cheating us for generations.

There are two kinds of solidarity – against social oppression and against natural calamities. The latter you cannot change. Last year's floods destroyed our fish-ponds. But unnatural calamities, human-made ones, give the poor greater grief.'

The cultural group were to perform. It was prayer-time. They did not want to provoke those who were praying. 'Of course', they said, 'they would not show us the same consideration. They are never silent, even for the sick and dying, since they serve Allah, not humanity.'

There is a harmonium player, a drummer, a *dothara* player. Some are young students; others farmers, mature women and men. The fundamentalists detest women and men singing and performing together. 'They hate our culture. They would like to silence it. Funda-mentalism is not religion – it is politics dressed up as religion.'

Even the poorest people find time to sing, to rejoice in the tradi-tional festivals and celebrations of their country. This would be inconceivable in the West. How would poor people in Britain celebrate their identity? Expressing hatred of asylum seekers, a loathing of Europe, support for the football team?

The first song commemorates the freedom-fighters, the blood-sacrifice of the people: 'even the instruments we play will remember you'. Then a traditional love-song; a man, far from his village, calls to the birds, the river, the animals, to take the message to his loved one: 'I am consumed by my love and my body is ashes'. A second song celebrates Bengal: 'This is a heaven on earth, which can produce fruits, paddy, trees, 120 million people in a land of plenty'. Azahar sings about Barisal, pride in its canals, rivers and fertile land – nowhere can compare with its sparkling waters, its fruit, its number-less kinds of banana, mango and papaya. Then a poem by Nazrul Islam, which, although written in the early 20th century, has a strong contemporary resonance: it laments the farmers' loss of land. Once Bengal was rich, the farmers happy, they had time to smile, but people came from afar to rule them, and they became poor. The motherland has been washed by our tears for hundreds of years, and now we have to fight for her. Then a song written by the group against dowry, divorce, confinement of women in the house. The last song is a traditional tune, with contemporary words by Abul Hossein, the complaint of the rickshaw-puller who is refused payment for his services.

All over Bangladesh, I met many such groups. The passionate feeling of the young women and men often brought me close to tears. At first I thought this was sentimentality, but as time went by it became something else. Here, an existential desolation is always close to the surface. Hunger, sickness, pain are public realities, have not been overlaid by the denial that comes with affluence. People live on the edge of survival. But they are rarely sad or depressed; they sing, celebrate and smile.

Azahar says the collaborators have made common cause with the fundamentalists. 'They feel they are now winning. The anti-liberation forces are united. We must give the people our vision, the dream we could not yet fulfil, the full development of women and poor people.'

The crowded countryside

The countryside of Bangladesh is crowded; not like towns, but full of purposeful activity. No one is not employed on some useful and necessary task. Pedal-vans are piled high with sweet local bananas, vegetables (gourds, red or green spinach), leaves for fodder, paddy, long bamboo poles. Everything moves towards the town and its market. Young boys and girls, in ragged trousers or dresses drained of colour, twig in hand, tend cows and goats. Young girls are bowed beneath the weight of head-loads of fodder. An adolescent is supervising labourers taking out the retted jute from a shallow canal beside the road: the silvery fibre is detached from the cane and tied in bundles for drying; the jute-sticks are then gathered into wigwams of golden spindles glinting in the sun. Some men stand in water, cutting the *kachuri panna* (water-hyacinths), for green manure, their spare bodies reflected in the water, above which the heads of the *shapla* (water-lilies) raise their spiky crimson crowns. A lean fawn cow, a blue-black crow on its spine, crops grass, while a girl of about eight watches it, jealous perhaps of its daily work of eating, while her own body is thin with hunger. An old woman carries a child, while her daughter holds a bundle of firewood in her arms as though it were a sacramental offering. Men carry logs on the back of a bicycle; cart-pullers run, their long vehicles loaded with bamboo, jointed like long olive-coloured bones; a sheaf of dark mango-leaves moves like a living creature, concealing the child whose slim arms clasp it above her; a child parts her mother's long sleek hair, searching for lice, which she cracks with her tiny fingernails; a man walks beside a cart in which a sick cow lies, covered with a jute sack, his anxiety evident, since this creature probably represents his sole wealth; women thread knobs of dung onto sharp sticks and lean them against the wall of a hut to dry for fuel; a cart of earthenware pots, another of aluminium vessels, another of red plastic bowls; a basket of fish from a pond, a harvest of vermilion chillis. A woman spreads unhusked paddy on the road for vehicles to winnow with their wheels; another repairs a fence to stop goats straying onto a vegetable patch; women weed the paddy, as coloured birds wheel above their shiny braided hair; the rasp of a sickle against thick fodder-grass; paddy ready for cutting, its red-gold grains drooping like a string of pearly ornaments. Bamboo sculptures over the river release fish-nets into the water; a boy spins jute into rope, using a tree to create friction to bind the fibre; children carry bamboo fishtraps which they leave for the fish simply to swim into captivity. Tribal people in conical bamboo hats are minding black-grey hogs scavenging by the roadside. No one is idle. A lean old man leads a leaner cow; a child stands beneath a tree, catching the fruits his brother shakes from the upper branches; a wandering musician with a single-stringed *ekthara* makes his way to another village.

Sometimes people still complain of the lack of a 'work-ethic' in Bangladesh. Clearly, they have never seen the relentless labour of the rural poor. Here, work needs no ethic, for work is life.

Sky, water and land create a vast open landscape; water invades earth and land emerges out of the floodwaters. Above it, towering, fleeting clouds create celestial cities that melt in the wind and pour their liquid substance into the ponds, which overflow and claim more land.

The village in the woods
The village of Charbaria is 20 kilometres from Barisal. The roads muddy, the landscape sings with the rain, a melting music of water falling on water, on stone, on leaves, on metal; the deliquescent cadences of the aftermath of a tropical cyclone. We followed a cause-way of slippery grey mud, where the motorcycle skidded and snarled impotently. It fell, and we had to jump clear, leaving it to spin and writhe on the ground, a wounded machine.

The village stands under a canopy of dripping trees. A small schoolroom of bamboo: the frame has begun to sprout indoors, so

21

that at the four corners of the room, leaves form capitals to bamboo pillars, a living architecture. This is a Proshika school for children who have had no previous schooling. Most aged 8 to 11, they sit on bamboo mats, a pile of schoolbooks before them. Their faith in what they are learning is absolute. The promise of education means the difference between certain poverty and possible improvement. The day is the same for every child: up at six a.m., work for their parents on the land, feeding cattle or goats, weeding; then school; then more work, looking after younger children; work in the fields; sleep at ten p.m. The children, being under Proshika's tutelage, know about Sheikh Mujib, when he was killed. They know the names of Nazrul Islam, Rabindranath, Rokeya Begum. Grave recitals of the life and death of Bangabandhu. But *how* do they know it? In what way? Does it mean more to them than the government schools' rote-learning of English nursery-rhymes and mathematical tables? It is hard to say.

I went with some children to their families' clearings beneath the trees, houses mainly of wood, an emanation of the forest. They were built by craftspeople – wooden balustrades, a carved pineapple, ornamental leaves and flowers, a solid wooden door. On raised platforms, the floors are of beaten earth, swept with sharp brooms that have left long parallel grooves. On the verandah covered with a metal roof, a cooking fire, utensils and brushes. Hens and ducks forage around the broad leaves of plantain, leaving arrow-mark footprints in the mud; flowering grasses with silky rose-white blooms, a red hibiscus, give a mud-trodden beauty to the area.

Shilpi is 10. Hosniyara, her mother, came from a nearby village after marriage. Hosniyara has five daughters and one son. Farzana, 12, and Sharmin, 7, are at home. Hosniyara's husband is a maker of mosaic floors. He is a supervisor, earning 5,000 taka a month. To feed seven people adequately costs 150 taka a day. Hosniyara's son, 14, is working with his father. The homestead occupies four decimals of land; the paddy-field of 20 decimals has been mortgaged. Hosniyara's husband was sick with heart disease, and during a month in hospital all income ceased. They received 6,000 taka for the land. She prays that her children will remain healthy, because they have nothing left to sell. Hosniyara's daughter was married at 15, and has gone to her husband's house 'far away'. Hosniyara has four ducks and four hens which provide eggs. She grows vegetables around the house. Firewood is bought in the market – 60 taka for 40 kg (one maund), which lasts 10–12 days. Electricity costs 400 taka a month.

Hosniyara says the rich oppress the poor, because they control loans and get their labour cheaply. She hopes her girls 'will get married to someone good from a good family, who will be handsome and well-off'. She sighs, saying that she has many problems, but cannot speak of them. One of these was sitting in the room within, preparing vegetables, listening to our conversation. Hosniyara's husband has taken a second wife, with whom she has no wish to quarrel. With five children at home, she does not want to be divorced, for their sake, as well as for her own. She says nothing, and pulls the orange scarf over her lined handsome face to hide a tear in the corner of her eye. Hosniyara's position is fragile. If she does not accept her husband's right to bring another woman into the home, she risks losing her children. By law, the permission of the first wife must be sought before a man introduces another into his home; but what woman would refuse permission when the alternative is so bleak?

There is a half-built bridge at Charbaria: concrete platforms from the riverbank reach half-way across the water; the ghost of a road rises to the phantom crossing; wild flowers grow in the crumbling structure. The bridge was planned by the BNP government, construction began under the Awami League and was abandoned. Did the funds run out? Where they misappropriated? 'Never mind', they say cheerfully, 'another election is coming. Maybe the funds will be found then.'

Organising the people
We visited the nearby village of Rarimahal, to meet the Proshika *thana* (area) committee. This first primary group was set up in 1980. At that time people were deeply in debt, their lands mortgaged, their labour exploited by landlords. Many discovered that they had sold rather than merely mortgaged the land. They could not even read the documents that robbed them. Their first act of resistance was to organise, the next to learn to read. This gave them confidence to attack other social evils, especially the dowry system. People were losing their land by borrowing for dowry 'demands' which were beyond their means. 'How can a day labourer afford to give dowry?' They have not succeeded in abolishing the system, but the amount

23

now expected has declined. They no longer incur a lifetime's debt for the marriage of a daughter.

This area was badly affected by the floods of 1998. 'Many people lost much of their property, crops and animals', says Morjina. 'Even now, we have still not recovered. Most have little land – 20 decimals on average. Some work as rickshaw-pullers, others as day labourers, construction-workers, seasonal traders, brick-makers and brick-breakers.' Here, the women judge it requires 100 taka a day to feed a family with three children. One of the benefits of Barisal is that its waterways provide plenty of fish – even among the dense growth of water-hyacinths, they can catch carp, *rui* or *pangash*, freshwater fish.

All children of members of the *thana* committee go to school, an advantage which most of those gathered in one member's small house never had. They remain poor: markets are still controlled by the local elite. Rice is 18 taka (33 US cents) a kilo, potatoes 12 taka, aubergines 14, onions 30, oil 40 a litre. They can afford bananas at 2 taka each. Meat is eaten only at festivals. Although many have taken loans over the years, the greatest benefit of solidarity has been not economic but social – learning to overcome customs and traditions which damage the humanity of the poor. 'Women were kept indoors. Men and women were not allowed to sit together as we are sitting now. Some fundamentalists object, but they cannot force women back into the houses.' Here, they say that 85 per cent of people are poor, 10 per cent middle-class and 5 per cent rich. 'No one can become rich through honest labour', said one woman. Some grassroots leaders were successful in the local elections. This is the long-term goal – direct democratic representation of the poor. 'Most people are poor. So when we are the majority, who will prevent us from going forward?'

Aliya Begum is a village committee chairwoman. Small, vivacious, in her mid-30s, she speaks with passion.

> Before we formed the primary group, I was not allowed out of the house. I had never visited the chief town of the *thana*, much less Dhaka. You do not know how limited your life is until you first see the vast beauty of the world. My life is transformed. I have one daughter, 13, and a son who is 7 months old. My husband has a betel-leaf shop. Our only land is the 8 decimals around the house, but we grow vegetables and use it intensively. We are still poor, but coming together to share our lives, our woes and joys,

makes us less poor. When I was younger, I never even entered the local market. When I began to study and became aware of oppression, my brother said, 'You should stay indoors. It is not proper for married women to move outside.' Why is it not proper? I challenged him, and he saw the truth of what I spoke. We are stronger now. The head and the heart work together.

The literary review

Next to the hotel in the centre of Barisal, a dark concrete passage and a flight of crumbling stairs lead to the office of *Anandalikhon*, a cultural magazine devoted to local poets, writers and interviews with Barisal people prominent in the wider world. Its editor is Syed Dulal, whose concern it is to maintain the regional temper and sensibility of his people. A cluttered room – swivel-chairs, upright wooden chairs and a big desk full of papers – the drab office looks like the clandestine headquarters of some seditious anti-Raj publication of the 1930s, or even the 1890s. The magazine itself is printed on recycled paper, and it too has the improvised appearance of the kind of document that might have been passed from hand to hand by those plotting the downfall of the Empire. The 'staff' consists of 8 or 10 young women volunteers, most studying social science, literature or Bengali culture at the Women's College of Barisal. This they regard as the strongest bulwark against an Islam in which they do not recognise their interests. The tender vulnerability and enthusiasm of the young women, their absence of cynicism, made me feel strangely ashamed.

Syed Dulal spent five years, 1987–91, in Japan, working as a truckdriver's mate. The nationalism there frightened him, the ferocious work-ethic and corporate sense of purpose far removed from the Bengali sensibility. With the money he earned in Japan, he subsidises the magazine, which sells 1,000 copies a month. It now has an established presence, but makes no profit. 'I cannot close it down now. After one year, I could perhaps have done. But now enough people look to it and see it as a source of hope to make closure impossible. It is part of a wider struggle, not against Islam, but against the joyless perversion that has become a substitute for *dhormo* [religion].' Perhaps he has more in common with his 19th-century predecessors than might first appear; he, too, feels he is fighting against an alien culture.

Cultural diversity in decline

We travelled to Agailjara, west of Barisal, where a relatively high proportion of Hindus remain – almost 40 per cent; there are 40 per cent Muslims and about 20 per cent Christians.

It was raining. The landscape displayed multiple shades of green: the glaucous green of tanks and ponds, the acid green algae in stagnant waters, the black-green of wet leaves, the bright green of reeds, the sombre green of *kachuri panna*, the water hyacinth. The area is heavily forested, and the fall of rain is delayed by leaves, so that even when the sky brightens, the rhythmic dripping of water continues on taut leaves, waxy leaves, thin ferny leaves, and the air is filled with sounds that seem to come from the delicate fingers of a phantom aerial drummer.

This was the site of an ancient university until the fifteenth century, and the Bengali poet Vijay Gupta was born here. His celebrated poem is to Manosha Mangal, who fought against the stranglehold of the Brahmins over the lower castes. Shrines to Manosha Devi were everywhere: as well as goddess of the outcast, she was also goddess of snakes, which flourish in these marshy places.

Fundamentalists are not active, but here, as everywhere, Gulf money is spent on *madrasas* (religious schools), mosques and libraries. We passed a mosque built with money from Kuwait. There are rich and poor Hindus and Muslims. Christians were converted by missionaries in the 19th century. The literacy rate is high, with the rare distinction of higher female than male literacy. Formerly, Hindus were dominant. In the British time, enlightened Hindu zamindars recognised the value of modern education, and the higher castes embraced it enthusiastically. The Muslims resisted, and although the zamindars and their descendants have long gone, their influence lingers. The emigration of Hindus from Bangladesh represents a decay of pluralism. The eclectic non-communal tradition is being replaced by the shriller monoculture of an exclusive Islamic identity.

This area produced many politicians, freedom fighters, academics and educationists. Although the Hindu zamindars started out as *chamchas* (servants) of the British, many later used their education in the service of the nationalist struggle and freedom movement.

I met Abdul Hakim, Assistant Professor of Bengali at Sher-e-Bangla College in Sirkarpur.

The British hated Bengal, because they had injured us more profoundly than any other part of the subcontinent. Calcutta was the port through which the wealth of Bengal was drained. Here, farmers were forced to grow indigo at the cost of their subsistence. Subhash Chandra Bose was Bengali, and when he threatened the British by supporting Japan in the war, they should not have been surprised. We were also in the middle of the famine of 1943–44, which was a replay of the Irish famine a century earlier. Food was exported from Bengal as the people starved. At the worst time, people chewed sugar-cane, and when they spat it out, someone would pick it up and chew it again; when there was no longer any juice in it, someone else would pick it up and chew it once more.

Abdul Hakim is from a middle-class family with two and a half acres of paddy-land. His parents and one of his brothers are strongly fundamentalist. He studied in Calcutta, where he lost his faith, and became committed to science and rationalism. This made him many enemies. Even at the college, they call him *nastik,* a man without faith. It is not easy to work for rationalism in present-day Bangladesh.

I also met Ajay Das Gupta, a journalist in Dhaka, home for the Durgapuja festival. He has observed the improvements that have come to Barisal since his childhood.

Durgapuja was the hungry season. There would have been hundreds of people begging at this time. They came to our door, and we gave them food. Now they ask for a different kind of charity – money to send their children to school, cash for the examination fee. The worst of poverty has been relieved by Government and NGOs. The Government now even gives 100 taka a month to widows and destitute women. The very needy are identified through the local government council. Of course this reaches only a few of the poor, but this is the first time the state in Bangladesh has acknowledged it has a duty to its poorest.

This raises another question. How far are the people organised by NGOs also beneficiaries of wider social and economic change, apart from the work of non-governmental and charitable givers? It is hard to assess the contribution of other factors. NGOs sometimes take credit for changes that occur for reasons other than their intervention.

27

The most important work of Proshika is that of popular organisation. Throughout the country, over the past 25 years, 100,000 primary groups of poor people have been formed, more than half women, each with an average of twenty members. The purpose of these groups is to further economic and social development of the members, to link material improvement with social awareness. The long-term aim is to create independent popular movements, which will play an active part in the democratic evolution of the country. Each village or community-level group sends representatives to district, *thana* and national organisations. It is a paradox that non-governmental organisations should be concerned in the long run with *governance*. Because existing democratic structures are weak, corrupt and dominated by elites, it is necessary to re-democratise the country from the base upwards.

The social emancipation of the people cannot happen if they are subject to traditional economic oppression. On the other hand, purely economic gains are readily cancelled if unaccompanied by programmes of social and civic education. It is this combination that gives Proshika's version of micro-credit its distinctive features.

Proshika started such schemes long before they were called micro-credit. In the early days, they were given the more homely name of 'revolving fund'. The Proshika model is different from the better-known version followed by Grameen Bank and other NGOs.

Micro-credit with a difference
Shiraj-ul-Islam is responsible for Proshika's field operations, including micro-credit. After the 1971 war, he worked with young people in his village near Koitta, site of Proshika's training centre and farm.

> After relief and rehabilitation, we came up with the idea of community development, building roads, planting trees, supplying water. This was how Proshika emerged. Its unique contribution was to identify the poor, and organise them into *samitis* or groups. The Government was by-passing the poor, benefiting the better-off. The Green Revolution, health, education, did not reach those for whom they were intended.
>
> We always believed that economic development without social empowerment serves little purpose. A poor woman alone in a village can do nothing. But when 20 poor women sit in a meeting, if they have some savings, they share problems and pool their

power. In a crisis the poor go to the moneylender, because they can get nothing from the bank. Moneylenders charge vast interest. The borrower must give her labour in the fields or sell her goods. But if she has her own savings, she can borrow from the collective fund. She can also take a loan to supplement her income. Agriculture is seasonal, so in the off-season, millions of people migrate. Most borrow to maintain the family while they are away. Thousands come from North Bengal to Dhaka, but when they go back, they have to pay all their wages to their creditors. If they can borrow from their own organisation, they will not have to migrate, especially if they also have a loan for income-generation.

Even the poorest save. In every village, women told us that each day, when they cook rice for the family, they set aside a handful in a separate pot. After 15 days they have saved a kilo, which they sell.

Proshika's credit system is different from the classic model.

We started savings groups. People spent what they saved for emergencies or their own consumption. But they also used a little for income-generation – raising a few chickens, fattening a cow. We took the idea from them, and started loans to help employment and income. Proshika began in 1976, and the credit programme followed two years later. We started before Grameen.

Grameen is very effective in its loans to the poor. Their idea is that money generates money. They are skilled at getting money back from the borrower, but providing credit and credit-realisation is the main business. How people use the money is not the concern of Grameen.

Proshika does it differently. The loan is to the group as a whole, and they distribute it to individuals within it. Among 20 women, two may take a milking cow, three invest in poultry, a group may share a small fishpond, one may sell vegetables, another make cakes. We also offer extension services – instruction from technical personnel in animal husbandry, fish-culture, bee-keeping. This ensures success of the enterprise. The use to which loans are put must be approved by Proshika: we do not support anything socially harmful.

But the most important thing is social development – understanding of relations between the village elite and the poor, men and women. The credit programme merges with a wider project of social awareness. We have what we call universal education: our teachers come mainly from those who have been through the primary groups. They are close to the people and know how to communicate. But the essential thing is for the people to organise – once they have their own organisation, development will take care of itself.

This was confirmed in the villages I visited. People said that although their economic status had risen, the most enduring effect of Proshika's intervention was the gain in status, the insight into social relationships, the ability to rise above the sense of inferiority which has been the inheritance of the rural poor.

There is one more significant element in Proshika's loan-scheme. The credit is 'soft'. Repayment is at a declining rate of interest. Most credit programmes charge a flat rate of interest: the loan is fully serviced to the last instalment, even though by that time only a fraction of the principal is outstanding. Proshika calculates the interest only on the remaining principal.

Micro-credit releases people from moneylenders, who enforce interest rates of 10 per cent per month. If people cannot pay, they sequester the goods, houses, cattle or labour of the poor. Micro-credit disturbs traditional patterns of hierarchy and dependence. Rural elites, seeing their power diminished, are then ready to ally themselves with fundamentalists to restore their control over the poor. Indeed, this is a significant element in the rise in fundamentalism. Collusion between the rural rich, students of *madrasas* and political activists of Islamic parties, is, in part, a response to the growing power of NGOs and civil society – human rights groups, women, the rural and urban poor, cultural groups. These now form a de facto opposition, filling spaces deserted by mainstream politics, which is reduced to disputes between factions of the rich over the spoils of power. This is why NGOs are the objects of the wrath of fundamentalists. Women, above all, are both the site of struggle and agents of resistance to a politicised version of Islam, which has little to do with religion, and everything to do with power.

The changing landscape

Around Agailjara, Proshika has been active in establishing roadside forestry. Wayside tree-planting now involves local government, non-governmental organisations and villagers. There are 63 kilometres of roadside plantation, a project which, within ten years, will produce significant income for those who take part. Proshika has planted almost 80 million trees in Bangladesh in the past twenty years.

Here, the trees form a long green nave over the road, which is little more than an embankment, flanked on both sides by stretches of water: rivers, canals, flooded rice-fields, all overbrimming in October.

A roadside tea-stall: a couple of benches on either side of a wooden shack, protected by a rusty tin roof. Taking shelter from the rain, we met Mr Md. Ali, president of the *Udayan* (Sunrise) group, founded in 1980 in the nearby village of Jopsen. Nearly all the groups have names suggesting optimism and hope.

Mr Ali had no schooling. At 5 years old he was working in the fields for five taka a day (ten US cents).

> At that time our houses were palm-leaves, no land for cultivation, just a homestead. We worked seasonally as day-labourers, and there was no work for women outside the home. Proshika had a contract in the Work for Food programme, digging ponds and making roads. We were paid in wheat. That laid the foundations for future improvements. We took a group loan from Proshika to rent agricultural land, to start fish culture, homestead gardening, reforestation. They gave us technical support and training. We constructed a shallow tubewell with equipment from Proshika, and now, during the *boro* crop (dry-season), we sell water for irrigation.
>
> Our lives have changed. We have tin roofs which offer better protection against wind and rain. We sometimes make a leaf canopy inside in the summer, so it is not so hot. We used to eat only roti and dal, but now we have rice, pulses, fish. Even the poor can drink tea. No one in the village is illiterate. With help from Proshika, I buy and sell cows. I make 3,000 taka a month. We also have one kilometre of trees. After ten years, we expect to sell them for 5,000 each, which will yield a profit of 1.25 lakh for the group.

Shobharani Halder is from a neighbouring village. Her group is *Asharalo* (ray of hope). She has a boy who has passed Higher School Certificate, a girl of 15 just married, and a boy in Class VI. All the

31

women in Shobharani's group used to live by daily labour. Now they have diverse livelihoods. Shobharani has two bee-hives, six hens, twelve ducks. The group also has a collective fishpond. Fourteen people took a loan for roadside forestry. When the trees mature, they will share 40,000 taka a year. The contract is for ten years. For the first five, there must be no cutting. Between the fifth and tenth years, they can take leaves and small branches for their own use and for sale at small profit, but they may not touch the main trunk or branches. The trees were planted in 1992, so they have now reached this stage.

The women are no longer poor. They have enough. How much is that? 'Enough to be able to stand up to the rich, to express our views to them, to be respected by those who once employed us in their fields. When we began wayside forestry, some influential people sent their agents to destroy the trees. They did not want to recognise the right of the poor to peaceful economic activity.'

The causeway was built only in 1990. This has also contributed towards the social progress of the poor. The area was 'remote'; it was impossible for poor people who had been cheated to get redress. This place is also haunted by the ghosts of the Liberation War. In the secret places, freedom fighters took sanctuary from the Pakistani army. There were massacres of people believed to be sheltering freedom fighters. Only they knew the system of canals and waterways. Some villages can still be reached only by boat. Ajay Das Gupta was at university then. He says, 'Children used to swim across the river to go to school. On their head they would carry their books and a dry *lunghi,* and they would change when they reached the other side.'

Shobharani says,

> Muslims and Hindus don't think about religious differences – we share our lives. Our house is made of tin, and I have four sarees! We own an *almirah* [cupboard] and chairs. Can you believe these were luxuries for us before? We have a fan and electric light. But the main improvement is not economic progress; we are now valued as members of society. Here, we say we are sisters and brothers first, then we are Bangali, then we are Hindu or Mussulman. There is no antagonism between us. Seventeen women and men who are members of Proshika were elected recently to the union parishad [the first tier of local government].

The freedom of women

We met Jutikona Halder in Sabikhardar village. The name 'Halder' indicates a former small zamindar, although most have now declined into poverty. Jutikona is Christian. She has been with Proshika for ten years, attracted by the idea of 'human development'.

Jutikona wears a pink saree, thin gold earrings, red bangles. There is an enclosed verandah; floral pink and green curtains hang at windows protected by metal bars. She sits on a bamboo mat, supported by a red bolster, on a broad wooden bed. Outside the rain drips with mournful persistence on the mud and algae of the slippery compound.

There are about a dozen homesteads, extensive older houses of rusty tin and weathered wood, shaded by soaring trees. Hens, ducks, goats move around freely. The village is set back from the road, reached by a decaying wooden bridge across a marshy ditch. It looks prosperous, but the structures are old and in need of renewal.

> The people are not well off. The rich exploited us, paying less for our labour than we needed to live. This is now changing.
>
> Everyone here has a little land, 40 decimals or so. This gives three months' security in the year. We laboured for the rich, but they want our labour at the time when our own fields are also calling us. We had to go to them, and get other family members to look after our land. After saving for a year, the group took a collective loan for lease of a fish-pond. The floods of 1998 simply flushed all the fish out of the pond. We lost all our *rui*, *kotla*, *pangash* and carp. But most years, we have a small profit, 5,000–10,000 taka a year. We were also trained in homestead gardening and wayside forestry. We started one kilometre of road in 1992. Vegetable gardens provide food for the home, with some for sale. We grow papaya, bananas, red spinach, okra, *paisak* (green-leaf), carrots.

Jutikona acknowledges the social respect that comes with economic advancement.

> The rich pressed us into domestic as well as field-work. When they didn't need us, we didn't exist. Women could not move freely, even though we are not Muslims. They tried to stop our roadside forestry. They said, 'This is not suitable work for women.' They

damaged our saplings. We fought for recognition of the right to improve our lives. Our families have been here for 200 years. We have no religious problems – the conflict is between rich and poor. Big landlords stay in Barisal town or Dhaka. But they control everything, administration, bureaucracy, the police.

Proshika has been the main factor in getting women out of the house, although education also helped. [Jutikona has three girls, who attend a 'missionary school', a private Christian school, which costs 500 taka a month]. Women are still exploited. They go to their husband's house, and you have to give dowry. The very idea that you should have to pay a man to take away your beloved daughter is difficult to accept once you understand relations between men and women.

I am a Bangali before I am a Christian. Before I was educated I was captive. I had neither views nor voice. We always knew there was injustice – you cannot be poor and be unaware of it – but we didn't know we could do something about it. I was captive, but my daughters will not be. At least they will not have that struggle.

Jutikona has a fine singing voice, but a recent operation on her throat has impaired her singing. She nevertheless takes out the harmonium and sings a song written by a Proshika worker: it is a sweet plaintive story, set to a traditional tune, of a woman who has lost everything to the Jamuna by river erosion: 'Only our lives remain'.

We walked into the muddy compound. The cloud was lighter and a diffuse warmth from an invisible sun could be felt through a ragged sky. She points out the trees – *amjam*, *chabuta*, which has a fruit rich in vitamin C, *kamranga* with a pink flower, *kafila* or gum-tree, mahogany, *kub*, also rich in vitamin C, arum stalks which are eaten as a vegetable, Bengali *kejur* or date-palm. Jutikona says that for all their economic improvements, dignity is by far the greatest achievement.

Keeping alive the spirit of liberation

In the evening it is still raining in Barisal. Durgapuja is at its zenith. The Hindu parts of town are illuminated with coloured stars, festoons of red and green bulbs: these cease abruptly in Muslim areas. The music has been playing for four days – a mixture of Bangali songs, Hindi film-music, devotional music that suddenly gives way to a disco-beat; then back to Bengali poetry. A haunting song about a

Bengali boy, Khudiram, hanged by the British for killin,
magistrate in the 1930s. The recording, resonant, passion.
Mangeshkar, was made about 35 years ago.

Rain-puddles made the road impassable. In a booksho_   _c to
the hotel, I found four books in English – *Gone with the Wind*, *The
Satanic Verses*, two Mills and Boon novels. I asked the owner for a
history of the Liberation War. 'Our young people do not know their
history. The struggle has been so quickly forgotten.'

The bookseller expressed one of the difficulties now facing radicals
in Bangladesh. The Liberation War was a momentous event. Those
who lived through it felt a passion and elation which they have never
known again. That can be neither recaptured nor easily transmitted to
people who were not even born at the time. That the hopes were so
quickly dashed, and followed by two decades of denial – this created
a sense of bitterness and betrayal in many freedom fighters. They
blame the indifference of the young on the years of silence and distortion, and they seek desperately to revive the days of glory of 1971. But
the context in which they live has changed beyond recognition. The
age of heroism has gone; the dream of socialist transformation has
been laid waste. The inheritors are the wielders of money-power; the
heroes are the rich; the hopes of a better world have been absorbed
into a global economy, which promotes it own version of salvation,
where collective striving and popular struggle now appear archaic.

But it was a moment of deliverance. My companion in Bangladesh
was Abdur Rob, who runs the Cultural Development Programme of
Proshika, and whose story itself exemplifies the psychological and
social journey through exultation, disillusion, and the hope of renewal.

Memories of Liberation 1

Barisal is Abdur Rob's home; his village is still accessible only by river-
launch. His father grew betel-nut, paddy and chillis for the market
and food for home consumption.

> We were self-reliant. In the market we bought only oil, kerosene
> and clothes. We never bought food. We had so many fruit-trees
> we didn't sell fruit, but gave it to the poor and neighbours. I had
> a secure childhood in a stable society. Of course, there was a
> problem with dacoits [robbers]. They used to attack houses, rob

them of ornaments and cash-money. We were robbed twice. In this remote area, law and order could not easily be enforced. They struck in the rainy season, when everywhere was waterlogged, neighbours could not help. They came by boat, in organised gangs.

I was the second of three brothers. My father was very liberal-minded. He said the prayers, but he was not fundamentalist. He carried religion lightly. Neither of my parents was academically educated; they were pious, but liberal, kind to the poor. Since the mid-1960s our family has been falling down. Since I was a student we have been ruined.

My younger brother married early, without consulting the family. My older brother died in 1988 at 54. He worked in the police department, which my father hated. He left, and came back to manage the family farm. He was also a liberal-minded man, had five sons and two daughters; at his death, he left one son in the army and the rest at school. I took responsibility for them. His wife died in the same year, as did my mother. My father died in 1973. I arranged the marriage of one of my brother's girls with an orphan boy, who was a very good man with a bookstall in Barisal town. He died in 1997, so my niece is now a widow with two daughters and one son. I look after them also. I have a network of dependants – that is family life in Bengal. I helped my younger brother, but he lost money gambling, drinking.

In 1968, there was a family crisis, so I joined the Pakistani Air Force. I was selected to go to Karachi Academy for training in armaments engineering. I hated it. Bangalis were badly treated by the Pakistani authorities. They didn't even consider us Muslims. They said, 'You are Hindus.' Barrack life was harsh. There were few Bangali senior officers. Only after the 1965 war with India did they begin to recruit in East Pakistan. They realised, a bit late, that it was prudent policy to employ Bangalis. It was a wrong decision, because Bangalis occupied only the lowest ranks. I was to train as an officer. But the war had started: we knew by then we would get our freedom, so it was irrelevant.

In the election of December 1970, I came home to vote. I made the mistake of going back to Pakistan. On my return, I told colleagues I had voted for Sheikh Mujib. They said, 'He will never be leader of Pakistan.' I said, 'We will get Independence.' On 26 March 1971, Pakistani Air Force Authority seized our work, and ordered us to stay in camp. They segregated Bangalis from Pakistanis. Many tried to escape. Some succeeded, most were arrested by the army at the border. They were taken to the cells and tortured. I was crazy to get out and join the liberation army. I had a civilian friend with Pakistani Airlines. I asked him to get me a ticket from Karachi to Dhaka under a false name. He booked me on Thai Airlines. I managed to cross the fence in darkness. I went to my friend's house, got the ticket, a civilian bag and clothes, and took a taxi to Karachi Airport. I was interrogated. Why are you going to Dhaka? I told them I was a shopkeeper, but the Awami League had burned everything, so I had come to Pakistan to get money from my brother. I was allowed to take the flight. When I reached Barisal, I sought out the freedom fighters. I was 23.

My parents told me the police were looking for me. The police auxiliary came and said 'Report to the police.' I said, 'Tell your officer to come if he needs to see me.' I knew he would not, because they were afraid of the freedom fighters. The area was full of fighters, but they had not yet organised. They had no arms. I called a meeting – about twenty of us met in a local school at night – ex-army, ex-air force, ex-police, ex-Border Security, some militant students. I suggested we should collect arms. There were armed people in the rural areas, but they were waiting for the volunteers to return from India. I suggested we should get those who had arms to surrender them to us, because we were prepared to fight. There were also arms in the hands of supporters of Pakistan – we had to get these too.

Within fifteen days we had .303 rifles, musket rifles, 12-bore guns. We threatened pro-Pakistanis to give what they had. One of our nearest neighbours was an honorary magistrate, who was of course pro-Pakistan. In mid-August an informer said, 'Tomorrow Chowdhury, the magistrate, is leaving for Barisal, and within three days Pakistani troops will come and camp here.' I was amazed. How will they come to this remote rural area? He showed me a letter: a Pakistani major had written to the magistrate telling him troops would arrive on a certain day to be billeted here. Then I believed. We made a plan to kill him.

Chowdhury had an armed bodyguard. He was due on the day

of the *hat*, the weekly market. We set up watch in the house of a supporter. We had knives and pencil revolvers. Six gunmen were to cover the boys who would attack him. He came into the market. We detonated a small bomb to distract attention. They attacked and killed him. They didn't use revolvers but knives. A crowd gathered. We declared over the microphones that freedom fighters had come, and were attacking Pakistan supporters. We told them we were friends and they should go about their business in peace. We showed ourselves. We said, 'Send your sons and brothers to join us.' Then we returned to our camp.

Next day, we went to Chowdhury's house and saw his wife and elder brother. We begged pardon of them for what we had had to do for the sake of the soil. They gave us three .303 rifles, two 12-bore guns. There was one 18-bore gun, a .45 revolver, a kris, other weapons and ammunition. We sent representatives of our small troop to India with letters asking for help with heavy arms, machine-guns, grenades and mines. We received only light arms and mines.

We fought the Pakistanis several times face-to-face. They were in the camp at the *thana* headquarters. We planned to confine them there. Sometimes, naval forces came from district head-quarters, because our area was surrounded by water. Then we fell back, coming forward only after they had gone. We had a hit-and-run policy. Late in September, 27th day of Ramadan, an important date in the Ramadan cycle, they sent a big force with naval support. We had to withdraw. They killed over a hundred people and burned thousands of houses. That continued until 16 December, Victory Day. On 20 December I went to Barisal to the headquarters, deposited our arms, and then came to Dhaka to join the new Bangladesh Air Force.

The exile of the freedom fighters

One of the most powerful feelings in testimonies of that time is a recurring sense of having been *cheated* of freedom by the coming to power of the military, and of unfinished business. The work of Proshika (and many other organisations in Bangladesh) is the con-tinuing expression of this. From the desire to recover the idealism of the early days of Independence stems commitment to the poor, to the minorities, to women and to labour. The greatest obstacles now are the apparent indifference of a new generation, concerned with individual advancement, making money, a career, getting out of Bangladesh, going abroad. The altruism that inspired the liberation fighters is hard to find. Proshika's emphasis by now on the 'training', 'education', 'conscientisation' of its new workers strikes at every turn against the fact that NGOs are now seen as a means of career and personal advancement. Although many young people are drawn to Proshika because they are shocked by the degeneration of politics and by extreme social injustice, they cannot feel the passion that animated those whose hands actually liberated the country.

In the office of the Freedom Fighters' Association, I met Saik Kutubuddin Ahmed, Vice-President of the Central Committee. The single-storey ochre-washed cement building is in a stony compound in the centre of Barisal town. A meeting hall with bamboo ceiling suspended below the tin roof to keep it cool, heroic pictures of fighters spaced around the wall; ceiling fans purr gently, moving the papers on glass-topped desks. He says,

> New freedom fighters are needed. We are still fighting for basic needs. We are fighting fundamentalism. Those who never supported the existence of Bangladesh have found succour in the BNP. They want to destroy the culture and heritage of Bengal, a history of a thousand years. They speak of 'Bangladeshi nationality', but they are pro-Pakistan. Their talk of 'Bangladeshi patriotism' confuses the young who do not know their own history.

The confusion of the young is the lament of many freedom fighters. One part of the story is 'We failed to communicate our vision', and second, 'They have been misled by those who do not want them to know their past.' There is truth in both parts. But the passage of time has also done its work. The social and economic changes have been determined not in Bangladesh, not even with the 'return to democracy' of 1991. It is easier to dwell on myths of conspiracy by anti-liberation forces than to confront the dwindling freedom of a Bangladesh forced to integrate into the global economy.

> Sixteen years of army rule spoiled our Constitution – the principles of socialism, democracy, secularism and nationalism. These ideological foundations were cancelled and replaced by an ideal of Islamic brotherhood. We could fight the Pakistanis, but

39

we could not resist military government from within. They killed four of our national leaders in the central jail in Dhaka in November 1975, and ever since then there has been a crisis of leadership in the national forces. They eliminated many freedom fighters, both civilian and armed.

It will be a long fight to regain the ideology of liberation, because we face two monsters – fundamentalism and imperialism. Our country is now a labour camp to serve Western interests. We know the West is powerful; we cannot fight them directly. Only the unity of the Third World can be effective against the World Bank, IMF, WTO. It is more difficult because the fundamentalists and the imperialists are also at war; sometimes they are allies, sometimes they operate separately. We try to inspire our young people to be proud of our Bangali culture.

A profound melancholy and exhaustion underlay many such meetings. The passion has been embalmed in a pietism of cancelled liberation. It was a bit like the sonorous platitudes of the moribund Soviet Union. As we left the Freedom Fighters', there seemed to be little trace on the streets of Barisal of the issues that concern them – the children living on the river terminal, the loudspeaker announcing that it is now time to apply for work-visas for the USA, the tangle of cycle-rickshaws. It has already become another world, the world of the past.

The beneficiaries of liberation
Many young people are unaware of the sacrifices of their elders.

At Madabpassa there is an ancient lake, with wide steps leading down to the placid water. All around, trees and paddy-fields, and beside the lake a tangled banyan-tree; actually, it is two trees, *bodh* and *ashato*, their trunks and branches intertwined. Local people say they are male and female – an inextricable marriage of trees. Migratory birds from Siberia will soon be arriving for the winter.

A government guest-house overlooks the water, with a verandah over a stone floor. Nizam, a young man in his 20s, sits cross-legged on a jute sack, selling biscuits from clear plastic jars, sweets, peanuts. A single packet of cigarettes, some crackers which he buys each morning from the bakery; *laru*, a mixture of coconut and gur; some *tetral*, a red paste rich in vitamin C, good for pregnant women. Nizam earns

30–50 taka a day. He lives with his joint family – parents, brother and sister, wife and child – on 12 decimals of land. They live in a small tin house. Nizam and his father take turns through the day. His father tends the little land, but he is also a fakir, who heals suffering with traditional charms and amulets. The family earns about 3,000 taka a month. They cannot save: Nizam says that twice as much would amount to a comfortable living. They eat *alu bhaji* in the morning, with roti, rice and fish at midday, and dal, vegetable and rice in the evening. There is fruit from the homestead garden, papaya at this time of year. Nizam never went to school. A neighbour taught him to write his name. As a child, he worked in other people's fields. Now he is married, he must provide a living for his family. He wants his child to be educated.

We are joined by the ubiquitous unoccupied young men of the villages. Mainul Islam left school after his intermediate certificate; his friend studied up to secondary school certificate (SSC). Both are unemployed. Mainul's family has two acres of land; his friend's family has three. The boys will not work in the fields. They explain solemnly 'Education means an office job. It is impossible to be a farmer when you have a qualification. Our fathers employ day labourers for that.' The disabling effect of education, or half-education, is clear: they are above working in the family's fields, and would rather do nothing than demean themselves. 'Isn't it un-economic for your parents to employ labourers when you could work for your family?' They are offended. 'You do not understand.'

Jamal Talukdar is 29, a smart man in blue-embroidered *kamiz*, and striped *lunghi*. 'I am a B.Com.', he says (not I *have* a B. Com: B.Com is clearly his identity). His family has almost enough land to be self-reliant. His uncle works on a rubber plantation in Malaysia. It is bleak, relentless work. He sends home 2,000 taka a month. Jamal wants to join him. He will pay 1,20,000 taka (US$2,200) to an agent for the job. He knows it is risky, but 'there is no point in investing in Bangladesh. There is no secure return, there is too much corruption.' He is a Bengali before Muslim, 'because we lost so much blood for our Bangladesh.' I tell him of the desolation I have seen of the Bangladeshi workers in Malaysia. 'It is money', he says simply. He would never do such work at home; abroad, no one sees the humiliation.

The fate of the Hindus: a remote village

There is no road to Goalbatan village, 'the place of stray cattle'. The paths are slippery. Most people go barefoot. This is a heavily wooded area. On the grey earth a mosaic of leaves torn from the trees by storms and pressed into the mud glisten like green stones. The trees shed a delayed water-shower. A canal follows the path with country boats carrying logs, some of them part of the private enterprise of Forestry Department officials, supplementing their income with produce of the forests they are appointed to protect.

The village is poor, on a muddy expanse of cleared land; chickens, hens, a cattle-shed. The wood of the houses is blanched and rotting. Nilurani and Renubala are members of the Jagrota Mohila Samiti, a Proshika women's group which means 'Awakening'. This meeting is strangely muted. The group has been working for fourteen years, and I expected to find a higher degree of self-confidence than is evident. The women are from the minority Hindu community. The Muslim leaders are dominant and highly visible. This was formerly a Hindu area, from which many well-to-do Hindus fled. There is bitterness and tension between the communities – a distant legacy of British divide-and-rule policy. Here Hindu zamindars oppressed the Muslim majority. People who had lived amicably for centuries began to identify their oppression not with the imperial authorities but with their agents. The damage echoes through the years, in the carnage of Partition, the post-Independence religious 'cleansing' of Bangladesh.

The women have made small economic gains with the help of Proshika. All have been here for generations, but are landless, owning only the homestead. Nilurani says 'other people' came and took possession of the houses of higher-caste Hindus who left after Partition. They took a loan for latrines and house-repairing, and there are three income-generating projects: five women have milking cows; there is a handicraft worker making traditional *boisha* (bamboo) household goods, like fish-traps, trays for winnowing rice, bamboo musical instruments. With fish-traps people catch prawns and fish for consumption and for sale in the market. Middlemen used to collect the handicraft items, but now they are sold directly in the market for 30 taka apiece.

Of the fifteen group members, ten took credit, the other five restricting their activity to savings. The income-generating project pays 5 per cent of its profit into a common fund, in which the other five also have a share. They started saving in the traditional way of all poor Bengali women – every time they prepare a meal, they take *ek mushti chaul*, a handful of rice, and place it in a pot. If they have hens, they set aside two or three eggs for sale. Most of the men work as day-labourers, for 70 taka a day. This work is six months in the year – building up the embankments around the paddy-fields, transplanting, weeding and harvesting rice. Some families also make bamboo goods in the lean season. A few men migrate. Income remains low (1,200 taka a month), but Renubala says 'We are rural people, so our budget is small.' They pay no rent, and there is some homestead production of vegetables or from livestock. All eat three times a day, although breakfast is *pantha* – rice with water from the day before.

They are still cheated by the rich. Wages are often paid in rice instead of cash, so it is not easy to prove that they have been under-paid. Illegal cases are filed against them, sometimes by those who want their land. The children go to school. The women can write their own names, although most do not read.

Men dominate village society. Hindus are subordinate to Muslims, so women Hindus are lowest in the hierarchy. They say 'Do not judge our poverty, but think how far we have come.' The greatest problem is the unemployment of grown-up boys. They pass Intermediate level, but the only work is day-labour in the fields, which they will not do.

They are conspicuous in all public spaces, the young men whose expectations and dreams have been raised by promises implicit in an idea of 'education' which cannot possibly be fulfilled. They sit in village squares, under trees; they lie on *charpais*, benches, concrete ledges, playing cards, ludo, *karam* with bottle-tops, talking, scheming, desperate to find work, to get out, to leave the village for Dhaka, to become drivers or domestics in the Gulf, ready to do any menial labour abroad which their (often rudimentary) education has rendered them unfit for at home; seething with energy and desire, spoiled for work they consider demeaning, their youthful powers are wasted by inactivity and a sterile longing to be elsewhere. Some will be recruited as political 'workers', *mastaans*, to intimidate the poor from whom they have sprung; or they find solace in fundamentalism, an outlet for the violence engendered by disappointment and rejection. It seems that 'education' was intended only to pacify another generation, to

43

postpone yet another day of reckoning for the rulers of the country. These young men are themselves as oppressed as the women they in their turn oppress; only it takes a different form, in the traffic in illusions and dreams. At least women have no illusions: if they cherish dreams, it is on behalf of the children.

The schoolteachers

We discussed these issues with young women primary-school teachers. These are the most committed people in Proshika, since they remain close to the communities they serve, sharing the same problems and pain. They do not leave their place of work at the end of the day: they live there. One teacher tells how her education was interrupted twice: taken out of school at eleven by her parents, she persuaded them to let her return; at 14, she was removed again, and made to work. Only later, through Proshika, could she make good what she called her 'lost years'. As she speaks, her eyes fill with tears at the memory of her disappointment. A sympathetic understanding creates strong bonds between teachers and taught. They see themselves in their pupils. It is far from the indifference of government functionaries, whose obsession with status ruins their contact with the children of the poor.

I asked what difference being literate makes in the life of a girl. One young woman said 'People think a girl is destined for marriage, she will go to the house of her husband, why should she read or write? Even at the most basic level, an illiterate woman may know how to cook, but an educated wife knows the nutritional value of what she cooks.' 'An educated woman will not accept dowry. Once she is educated, her vision changes, a new consciousness comes.'

These young rural women have learned a precious truth – the irreversibility of consciousness. 'This is our most powerful weapon for change. You cannot go back. You cannot return to *pardah*, you cannot put on the *burkha*, you cannot unlearn what you know.' They are opposed to the dowry system. 'In Muslim culture earlier, it was not the bride's family which paid dowry, but the husband's. Among the *Ashraf* (the faithful), men would not pay an *Atraf* (non-Muslim) family for a bride. So if a family wanted their daughter to become *Ashraf*, they began to pay dowry. Although Muslims claim there is no caste in Islam, this shows that a form of caste does exist.'

Most of their pupils work in the fields. They feed cows, goats and buffaloes, collect fodder and water, move the animals to pastures. Others work in small shops, tea-stalls, in workshops, repairing cycle-rickshaws, baby-taxis, making metal gates and windows. Some sell fruit, pens, water; some work on the passenger-ferries. Repeatedly, we hear of girls taken out of school, mainly to work in the home, to look after younger children, to cook and clean. Sometimes one is 'given' in marriage, from a fear that she may be 'spoiled', abused or raped, ruining her marriage-prospects.

The privileges of young men

The privileges of boys were evident in the young men who work in the hotel. They live there, sleep in small dormitories. Rashid is 25, earning 800 taka a month. He has five sisters and two brothers, and is married with two small children. He lives only an hour away, but goes home once a month. He sends home 700 taka, and earns almost as much again in tips. Why does he prefer to stay here? At home, he has land, his family. The answer to this question became clear during the week. He enjoys the friendship of his companions and fellow-workers. Their duties are not too arduous. Rashid gets commission on food and drink he buys for the guests. But the freedom he enjoys with his friends is the main thing. They are always laughing. They chase one another along the corridors of the hotel, or sit on each other's knees, arms and legs physically entangled, innocent homo-affective relation-ships, where they find a different self from that defined by relationships of son, brother, father, husband. It is a release from the constraints and duties of home. Is something similar available for women within the secret enclosures of family? No one was able to tell me.

Child marriage

I cannot forget a recurring story from all over the country; a story of girls married at 12 or 13. In village after village, women told of their anxiety and terror at the time of marriage. Some spoke with a frankness which surprised me. Often, they were married to much older men. They may have been his second or third wife. Some felt revulsion. Many were not ready for sexual relations. They knew, from the most bitter experience, that early marriage is an affliction.

Yet, repeatedly, it emerged that they had married their own daughters at the same age. Why, when they knew it was horrific to young girls? When they themselves had been made ill by premature sexual assault, bearing a child at 13 or 14, suffered anaemia, mal-nutrition, trauma – why had they put their daughters through the same thing? 'What to do?' They shrugged, lowered their eyes, turned up their palms.

We sat in a village near Bogra in north Bengal. Half a dozen women, close to a stove where husked paddy was boiled. An idyllic scene: the sun lemon-yellow on pale grey clay, a tethered cow, bronze chickens running around the yard; aluminium vessels cleaned with grit, glinting in the sunlight; a rick of golden straw for cattle-food, a store of kindling for cooking-fires. A creeper on the roof of an out-house, heavy with yellow flowers and green gourds. A jackfruit tree, with its flaking orange-red bark. Newly harvested potatoes, a pyramid of purple, waiting for prices to rise before being sold in the market. A fragile prosperity and well-being. Why this sacrifice of daughters?

The children are given in marriage – which suggests the reality, that they are not agents in the process at all. But it is not indifference that makes poor families dispose of their daughters in this way. They are given, not only because this is their destiny, but also because it is believed to be *safe*. Once a girl has gone to her husband's house, she is thought to be out of danger. While she remains unprotected, she is vulnerable. In this predatory male society, she is at constant risk of being teased, abused, humiliated, raped. And if that happens, she is *noshto*, spoiled. Her chances of marriage are ruined. She will become an embarrassment and an encumbrance, a source of perpetual shame.

Some poor village families send their daughters – as young as 8 or 9 – as domestic servants to middle-class homes in Dhaka and other cities. They often work for no salary, simply for food and second-hand clothes. Parents believe the girls will be secure from the attentions of men. A place of safety – this is the first concern, even though in the city they are often abused, overworked, and even sexually assaulted by the house-owner or his sons. The mothers of the little maids who sleep on verandahs or in corridors hope that their employers will find a husband for them, perhaps a driver or cook from their own household.

But marriage is the safest place of all. In the villages, many girls put on the *burkha*, which covers them from head to foot, denoting her status as belonging to a man, and therefore beyond the reach of others. Unhappily, marriage often proves as insecure a shelter as the fragile bamboo and tin of home, liable to be smashed to firewood by storms and cyclones. The girl-wives may well be beaten or abandoned; demands for more dowry sometimes follow, and punishment if her family fails to deliver – violence, divorce or rejection.

Many NGOs work with poor women, to raise consciousness, make women aware of their rights, teach them literacy, empower them, give them confidence to resist their destiny. But it isn't a question only of education. Women know. They need no instruction. Women are both site and victims of the profound struggle between religion and fundamentalism. It is a question of culture. Consciousness does not necessarily change culture, as the women in the sunlit yard testify: they know the virtues of solidarity, the wrong that is child-marriage; but they find it a lesser evil than any alternative yet open to them.

A pioneer of women's education

We returned repeatedly to this theme. The most revealing insight came in a long conversation with Umratul Faisal in Chittagong. Now in her late 70s, she is a significant figure in the national movement for the emancipation of women.

She lives in a house from the British period on a busy road opposite Chittagong Stadium, a sunken ground floor below street level, palms and shrubs providing a screen from the traffic. The brown-painted shutters are closed, so the front of the house forms a protective façade against pollution and noise. The back of the building is cool, the afternoon sunlight filtered through light white curtains.

Umratul Faisal is the widow of a poet, a former MP in Zia ur-Rahman's government. Her story reflects that of the women of her country. She spoke with the frankness and vigour of a woman who will not be silenced. Her eyes were bright as she recalled her triumphs, and expressed her anger at the resurgence of fundamentalism.

> I remember clearly the famine of 1943–44. The British kept food back for the soldiers. They also wanted to punish Bengal, because of Subhash Chandra Bose, who joined with Japan to rid India of British rule. Hundreds of thousands starved to death. Even those who had money could not buy – they fought each other for food that had been thrown away. Of course there was hatred of the British.

47

My father was extraordinary, an enlightened man. He fought in the First War, in Mesopotamia – Iran, Iraq. He was a novelist, one of four brothers, all writers. My mother was 13 when he married her, but he went to the war, so she was 16 before he brought her to his house.

As a child I lived about 25 kilometres from Chittagong. After the war, my father joined the Land Registry Office. Preferential treatment was given to those who had served in the British army. I was married at 16. My husband was 18 years older. My life was unusual – I chose him.

Only in mid-life did I start my own social and educational work for women. The great Sufia Kamal – who died last year – was a distant relative, and I was close to her. Her *Mohila Parishad* (Women's Society) was an inspiration to us. She herself had been inspired by Begum Rokeya, so there is direct continuity. She gave us courage to see that women should be educated to achieve economic freedom, personal self-reliance, and especially freedom of thought. This would make them conscious of their dependence on men. She encouraged the women who came to Mohila Parishad to work outside the home.

I started in 1972. Educated people said bad things about the Mohila Parishad, and the uneducated echoed them. I started an Adult Literacy School. I encouraged women of the neighbourhood to study and learn. Men protested. They said, 'What need have women of education?' They placed every conceivable obstacle in my way. One morning, when I arrived at school, I saw a dead snake on the path at the gate – a warning to me to desist. When the women came to study, people threw stones and thornbushes to disturb their activities.

One day I arrived at school, and no students had come. Not one. I thought, 'What has happened?' A young girl had written a love letter to a boy. Her parents had intercepted it and beaten her up. They were angry that her education had enabled her to write a love letter. This is what education does for girls! So no one had come to school, for fear that all the girls would be writing love letters.

The boy she had written to was a BA from an eminent college. I went to the girl's father and said, 'Your girl didn't write to a rickshaw-wala, to some uneducated person. Why did you beat her?' The father said, 'Now she is a bad girl.' The words he used were '*noshto ho giyeche*', which means ruined. I persuaded him. I went to all the parents, asked them to return their girls to school. They came back. I taught them to Class V. They wanted to go on, but it wasn't possible at that time.

We protested when police took no action on violence against women. We had rallies and processions to shame men who had beaten up wives or sent them from home. We inspired women with speeches. Big crowds came. Even male leaders came to listen, and we convinced them the future of our country lay in the emancipation of women.

After liberation, we had high hopes of our freedom. But after Sheikh Mujib was killed, such disillusionment! We had lost so many freedom fighters, the massacre of Bangalis ran into millions. We struggled to rebuild our broken country, homes, bridges, roads. But to us, the role of women was crucial, because we were responsible for a new generation. My mother and aunties could read but not write – and they were relatively privileged.

I wanted so much to be educated! I persuaded my father to let my grandmother take me to Chittagong, where she could bring me to and from school. This was the only place I could get an education. But my grandmother fell sick, and no one else could take care of me. We went back to the village. I was bitterly disappointed. My father sent for all the newspapers and journals, and my Auntie looked after me. She was a pious woman. I was very bored. One day, I got the name of a school from a news-paper – Ideal Home School, English and Bangla medium. But there was no boarding facility for girls. My father looked at the school. It was good, but I had nowhere to stay in Chittagong.

My father contacted a friend, a teacher in a boys' school. He asked the family if I could board with them. That was when I first came to this house, for this was their family home. My father's friend had a wife and family, but his wife died. It was he who later became my husband.

He was 18 years my senior. I came here at 14. Within two years, his wife died, and then he asked my father to give me in marriage. Many families had made an approach, but he considered I was too young. Abul had in fact been married twice, but both wives had died. My father said he did not advise marriage to a girl so much younger – he already had a child about my age. But Abul was very determined.

Later, I asked Abul why he had been so set on marrying me. He said, 'I could think only of you.' His friends suggested many other girls, but he would not accept. He wrote to my father, and my father asked what I wanted to do. No parents ever consulted their daughters on such matters at that time! He gave me Abul's letter. He said, 'Now you read this, and after half an hour tell me what you want to do.'

I read his letter five times. I felt like a queen! The feeling he had for me he poured into that letter, and I was moved by his words and his sincerity. After the half-hour, I went to my father and said yes.

On the wall is a photograph of Umratul and Abul; a faded, greying image in which she looks frail and youthful, although she was then in her 30s, her husband over 50, with a square white beard at his chin.

He said to me on our marriage-day, 'You are not a housewife, you are my beloved.' You cannot imagine how happy we were.

When I went to the village after marriage, 1936, with my husband, I went without *burkha*. It was a sensation. I told them my husband said I should not wear it. I was laughing at something and talking in a loud voice. In that village it was not allowed. I said, 'Why can a young woman not laugh?' A young wife was not supposed to make a loud sound in case a stranger should hear.

Now men and women are more reasonable. They understand better how to live together. Girls work, women have economic independence. Such changes were unthinkable 40 years ago. I have five sons and one daughter: she and all my daughters-in-law work outside.

I asked Umratul about the rise of fundamentalism.

I am furious. As President of the Mohila Parishad in Chittagong, I have been to many meetings. I went to Dhaka, to protest at a conference against violence by these people against women. At the time of the UDICHI bombing (see pages 91–3) in March 1999, I stood on a platform and said, 'The man who does not love songs has no feeling for humanity.' This is their culture of joylessness – no wonder it feeds hatred. On that day I wrote no speech, I spoke from the heart. People came afterwards and asked for a copy. I said, 'There is none.' It was uttered spontaneously.

This is now the biggest threat. If we fail to build barriers against it, it will engulf us. When young women come to me, I say 'Fight fundamentalism now, or nothing will change.' When I was young, there was bigotry and conservatism, but they were not mixed up with politics as they are now. When it is involved in politics, it is much worse.

My father encouraged my independence of spirit. But there was also something in me. Before I married, a proposal came from a feudal family. They promised dowry enough to cover my whole body in gold. My father was inclined to consider the proposal. I rejected it. That became quite famous – how can a girl deny such a proposal?

My father and uncles were enlightened. Poets and writers came to our house. Nazrul Islam was fond of my uncle, who was known as a writer at a young age. Nazrul wrote one of his most celebrated poems in our house. My uncle died at 26, but he had written some lasting things.

Bengali or Bangladeshi identity

DR FARUQUE:

Bangali identity precedes Bangladeshi identity. If you say you are Bangladeshi, this implies you had no beginning prior to the existence of Bangladesh. This is historically and culturally quite wrong. If you are Bangali, you are connected to a past, a history, a tradition and culture. But if you are Bangladeshi, your life began only in 1971.

Bangladesh was not created only for Bangladeshis. It was created on the grounds of Bangali nationalism, rooted in language and all forms of culture; most of all distinguished by its humanism. Bangali literature you can trace over centuries. It has tolerance for all religions, a secular humanistic spirit, which you can see at its best in the Baul tradition.

The Bauls were a religious sect, a fusion of Muslim and Hindu belief, and their culture was characterised by mystic songs which, although devotional, are also sensuous, a celebration of nature and life. Tagore was influenced by Baul songs, and the Bangla-desh national anthem is based on a Baul melody he heard. The Bauls were rooted in the south-west, around the present India–Bangladesh border. The best-known representative of the tradition is Lalon, who was born in 1800 and died in 1880. His devotional songs are the supreme expression of an eclectic Bangali spiritual-ity. No one knows whether his parents were Muslim or Hindu. At the age of 11 or 12, he had smallpox, and was left on the road for dead. He was picked up by a Baul family, who adopted him. He lost the sight of one eye. His influence pervades 19th- and 20th-century Bangali culture.

To be Bangali is to be rooted in the soil like a tree, but with branches and leaves reaching towards the sky. Bangali culture is not static, but interacts with others without losing its identity. Bangali nationalism is based in the culture, although of course the political aspect is important. As a Bangladeshi, you identify your-self in terms of citizenship only, a truncated form of identity. You can write it on a form when you are travelling, but as a compre-hensive identity it is slim. In all other spheres, I want to be known as a Bangali, because this has been given over generations, over centuries.

Ideologically, its values are non-communalism, respect for other cultures, non-discrimination on the basis of race or religion, peaceful development. If you don't believe in secularism, you believe in communalism: that means domination of others and conflict. And that is a potent poison in society. It can destroy not only development, but society itself. Bangladeshi nationalism is against the spirit of the movement for liberation. It emphasizes Muslim identity, which was part and parcel of Pakistani national-ism. That is what we struggled against, because it is draconian, inflexible and exclusive. What was the point of Bangladesh if we are now to emphasize our Muslim nationhood? To do so is both unpatriotic and communal. It is to deny the whole purpose of the Liberation War. The slogan '*Jai Bangla*' was not for nothing – it claimed victory for Bengal. Bangalis were oppressed. We are majority Muslim, yes, that is part of us, but that part was exploited by Pakistan. We shook that off with Independence.

We can't deny the kinship or history which we share with West Bengal. We have a separate state, but that doesn't deny other linkages. It doesn't have to be a merger of political entities. Cultural and economic union, better exchanges, a freer flow of ideas – that doesn't threaten our existence. As it is, the only people who travel unhindered across our borders are criminals. Innocent people visiting families, doing business, need a visa. There should be mobility of labour. Are they afraid that if we call ourselves Bangalis, we shall have to merge with West Bengal? Rabindranath Tagore is our national poet, our anthem is by him – great talent doesn't recognise boundaries. You cannot partition the soul, the great festivals. We always used to celebrate Hindu as well as Muslim festivals. The British tried to divide us, they couldn't do it, especially in the rural areas. With Partition they succeeded, but only the ruling elites of India and Pakistan benefited.

I am not saying give up religion to remain Bangali, just keep it in its proper place. Bangladeshi nationalists use religion for political purposes, while the fundamentalists use politics for religious purposes.

In our culture, there is a history of *udarshin*, which means a kind of nonchalance, immobilism, not taking responsibility; life has to be passed somehow. The Bangali environment has something to do with this development of the psyche – the long monsoon, the fluidity of the landscape, the water, storms and floods. But that melancholy is of the *bhadralok,* not of the labouring poor. On the other hand, you have the energy of Nazrul Islam, a man of action, tearing down injustice and oppression, breaking through apathy, dissipating this melancholic mood of the gentility. He was also an inspiration against the fundamentalists. Tagore's was much more sedate, powerful not in a revolutionary way, but reflective. Bengal, after all, was the first to rise in armed resistance to the British. The struggle against indigo plantation, the *svadeshi* movement, all had deep roots in Bengal.

We celebrated a hundred years of Nazrul last year. The year 2001 is Tagore's 140th birth anniversary. Tagore is usually thought of as philosophical, rather sedate, but he was the first development worker in Bengal. He wrote a book on rural development; he set up Santiniketan to develop the villages, he sent his son for agricultural training in Japan, so he should come back and do farming. In that sense, we are all disciples of Tagore. He

53

expressed the need for organisations of the rural poor, for preventing the flow of resources from village to city.

For a development organisation, issues of Bangali or Bangladeshi nationalism should not matter, but I tell you, they matter a great deal. The spirit of the Liberation War is vital to the development of Bangladesh, for it was infomed by secularism, social justice, democracy and non-discrimination. Bangladesh was created to establish justice and to free Bangalis from exploitation, particularly from outside foreign exploitation. But it needs another step. And that step is to remove injustice within. That is now our task. It is continuous with the War of Liberation. We are not disconnected historically from that process, and to deny it is like saying the river has no source.

Development is not just economic growth. Development means justice between rich and poor, men and women, different religions and ethnicities. If you achieve fairness in these relationships you have cut the roots of poverty. Economic, social, cultural, environmental, political improvement are indivisible. To see development as holistic – this is to recover the values and spirit of the liberation struggle.

Despair and frustration came in 1975, when we saw the failure of our hopes. We were disillusioned, but we decided we should not sit and lament what others were not doing, but see what we could do. And what we could do – that is what has become Proshika.

A theatre group
Dedication to Bangali culture is a noble idea. On the ground, it is sometimes more modest. In Barisal, we met a student theatre group in a derelict building next to the police barracks. The ceiling has peeled away, the green wall-paint disintegrated into a chalky dust; the iron at the windows is rusty. A tattered blue cloth protects the open door from the street, a broken window-shutter clatters, a single light-bulb is looped by a long flex over a nail in the wall. The floor is concrete, the chairs broken plastic and gaping foam. On the wall hangs a portrait of Nazrul Islam and some photographs of the group's productions.

The students are idealistic and energetic. Riaz Mohammed Khan is doing Islamic Studies. It sounds an unlikely subject for Bengali drama enthusiasts. 'I am doing that only to get a certificate. My real interest is law, which I am studying so I can help the poor. It is easier to get a place for Islamic Studies. The progressive forces are not reaching the young generation because we are not united. The Awami League is in power, but it takes no steps to empower the people.' Kamruzzaman Miraj is angry with the leaders of the Awami League: 'They want power for themselves, they do not take seriously the young people coming up. They are in crisis – even their members do not come out onto the streets to challenge the BNP. They do not support us.'

One of the reasons for this, of course, is that the government itself is caught up in the necessities of globalisation; so as well as conciliating its political opponents, it is also busy following the 'advice' of its Western 'partners', 'inward investors', 'sponsors' and all the other agents of dominance holding seminars in the muted luxury of the Sonargaon Hotel. There is little chance that they will listen to the representations of these young people in their desolate Barisal meeting-place.

Riaz Mohammed Khan looks to the poor to preserve Bengali culture.

> The fundamentalists provide programmes for the young. They have networks all over the country. And the Western interests are also busy, promoting their values through satellite dishes, pop culture and consumerism. Bangali culture must be protected, against the attack by fundamentalism on one side and Western culture on the other, not to mention India and its cultural junk. Our hope is among the poor. Most cannot afford TV. They still live Bangali culure and it lives in them. The rich do not love their country. The new rich class are culturally very backward. Even in India, the Tatas and Birlas [two of the richest industrial families] look after their national interest. Our rich do not. They look to America, Europe or Saudi Arabia. Even if our Minister of Culture is good, the bureaucrats who work for him may be fundamentalist. How will they help cultural activists? Uncultured people sit in high places administering culture – what can we expect from them?

A slum settlement

We went to Polaspur slum, a world away from such preoccupations. This low-lying area is on the edge of Barisal town, reached by a brick path, raised to avoid waterlogging. Even so, it has been partly submerged, and is heavy with grey mud. On either side, the water laps at the threshold of houses built on earthen platforms. Some are substantial – brick, concrete and tin – while others remain poor things of *chetai* and *golpatta* (bamboo and reeds) in urgent need of replacement. This slum, built on government land, has been legalised by the local authority. As soon as they had security, some poor people sold their plot to the rich, who have built superior houses.

As the path goes on it becomes more decrepit, and the houses more uniformly poor – rusty tin, rotting wood, plastic and bamboo. On either side of the path, wide stretches of water coloured by algae, water-hyacinths and *shapla* (water-lilies); here and there a stone slab with a deep-well pump. We reach Polaspur Number Seven, in the grim naming system of these settlements. This area has not been regularised. Everything is sodden, mud-stained, pervaded by a smell of soaked earth and wet wood, a chaotic eruption of mildewy life over all surfaces – spindly, pale mushrooms growing out of bamboo poles, and even blooming on the sandbags placed to contain rising water levels.

A fragile bridge of three bamboo poles tied together, and we are on a slightly elevated island of half a dozen houses. Here is the house of Mofazell Haulader: a roof of reeds, so low I have to bend double to enter, no window, a beaten earth floor. We sit on jute sacks. Clothes are strung across the room; food hangs in plastic bags out of reach of rats. There is a battered cupboard. In front of the house black water licks the toes of the women as they crouch over a clay stove.

There are six in the family. They lost their land in Jhalokati village ten years ago and came to Barisal. Monir, 17, has been married for two years. His mother is a maidservant. Monir and his father pedal the same rickshaw six hours each a day, paying the owner 40 taka daily. They earn about 80 taka between them. Monir does not like it. Passengers do not give respect.

Mofazell Haulader bought the house, even though he knew it was insecure, on government land, not the seller's to dispose of. From Polaspur One to Six, the dwellers have been allotted the land. Many have sold it and gone back to the villages. Monir says that slum life is bad, but they are, by the Grace of Allah, better off economically, although socially things have become worse. Drugs, hold-ups, muscle-men and gangs operate, there is no peace. During the *hartals,* boys paid by the political parties fight. About 5,000 people live here. Monir's mother says they spend 15 taka daily per person for food.

Monir's father arrives, a handsome, dignifed man in his mid-50s, white squared beard. He apologises for the poor hospitality, even though we more or less invited ourselves into his house. Even in the poorest place, biscuits appear, china cups of sweet tea; in the back-ground, an urgent whispering of women, as they borrow cups from a neighbour.

Mofazell was born in Khulna.

> My forefathers owned land. But a generation came when there was only one son. Most of the land was distributed to poor people. My father retained only a small piece, so after his death we received very little. One of my brothers was weak in the head, and was cheated of his land by a local rich man who paid him nothing. He was then landless. My father sold five decimals of land in 1970 and sent me to Khulna, where I shared a small shop with my brother-in-law. I was betrayed by him. I left Khulna to pull rickshaws in Dhaka. In 1988 I came back to Barisal because my parents were old, and had no one to look after them. In Dhaka, I became a rickshaw-owner. By paying 20 taka daily I came to own the vehicle. Here, I am paying for the rickshaw. I owe only 300 now.
>
> My boy married very young. He thinks Allah will give us food. I planned to marry my daughter first, then save some money to settle him. Young people will not wait. I could not make him understand. Rickshaw-pullers can earn money, but they do not always use it wisely; and in saving it, you waste yourself, you use up all your strength.

The gym
Each day in Barisal town, I passed a gymnasium. Athletic young men exercise in a large hall with white strip-lighting: parallel bars, a vaulting horse, weights. I was struck by these well-to-do boys developing their bodies in a place where muscle-power (in the most literal sense) is in

57

such relentless daily use for the sake of survival – the rickshaw-drivers' sweat gleaming on bare skin, the straining of the calf muscles, the lean muscularity, the spare ribcage; while these leisured young men simulate the same arduous effort to preserve self-respect in the face of under-activity and functionlessness. It would not occur to them to work as rickshaw-drivers to keep fit, but they spend many hours perfecting their body in purposeless exercise.

The local lawyer

Fazlul Haq is a lawyer who returned to his native Barisal to practise. He says that the Government could change the judicial system. After all, it has reformed the law in the industrial and commerical sectors, where privatisation has been rushed through.

> The separation of the judiciary from the executive is not necessarily a noble thing if the judiciary is corrupt. The judiciary supported dictatorship and arbitrary rule.
>
> There has been some social legislation in recent years which creates a framework for improving the condition of women. Cases are usually initiated by NGOs or human rights lawyers. Women's illiteracy, child marriage, the Muslim family system, all bind women to men in ways that give them little chance to escape. In 1961, Ayub Khan issued an Ordinance, the Muslim Family Act, which actually went against Islamic law in two important ways. According to Islamic law, a Muslim man may have up to four wives. Ayub Khan wanted to abolish this aspect of feudal law. Secondly, he amended the inheritance law. In Muslim society, if your father dies before your grandfather, you will inherit no property from the family. Both these were abolished by the same Ordinance. Because there was martial law at the time, no one protested. In the eyes of the state law, marriage is a civil contract, registration is compulsory. Islamic law also states that a civil contract is created by two parties, but some traditional Muslims require a ceremony by a Kazi or Imam. The defect is that illiterate people often fail to register their marriage, so when they try to file a case in the court, they cannot do so. One party can deny that a marriage contract was made. You can no longer marry four women, but a man may take a second wife if he gets permission from the first. In Islamic law of course, no permission is needed.

Literate middle-class women can now oppose the will of men. In poor and feudal families, it does not happen, because there is no modern education – even among rich landlord families. The feudal sensibility also emerges in other ways. Industrialists will employ children as maids or as workers. Feudalism is an attitude of mind, and it cannot be abolished by statute.

Barisal – remote no more

The sun eventually re-appeared in Barisal. It turned the puddles into steamy ghosts that evaporated in the bright streets, and the town lost its blighted, mildewed appearance.

Barisal town breathes melancholy and longing. Young men look into a shop window where a colour TV throws its vibrant soundless images into the rainy dusk. The presence of many products from transnational companies – Kellogg's, Benson and Hedges, Marlboro, Cadbury's, Toshiba, Sony, Mitsubishi – demonstrate that the goods may reach the people in this poor remote place, even if the people cannot reach the goods. These remain in the realm of spectacle, inanimate emissaries of promise, haloed with their mysterious otherness. What effect this has on those who must make their lives here, it is difficult to say; but as well as spurring people to competitive effort, it may also confirm them in a determination to do anything, even cheat and steal, to gain access to objects which speak of transformation to their pinched, hungry existence.

The critical economist

Before leaving Barisal, I met Md Hanif, economics professor, in his elegant Hindu zamindar's house, set with its shrubs of *rangan* and scarlet hibiscus. Well into his 60s, he is lively and energetic. He began by inveighing against micro-credit.

> Why is this now so fashionable? It is just another fad of the development industry. The benefits do not accrue to the borrowers, because of the high rate of interest. The socio-economic programmes undertaken by 'beneficiaries' do not yield the anticipated fruits, so they cannot keep up the interest on their loans. They take a loan from one NGO, then the next year take from another NGO to repay the first. Or they go back to traditional money-lenders to pay off their debt. Of course, NGOs do not

take bribes, as the banks do; that is good. But too many things go wrong with schemes undertaken by the beneficiaries. Proshika gives technical help with poultry and cattle, but how much does it cost to give this professional support? They are subsidising the credit they give. NGOs should restrict themselves to providing social services.

Abdur Rob defends Proshika's micro-credit system, saying this is the only NGO to combine micro-credit with social development. 'Credit alone is not enough. Proshika defers repayment until the project is implemented. Production starts before repayment is required.'

Md Hanif says,

Poverty is a vicious circle. Poverty breeds poverty. A country is poor because she is poor. We see we are a little better off. I am enjoying amenities now which I did not enjoy earlier. But my costs have also risen. I have become poorer. Or rather, I feel poorer. This is the demonstration effect – desires and wants become released, and this brings other social effects which become economic costs. The US has the highest income, but it cannot be said to be the happiest society – violence, guns, drugs, crime. These impose high costs which make everyone feel they must become richer, in order to cure them, and you are back in the same vicious circle.

It was raining again when we left Barisal. The swell of greenish water in the tank of the main square reflected the hoardings around it: trembling images of imperial products no longer sold in the West – Player's Navy Cut, Lipton's Tea, Finlay's Tea; but also for Danish condensed milk, Marlboro, Coca Cola, Lifebuoy Soap.

Reclaiming the socially degraded environment
On the way to Khulna we stopped at Jhalakoti to visit 'a social and cultural club'. A crowded township, a narrow concrete road, and in a small compound a sizeable brick building. Long tables with wooden chairs, and on the walls pictures of Tagore, Tolstoy, Helen Keller, Nazrul Islam, Gandhi, John Ruskin.

Jhalakoti was known 15 years ago as an alcohol- and drug-addicted community, a place of 'unsocial activities' and 'bad elements', as the residents unilluminatingly told me. I asked what this meant. I thought it must be too dreadful to talk about. It involved smuggling, robbing the river-boats, dealing in Phensidyl from India.

Some young people decided to do something about the reputation of the place. There was no work for young men, so they started a night school to compete with the allure of drugs and *Bangla math*, local alcohol made of fermented rice. A benefactor gave the land for the building; someone else gave a site for the night school, and the municipality offered five acres on lease, where an extensive fishpond has been excavated. Around it they raised the land, and created a garden and nursery where saplings are grown for reforestation. This is in the heart of the town: the fishpond and greenery around it provide an amenity for the community. There are places to sit; women come to talk, boys and girls mix freely. This is an achievement in an area known for social backwardness, lawlessness and fundamentalism.

The whole town enjoys the advantages the club has created. At first, residents were threatened by drug-addicts and gun-wielding gangs. Why was the area so degraded? It is close to the river *ghat*, at the confluence of several waterways. Outsiders came to service travellers, living in slums and makeshift shelters. There were no facilities, and much economic activity was illegal – drugs, drink, prostitution. Robbers stole from people coming to and from the ghat, and since the police scarcely functioned, they got away with it. Unemployment and illiteracy contributed towards the general lawlessness.

The work of the original students has inspired a new generation. 'We are highly political, but non-party political', says Kazi Kalilur Rahman, general secretary and local correspondent of a national Bengali newspaper.

> The drug business was controlled by politicians. Unemployed boys got money by snatching bags and robbery, and they bought drugs. If the political 'activists' stopped their illicit activities, it would be easier for us to encourage the young people to give up drugs. The unemployed were their captives, because they got hooked on brown sugar, Phensidyl, heroin. Of course the political organisations were stronger than we were. We persuaded some of the young people to join us, but you cannot change

corruption. We couldn't give monetary help to the young people, only encouragement, advice, friendship. We can now offer training in poultry production, fish-culture, gardening, which gives them a hope of becoming self-employed. We do this through the government youth ministry. There is a training centre in every district, but even those who are trained cannot always put it to practical use. To get a loan from the government you have to give 5–10 per cent of the value of the loan as a bribe.

There are other problems. 'The *maulavadi* (fundamentalists) do not help because they disapprove of many of the programmes, and won't accept participation of women. They will not tolerate dancing. They prefer dacoits and drugs to cultural programmes.'

The club holds gatherings around the pond at times of religious and other celebrations – Eid ul Fitr, Durgapuja, Language Day, Victory Day. 'The fundamentalists complained to the police that our activities are contrary to the values of Islam. There is a leader at the mosque near our park who says our programme interferes with prayers. But even fundamentalists do not pray all day. Bangali culture is a problem for them, because the Bangali spirit teaches tolerance and humanism.'

I asked whether addiction or fundamentalism was the worse problem. They considered the question seriously for a few minutes, and then decided that drugs were less damaging, because you can be cured of drug-taking, everybody knows it is bad for you. But fundamentalism is also a drug, which nobody recognises, and there is no known cure.

Among the young men assembled on that day were a journalist, an insurance clerk, a government servant, a salesman, a businessman, some students. 'There are many religions, but we are all Bangalis', said one young man. 'The making of Bengal has a history of a thousand years. We think in Bangali and we dream in Bangali.' In this area there is a folk-tradition, neither theatre nor song, but a form of story-telling with songs and action. They continue the tradition.

There was usually one main actor, and most of the stories had religious themes. Sometimes, there were two storytellers, one Muslim, one Hindu, and they fought – poetically, metaphorically. Since the founding of Bangladesh, these religious fights have gone. Instead, we express political and social problems using this traditional adversarial form. We also revive traditional dramas, one of which was made into a cinema-film. This is a love story from about two hundred years ago. A young girl, a student, is loved by a boy who wants to marry her. But the girl's uncle, who is also her guardian, does not like it. The father of the girl is dead. If she marries without her uncle's permission, she will lose all her property. The uncle does a cruel thing. He invites the boy to work with him in his wood-cutting business. The boy does so. The uncle gets some people to kill the boy. As the tree is felled, they push the boy under it so it crushes him. But they got the wrong boy. The uncle tells the authorities that it was the suitor who caused the death. The young man is jailed, and the uncle marries the girl himself.

With the money from the fishpond, the club maintains the park, an office, a library and night-school for working children. The school is in a series of rusty tin sheds; it is shortly to move to a new brick building, which has largely been constructed out of individual donations. Proshika is committed to help.

We went out to the pond, an open space of several acres, *rangan* and bright blue *aparajita*, mango and jackfruit trees, palms and *amlok*. We crossed a wooden bridge held up by oil drums to an island floating in the water. Someone throws puffed rice into the water, and instantly it is alive with silver carp and rui. The pond makes a profit of 40–45,000 taka a year. I was given a bunch of pink and red *deshi* roses from the garden. Members of the club guard the pond day and night. At the edge, there is a modest memorial sculpture to the language struggle. Proshika sees in this club at Jhalakati a model of self-help, an example of youthful energy harnessed to constructive purpose. Here, the gap between the generations, deplored by the old freedom-fighters, has to some extend been bridged.

3 ❀ South-West

Encounters by the river

The journey to Khulna was long and wet. We waited at the ferry terminal in a tea-shop, watching drifts of uprooted water hyacinths rush purposefully in the swollen Kocha river. Abdul Monan, 17, ferries passengers across the river in a small outboard motor boat. He charges 5 taka, and makes the crossing several times a day, a thin boy, far too fragile to negotiate the river with such a small craft. He says, 'I know the river, I grew up with it, the river is my friend because it gives me work.' He gives me two sweet *deshi* bananas, asks me to write to him. He came with us on the ferry to make sure we crossed safely. I felt touched and confused: we are not accustomed to such protectiveness towards elders.

On the ferry, I met a construction contractor in his early 30s, a Bangladeshi nationalist, who says emphatically he is Bangladeshi before he is Bengali. He said, 'We hate the British because they cheated us for 200 years. Now other foreign powers want to prevent us from being free. India wants the mineral wealth of our Chittagong Hill Tracts.' He asserts that there is every conceivable treasure in the hills – diamonds, gold, gas, oil. The government is 'giving them away' to India. This is the view of the BNP. He is Bengali before Muslim, but above all a Bangladeshi nationalist. I asked how Bangladeshi nationalism expressed itself. He said, 'Stand up to India. Stop them dumping their goods on us, damaging our industry. They dictate their terms in all bilateral negotiations.'

Bangladeshi identity

I heard a more considered version of the BNP in Dhaka, when I met barrister Zia ur Rahman Khan in his chambers in Dhanmondi. It was a day of *hartal*, called by the BNP and its allies in support of a 'one-point programme' of ousting the government of Sheikh Hasina. Police firing rubber bullets slightly injured two prominent BNP MPs. This raised the feeling against the Government close to hysteria: 'an attempt by the fascist government to murder Opposition MPs'. As a result, another shut-down is called for the following day.

The *hartal* is over by dusk, but young men who have heard exaggerated rumours of the 'shootings' wander menacingly through the streets. During our conversation, the phone rang constantly – a sense of urgency and high excitement.

Mr Zia is an urbane, sophisticated man, on the liberal wing of the BNP. He does not agree with use of the *hartal* as a political weapon. This not only deprives people of their daily earnings, but keeps them indoors. He thinks Khaleda Zia should address mass meetings. 'Bring people to you; do not separate them, and do not destroy their livelihood.'

We discussed the implacable hatred of the two women, each of whom sees herself as an avatar of the spirit of Bengal. Both sides have spun irreconcilable myths about the Independence struggle. 'Sheikh Mujib was the undisputed leader of East Pakistan – his party won decisively in December 1970. But it was the then unknown Major Zia ur-Rahman who announced the liberation of Bangladesh over Chittagong Radio while Sheikh Mujib was still held in West Pakistan.'

At that time, Zia ur-Rahman spoke in the name of Mujib, but when he later seized power, according to the BNP myth, his heroic announcement became something more – he embodied the courage of the ordinary soldiers, the voice of the people. He opened the way to another version of history. After the assassination of Zia himself in 1982 and the ensuing military dictatorship of Ershad, Zia's life and death, and his BNP, became invested with an aura of patriotic achievement and progress, yet another promise unfulfilled.

The orphaned daughter and the bereaved wife represent different forces in Bangladeshi society, but the hardening of their old grief into mutual loathing has led to paralysis, a dynastic rivalry for possession, even ownership, of Bengali/Bangladeshi identity. They are like feudal monarchs disputing territory; and behind their sterile struggle, in which neither is assured of 'victory', politicians, businesspeople and opportunists enrich themselves. The people, in whose name this is waged, are spectators of their own dispossession.

Zia ur Rahman Khan says

The Awami League tells that they brought Independence to Bangladesh. In fact, Sheikh Mujib was probably as shocked as the Pakistanis when Zia announced Independence. Sheikh Mujib still wanted to become Prime Minister of Pakistan. He was claiming the right to form a government after the elections of December 1970, although the junta was trying to put it off. He had a dialogue with Bhutto in Dhaka as late as 24 March 1971. He was not fighting for freedom then. The crackdown came two days later. I was in London at the time. In my letters to my father, I showed I had no love for Pakistan. Mujib could never have run Pakistan. He may have thought he could make a deal with the military – you quell the unrest, Bhutto and I will sort out our differences and form a government jointly. Even when he went from here, he was still saying 'Pakistan Zindabad'. If the crackdown had not been so brutal, the final break with Pakistan would not have been inevitable.

The idea of a national government uniting East and West remained possible until the 26 March crackdown, when many leading intellectuals were murdered. That made up our minds. I object severely to the Awami League's contention that they had been working at it for years. If that had been the case, they would have been traitors. No one in our party denies the place of Sheikh Mujib. The Awami League claims it is a grassroots party and the BNP a product of the cantonment. But BNP achieved its success because it appealed to many educated and intelligent people, those who could not tolerate it when the Awami League declared a one-party state in 1975.

The AL depends upon rabid Bangali jingoism. The BNP, Bangladeshi nationalism, is more inclusive. At the time of the 1972 Constitutional Conference, it was stated that all citizens should be called Bangalis. A Chakma tribal from the Chittagong Hill Tracts objected to being called Bangali. He had to flee the country, because Sheikh Mujib said he must accept. The agenda of the Bangali nationalists also extends to West Bengal. West Bengal is now called Bangla – they have a hidden project of re-uniting East and West Bengal. In the south-west, there is a Banga Bhoomi Movement, which suggests the division of Bengal is only a temporary arrangement. In 1971, Mountbatten said he always knew Partition would last no more than 20 years.

Our Bangladeshi nationalism accommodates the tribals; by 'deshi', I mean this country, not Calcutta. I am reminded of the Mexican President, who said, 'So far from God, so close to the United States.' We are the damp armpit of India. We have nowhere to go. With India next door, we have every reason to be sceptical. Co-operation? On whose terms? The water-sharing treaty – the Indus rises in Pakistan, the Ganga in India – we get the last leg of the Ganga, they are trying to interfere even in that. It is India's intent to cripple industry here. What do we produce? Nothing. Everything is from India – electronic goods, cloth, cattle, fertiliser, sugar, drugs, even unwanted army trucks. We make only garments, which yield 75 per cent of our foreign export earnings.

But India has a profounder reason to cripple Bangladesh. They want a corridor through our country to tackle the insurgency in their north-east. I once discussed with George Fernandes, their Defence Minister, and he gave me the hint that it would be easier for them if they could pass through Bangladesh to reach the north-east.

Hindus are leaving Bangladesh. I'm happy to see them go. They do not support the interests of this country. Hasina herself said they cannot have a foot in both camps. I have nowhere else to go; they do. That is why they do as they wish. The Awami League pampers them. They are now 7 per cent of the population, but they have government jobs far in excess of their numerical presence.

The BNP also supports entrepreneurship. Between 1977 and 1980 many state corporations were disinvested – everything had been nationalised by Mujib. This was reversed by Zia. There has been a so-called disinvestment programme over the past three and a half years. So far they have done virtually nothing. They do not believe in the free market; only in personal aggrandisement.

The version of the country purveyed by the AL is not

compatible with ours. One Awami League MP said in Parliament that Sheikh Mujib is Father of the Nation, and those who do not accept this are committing a crime. It was a farcical exchange. We left the chamber. In our 1972 Constitution, there was no mention of Father of the Nation. In 1975, after the introduction of a one-party state, the Fourth Amendment stated that the President shall cease to exist, and the post shall be held by Sheikh Mujib, Father of the Nation.

Hatred is a real factor. Hatred of Hasina is a test of loyalty to Begum Khaleda Zia and vice versa. If I speak of reconciliation, I get called *dalal*, traitor, saboteur. Begum Zia has a free hand with her party as Hasina does with hers. They will bow to no pressure, they surround themselves with people who say only what they want to hear.

We have formed a coalition with the opposition parties to oust the government. It is not exactly a natural alliance, but I think the BNP will have a majority to govern alone, not be too concerned with the sensibility of its partners. Of course, if the BNP get a majority, they'll be just as autocratic as the Awami League. Everyone in Bangladesh invokes 'the poor', but nobody knows what they really think. Their electoral support is sought, but that is as far as it goes.

There can be no reconciliation in the present context. When Hasina came to power in 1996, she behaved as though nothing had happened in the preceding 21 years. She took up where her father left off. They are living in a time-warp. I think, however, that our campaign on the streets is premature. It plays into the hands of the government. They want to exhaust and arrest us, harass our activists, use jail and detention to demoralise us.

Arrival in Khulna

We came to Khulna in the early evening under dripping grey skies. Everywhere the fields were a swimming emerald, the trees formed a green canopy on bone-white pillars; a flash of yellow birds, white cranes and herons reflected in the glassy surface water.

The ferry to Khulna was an inferno of trucks, buses with dented bodies and glass-free windows, overloaded lorries, beggars besieging the jetties. A young girl, barefoot, ankle-deep in grey mud, in a sodden red dress, her hair sticking to her head, pirouetted like a dancer, miming hunger to drivers skidding and slithering in the mud.

The shrimp factories are the most modern buildings, ice-white rectangles, as befits places for the instant refrigeration of wealth destined for elsewhere. A rift appears in the sky, and a gold bar appears over Khulna, pouring sunshine like another liquid over the half-drowned city.

It was dark when we got into the third city of Bangladesh. Arrivals in darkness are always intimidating, especially in congested streets, blacked out by electricity breakdown. Kerosene lamps and orange candle-flames throw sinister shadows on uneven textures of surfaces, illuminating stones and potholes in the road. The Besundhera Hotel, at the top of a ceremonial staircase above some shops, is not very clean. I sat in a cavernous chamber, listening to the hum of strip lighting, watching spiders spin their sticky webs in the corners. Outside, power lines looped across the street, an improvised skein of wires, cables wound on ceramic spools atop metal poles.

The village in the city: memories of rural life
In the centre of Khulna, a village called Gobarchaka is an insecure rural enclave surrounded by middle-class flats. The houses are bamboo-framed on raised platforms of beaten earth, *chetai* walls, roofs of rice-straw. Latrines, a few metres from the house, are bamboo skeletons with jute sacking for privacy. The spaces between the houses are muddy, with bricks for stepping stones. In the centre of the community there is a traditional rice-husking mill; a plank on a hinge, attached to a pole, operated by foot like a see-saw, with a metal stump which pounds rice in a bucket set in the earth.

The women's primary group started four years ago. Many have been here for twenty years, when it was still a rural environment. They began by saving 10 taka a week. After eighteen months, they were entitled to a loan, which has been used for a variety of livelihoods – buying and selling old clothes, sewing by machine, building a house for rent, investing in a husband's metal-shop or tyre-repairing business. One woman rears hens, another bought a cart, so her husband now rents it daily from her and not from an outside owner.

Many had only one or two years' schooling, leaving at 10 or 11. Two studied to intermediate level. Now, after universal education classes, all read and write. Most came to Khulna with their parents,

69

who had become landless – some dispossessed by river erosion, others by the sale of land for survival, for dowry, for medical treatment.

They are used to city life now. Comfortable without being rich, resentment at the loss of land still smoulders. It is clear that their archaic country-like village cannot survive in the middle of Khulna. Rents are increasing; growing insecurity has invaded this little enclosure of village life. The spectre of impoverishment, which drove them from the rural areas, threatens to pursue them here, where what was useless land has now become valuable real-estate. They also fear for the children: lack of work tempts them to join gangs, to use drugs. All the women say they are Muslim before Bengali.

Hazira Bibi invited us to visit her 'cake-shop' beside the main road opposite the village. On the way, we paused at the rice-mill. Maksuda, a woman in her early 30s, shows how it works. She balances on the see-saw, and the metal pole crushes the grain in the sunken bucket. I asked if they sang as they used the mill in the village. They laugh – yes, there were songs. 'Please sing.' Maksuda hesitates; but she operates the *dekhi*, as it is called, and sings a few lines of an old village work-song. The others join in – 'I dance with the *dekhi*', they sing, in rhythmic accompaniment to the work. The little demonstration lasts only a minute, but they become, briefly, the village-girls they once were, eyes bright as they re-enact a culture of work alleviated by collective song and ritual. It is a poignant moment, where the light in their eyes illuminates the depth of exile from a village life which shaped their sensibility. That life is briefly restored; then they dissolve in laughter, a laughter of regret and embarrassment.

Hazira Bibi is a big forthright woman in her 40s. She took us to her house, for which she pays 800 taka a month. Her oldest boy is a motor-cycle (*mistri*) mechanic, who earns well. Her youngest is an apprentice in a garage, not yet earning a wage. She has three daughters and two sons. She and her husband make 50–80 taka a day from the cake-shop.

The 'cake-shop' is not quite what it sounds: a blue polythene sheet tied from two neighbouring trees in the road to the back of the open-air 'shop': a platform over a drain with a big pot simmering over a constant fire. It is very hot. The smoke stagnates beneath the poly-thene. On a little wooden counter – a couple of boxes – the cakes are piled on tin plates. They are made with rice-flour, coconut, sugar and water. Hazira presides over the business proprietorially, as her husband rearranges the cakes in a white pyramid on the tray. The business gives her status and self-confidence.

Schooling in the slums

A slum on the edge of Khulna, between well-maintained flats and an extensive pond. The road peters out into a mud embankment, and, on the left, a settlement of bamboo and tin, a waterlogged path between the houses, unstable bricks for stepping-stones. Here is a Proshika primary school. Whatever its intention, it has also kindled high ambitions among the children, who want to be 'doctors' or 'teachers'. It is difficult to know whether they believe in the possibility, or whether this is only a symbolic response: a hope of higher status that will be achieved through literacy.

They know about Bangabandhu, Nazrul, Tagore. But what does such 'knowing' mean, when their experience as been shaped by migration, landlessness, menial labour, subordination? There is a dilemma here. Humanism, eclecticism and tolerance are not dogmatic: there is no revealed dogma, no Koran of humanism, no Bible of tolerance, no sacred text of unity in diversity. How to promote such sentiments, without falling into arid formulae? I could not help comparing these beautiful, excited children with those I had seen earlier in the morning, proceeding, solemn and serious, to the *madrasa* in their white *topee* and *kurta*. In some places almost half the children who attend school go to the *madrasas*. Some of these schools offer the government curriculum as well as Koranic recitation and learning. Others are the site of fundamentalist teachings, where *jihad* is promoted.

Noyon, a lively 10-year-old, lives a few metres from the school. He ran to tell his mother we were coming. I was uncomfortable with these unannounced arrivals, which left people little space to refuse; but no one, however poor, failed to extend the characteristic Bengali civilities.

Rohima, Noyon's mother, has another boy who left school at 11 to work in a meat-shop three days a week for 10 taka a day. Rohima works in a private clinic as cleaner and caretaker, earning 500 taka a month. Her own one-roomed house is very tidy: a wooden table covered with a newspaper, a plastic jug of drinking water with metal tumblers, a large bed covered with a bamboo mat for daytime use, a trunk under the bed for belongings and valuables.

Rohima's husband works in the shop with his son one day a week. For three years, he could not work because he was mentally sick. They endured great hardship. He caused disturbances with the neighbours. They came here a year ago because life had become intolerable. Here, although the rent is higher, the house is inferior. Rohima stayed in the hostile neighbourhood to pay for her husband's medical treatment, in both a government hospital and a private clinic. To eat adequately, Rohima estimates that they need 100 taka a day, but they can afford half this. House-rent is 250 taka a month. This is private land, but it is passing into the hands of developers, as new apartments come up. Noyon wants to be a doctor, and his mother seems to believe this is possible.

The faith that the unlettered place in the redemptive power of education is poignant: no one has warned them that economic necessity weighs upon even the most educated with irresistible force. Bangladesh is full of the half-educated who despise farming, graduates who have no function. Meanwhile, the labouring poor continue to do the work of society, ill-rewarded and unrecognised.

Education for social organisation, solidarity and self-emancipation of the poor – these lessons are the long-term goal of Proshika, although they are inhibited by corruption, collusion of rich against poor, oppression of women, the modernising of the feudal mentality. All this represses consciousness, which still slumbers at a sub-political level.

Babi, 12, took us to her house just outside the slum, built on a raised tongue of earth at the water's edge. It is open in the front, with a verandah covered with rice-straw. Babi's mother is also called Rohima Begum. She has two girls and a boy. When her husband's father fell sick, his brother quarrelled and demanded money. They made a contract, but the brother cheated him: the document was not legal, and the land was lost. Rohima's husband is a pipe-*mistri*, laying sewerage and water pipes for construction contractors. He earns 100–120 taka daily, but there is no work in the rainy season. Rohima's older daughter left school at 11, because of 'social problems'. This means: 'growing girls should not go to school'. Many girls here drop out at the age of 11 or 12 for the same reason, namely that the onset of puberty makes them vulnerable to sexual approaches by young men. They have to remain in the house. Babi listens as I ask if she will be taken out of school now she is 12. Her mother says, 'No, the school is very near.' She can watch her come and go, so the danger of being molested is small.

The dwellers on the river-terminal

From here, we went to the river terminal in Khulna. Immobilised convoys of trucks, carts, vans carrying goods to or from the river. It takes half an hour to cover a few hundred metres to the clearing between railway station and ferry-*ghat*. In front of the terminal, a large consignment of bananas, green and gold stalks, spherical bunches of fingers clutching thick stems; grain, in bulging nylon sacks and jute bags; baskets of purple aubergines; bulbous globes of arum-root; bouquets of red spinach on crimson stalks. A stone-built entrance leads to the *ghat*, and 3 taka gains entry to the wharves: a long stone corridor, from which walkways lead to where boats of all kinds are moored – steamers, freighters, ferries, country-boats, improvised rafts that look incapable of staying afloat.

Along the wall of the stone corridor whole families live. A woman in a red saree sits on a jute sack, a dingy mosquito net protecting the grubby layette where the tiny child she is breast-feeding will sleep. She was living in Khulna, but when her husband took a second wife, he evicted her and the baby, then only a few days old. 'I was left crying on the road with nothing.' She has lived here for eight months, depending upon the charity of passers-by, travellers and workers on the *ghat*. She has one brother, who is workless. A second woman, also abandoned by her husband, returned to her father's house in Bagherat. When he lost a leg in an accident and could no longer help her, she came here with her child. Another child, a boy of about 8, Sheikh Khayum, in a worn-out pair of red pants and no shoes, is chewing a fibrous piece of sugar-cane. He lives on the *ghat*, begging, picking up a livelihood as he can, carrying, loading and unloading small articles from time to time. He has a sister in Bagherat who is blind. His father is dead, and his mother also lives on the terminal.

A gang of labourers unloads grain, passing heavy sacks hand to hand, on to a waiting truck. Mr Md Akkas says they are employed by a contractor appointed by the government. This recent development follows the arrest of Ershad Ali Shikder, extortioner, serial murderer and gang leader, who formerly controlled the *ghat* here, his power base and source of his vast fortune. In spite of the arrest of Shikder, the workers still receive only a portion of the money they earn. They are supposed to be paid 5 taka for each sack unloaded, but they get only two and a half – the same as when Shikder ran the port. Are the new contractors taking the same tribute? Md Akkas does not reply.

How criminals are made

The papers are full of the story of Shikder. Everyone in Khulna is familiar with his reign of terror in the area. His activities illuminate something of the shadowy nexus between politics, business and crime – that parody of the enterprise and initiative that are supposed to be the finest expression of the market economy.

His history is a metaphor for 'success' in Bangladesh, and illustrates one way out of poverty. Born in Barisal, his father died when he was a child. He came with his mother to Khulna. He had no schooling. He lived as a street-boy by petty thieving around the ferry-*ghat*. He became a worker, then leader of a labour-gang in the port. He specialised in smuggled goods from India. He was also a psychopathic personality, and is said to have killed a rival when he was 12 or 13.

He joined Ershad's Jatiya Party in the 1980s. His gang levied an informal tax on goods brought illegally from India. The police were paid a monthly bribe. Shikder joined the BNP when they came to power in 1991, and transferred his allegiance to the Awami League in 1996, but for some reason this proved unacceptable. Control of the ferry-*ghat* remained the source of his power. The government offered the lease of the *ghat* contract to his rivals. Shikder invited some Awami League officials to his cold store to talk about it. He became angry, beat them and had them tied up in his godown. One of the officials died, another was severely injured. The government ordered Shikder to surrender. He refused, and called rallies and processions in Khulna, attended by any who owed him their livelihood. It is said 25,000 depend upon him directly or indirectly.

Shikder is said to have killed more than 60 people – rivals and competitors – since he controlled the *ghat*. He took the wife of a local Awami League leader into his luxurious mansion, Sornokomal, the palace of gold, where he installed her as his mistress.

Shikder's close companions are now revealing everything, and the relatives of his victims call for justice. A newspaper carries a photograph of Shikder on bail, bathing in milk to protest his innocence. He was eventually put on trial and sentenced to death. The appeals are still going through the court.

We didn't have to look far to find victims of Shikder. A member of a Proshika group told how his small piece of land had been seized by Shikder's hirelings. Jahangir's father was working for the railway. He built his house on land close to the track. Soon after, Shikder's men took it. Jahangir said, 'We have no gang, how can we get our land back? We couldn't file a case for fear of being killed. No one resists his will. Even now, we cannot go back, because his beneficiaries are still there, and anyway, he may be freed.' Shikder had corrupted ten of the twelve police commissioners who served during his reign on the *ghat*.

The context of corruption

This is the context in which Proshika works in the slums of Khulna. We met a group being trained in development and education, comprising one representative from each primary group in the area. Most of these were formed recently. Within the last year a group was set up among workers on country-made engine boats. Of the others, one man works in a match factory, another buys reject export garments for sale in the local market. Most are from outside Khulna. Kader, who represents the country-boat workers, came to Khulna for work in 1996. He was a victim of the Islamic law stating that if a father dies before a grandfather, the son cannot inherit. This occurred before Ayub Khan amended the Islamic law. I asked what prompted the boat-workers to organise. Kader says no trawler-worker owns his boat. They rent the vessel for 60 taka daily from fleet-owners. Within a short time of organising, they began to save. Now they have 7 trawlers constructed with a loan of 1,20,000 from Proshika and a further 1,00,000 from their savings. The trawlers will be group-owned and rented out to members, freeing them from the big owners. They will still pay 60 taka daily, but this will go back to the common fund. Their earnings fluctuate – up to 200 taka, but they go out only on alternate days, since they spend 18 hours on the water.

Amiron says that in her area the fundamentalists forbade women to organise. Some mosques declared *fatwa* against them. In Zubair's village the imams and local leaders also opposed women's organisation. A group invited the fundamentalists to sit and discuss the issues. They said, 'You are creating problems by asking women to attend meetings.' The women said, 'We go outside whenever we choose. You do your work and leave us to do ours.' 'They accepted the compromise, but made us understand that the situation will not last for ever.' Rizia said the rich people in her village warned them not to trust the NGOs, because they would ask for money. 'We did not listen to them.' 'We organise because we are poor', said Reeta, 'we have no shelter, no proper education, no health care; since society gives no benefit and government no help, we must use our own resources.' Maqsuda said that to get jobs for their sons, they pay large bribes. 'Where shall we find such money?' 'Women have no role in society, we are not allowed outside to work, many women must endure *pardah*.' Hamida complained that with low wages day labourers can afford only inferior food. 'This weakens their body so they cannot work properly.' Kader spoke of the problem of *mastaans* (strong-arm men), and then Jehangir told of his family's victimisation by Shikder's gang. Salt water has damaged many tubewells – they have to go down 900 feet to reach fresh water.

When I asked if they were primarily Muslim or Bengali, most placed religion as the first element of identity. Eight said they were Bengali first, twenty Muslim. Is anything worse than being poor? Kader said politics is worse than poverty. Rizia insisted, 'Poverty is worst.' Are the rich happy? Maqsuda said the rich are always fighting. 'They are afraid of losing what they have. How can they be happy?' 'It isn't happiness, but power. If power is happiness, they are happy.'

This training lasts six days. We sat with them for about 90 minutes. The process is very different from anything in the West. Members of a group will listen patiently to each other before considering their response. They are courteous and their disagreements not personalised, although, since these are from recently formed groups, the men – only 6 in a group of 28 – dominated. Here, we heard one chilling assessment of the fundamentalists. 'They speak brotherhood, but they mean murder.'

The pessimism of the intellectual
I sat one sunny afternoon in the Basundhera Hotel with Advocate
Firoz Ahmed, general secretary of the Khulna District Bar Associa-
tion, and one of the most pessimistic of the intellectuals I met in
Bangladesh.

Our Sunderban mangrove forest is being destroyed by the corruption of the Forestry Department. There is illegal felling,
destruction of wildlife. Water has become saline through shrimp
cultivation. They have cut embankments for shrimp cultivation,
so salt water comes inland. They get their money, but they ruin
paddy-land. No trees, no flowers, no plants grow. Our industrial
base – jute and paper-mills – is closing. After liberation, these
were nationalised, because the owners were Pakistanis. Now they
are selling them off to rich Bangalis, who take a bank loan as
credit, buy the mill, close it down, then sell the land. fifteen
thousand jute workers are unemployed.

In this environment new Shikders are coming up. Terrorist
gangs ally themselves to the party is power. In this region, what
remains of the old leftist parties continue armed struggle. The
Left was outlawed, and degenerated into criminal gangs. Faith
and ideology are lost. There are many opportunities for smuggling
from India: drugs, illicit goods. Our city is ringed by slums as
more landless people come in.

When Shikder was arrested, a warning was issued to all advocates. One lawyer was killed by Shikder's people. No formal
decision was taken by advocates not to represent him in court,
but in practice they resolved not to. No one dared speak against
him – you cannot imagine the extent of his power and the number
of his supporters. Gangs rival the government in their power. A
slum of 10,000 people controlled by Shikder had a paid staff of
200. Ten per cent of all goods coming through Khulna were
stolen by him, cement, food, even railway sleepers and carriages.

Left politics is now spoiled in Bangladesh. In the 1960s, there
was one Communist Party (CP) until the China–Russia split. The
pro-China faction was against the Liberation War, because China
was against it. It became isolated from the people. I was in the
pro-Moscow group. After the war, we became part of the Awami
League, which was pro-poor then. After the killing of Sheikh

Mujib, the Awami League became like any other party. With the death of the USSR, the remains of the CP also submerged its identity in the Awami League. The leftist movement of the freedom fighters is finished. There is no Left movement with a mass base.

It was not that social injustice ceased, or the terrible poverty of a majority of the people ended: the Left decayed because it was not indigenous, it had depended crucially upon influences from elsewhere. If internal patterns of exploitation and inequality cannot generate their own resistance from within, this illuminates, perhaps, one of the greatest historical weaknesses of Bengal – its dependence on external ideological inspiration. And yet Bengal produced some of the most powerful leaders against alien rule. The human rights movement, civil society and other NGOs have taken forward this sensibility: they represent grassroot resistance, although at a sub-political level.

'NGOS are funded by the West to fight fundamentalism. Their work is against Islamic fundamentalism, but this is only to make way for Western economic fundamentalism. Proshika is pro-Bangali, but it still accepts Western money. There is a problem with NGO beneficiaries – they speak as they do, not from the heart, but as "beneficiaries".'

Firoz Ahmed, a man of the Left, represents a mass movement now without people. 'Proshika has people, but they are tethered by patronage.' There is no doubt that 'beneficiaries' are inclined to echo the lessons taught by those who 'empower' them. In this sense, 'conscientisation' is a more subtle idea than it may at first appear.

The cultural struggle

The gloom of Firoz was dispelled that evening when we went to Rupantar, a cultural organisation committed to democracy, anti-corruption and social justice. Members of Rupantar are young and enthusiastic. The cruelty of the Ershad Shikders calls forth its opposite – the energy and delight of the young people in their work.

Rupantar is a big organisation, funded partly by the Asia Foundation and USAID. That a Bengali cultural group should be funded by the US government comes as no surprise. The US makes strategic alliances against fundamentalism wherever the opportunity to do so arises. It is not that the US has any love for Bengali culture – most Americans scarcely know of its existence. Rupantar has no illusions over t purposes of the US, but sees no reason to reject help when it is offered.

Rupantar has a sizeable concrete building in Khulna. Yellow-washed, two storey, extensive space for rehearsal, study and adminis-tration, unlike most cultural groups I had met, which were struggling and impoverished. I sat on a bamboo mat against the wall in a small performing space. They put on a programme for my benefit. They present me – as though I were the performer (and maybe, in my way, I am) – with a bunch of red roses and green-white *rajanivanda*.

The performance springs to life with a *pot* song – a traditional form of instruction in the villages. The dozen or so actors, singers and drummers march around the little hall, which becomes a village. They carry a large scroll which they unfurl as the song and its story proceeds. It depicts, in stylised imagery, the plight of women in the rural areas, their oppression, sorrows and resistance, and it is sung to a resonant traditional tune which, just as you begin to recognise it and get carried away by its stirring melody, changes abruptly into a faster, more urgent rhythm. Two actors unroll the big parchment between its wooden spindles, showing girl-children working in the house, in the fields, looking after younger children, fetching water, minding goats, cutting fodder. At the same time, scenes from village life are acted out; women are disposed of in marriage like cattle. Prospective grooms come to inspect their teeth, hair, eyes and legs. The main singer is a woman, who, like an insistent schoolmistress, points to the scenes unrolling on the cloth with a long stick. There is an image of women with a dozen pairs of hands, milling, feeding hens, making *parathas*, fetching grass, dressing children, milking cows, cutting rice. A woman, mistreated by men, hangs herself; the rhythm becomes more fierce, the text more overtly anti-fundamentalist.

It dissolves into a balletic version of the same story. Men and women carry multicoloured scarves, which they use, now as chains to block the movement of women, now as banners of hope and emancipation. The dance is highly ritualised, showing child marriage, divorce, polygamy, dowry-abuse of women; a mixture of dreamlike stylisation and moments of brutal reality. It is also – for Bangladesh – shocking, as the women become immobilised, entangled in the limbs of the men; they then break free, celebrate a moment of triumph, only to be held fast again. The stoles are woven around their neck like

ied like animals. Then they are ground between the
le bodies. The women revolt and enslave the men for
e inextricable mingling of male and female bodies is
but what it communicates is uncompromising and
s.

Tradi... al folk-tunes and dramatic styles are invested with a radical contemporary message – a powerful assertion of the Bengali heritage combined with a will for social reform and liberation.

The performance evolves as a collective, imaginative act of creation. This is 'alternative living theatre', as they call it. They say they will 'never' lose the vitality and commitment they bring to their desire to transform the country. Then they ride off into the night on bicycles. Even the women ride bikes, although they are accompanied by men to their homes. It is still not considered proper for women to cycle.

The technical workers

In Khalispur, on the outskirts of Khulna, I met a group of technical personnel and economic development workers. These support with their expertise the economic activities of groups receiving loans. The projects include poultry-raising, cattle-fattening, milk-cows, fish-ponds, paddy-growing, roadside forestry, well-making, bee-keeping, homestead gardening. Many are recently appointed, since Proshika has been here only five years. They are taken on for their technical skills. Most are graduates; many will not have met Proshika before they were employed. This illustrates a dilemma with what Proshika calls 'the third generation'.

Getting a job is a major concern of graduates, and Proshika offers opportunities which the private sector does not, although salary is not the main attraction. Security and status are now associated with NGOs. That this leads to a dilution of idealism is inevitable. Some new employees regard the work as a stop-gap, pending something better, a chance to enhance skills with a view to a more lucrative occupation. Many are from the middle class, and have had little contact with the poor. However, given the disillusionment with politics, many honest and sincere young people want to enter a sector which is, in general, corruption-free. For some, NGOs are a last hopeful enclave of radicalism, and a springboard for new kinds of social action.

Most said they were from relatively privileged backgrounds. 'Why work for Proshika?', I asked. 'Why not get rich like the shrimp-mafia or building developers?' They were shocked. Their parents have given them high ethical standards. One man said, 'We could become like Shikder, but if we do, a generation will be lost in evil.' Some wanted to help society, but could not do it as individuals. Proshika offered others personal security, a job and income as well as a chance to do good. I asked if their desire to do good came from religion. No. Their motives? 'Education', 'society', 'inspiration from the lives of great men and women', 'the family'. Are religion and fundamentalism the same thing? An emphatic no – fundamentalists use religion for political purposes; religion is a reflection of an individual's wish to lead a moral life.

I asked why Bangladesh, a beautiful country with many good people, should be perceived by the world in the negative light in which it is portrayed. 'Economic freedom has not yet come.' 'Oppression is still there.' 'The West tells the world we are hopeless.' 'We have no discipline.' 'We suffer from political instability.' 'There are many who wish to tarnish the image of Bangladesh.' 'The international media.'

What qualities do they see in those they work with? 'Dignity', 'friendship', 'humanity', 'unity', 'love of country', 'simplicity'. 'The poor bear the traditional culture of Bengal as educated people do not.' The group as a whole identified Western economic fundamentalism as a greater long-term threat than Islamic fundamentalism. I asked 'What is the opposite of poverty?' Many said 'self-reliance', 'sufficiency'. A few mentioned 'wealth', but a majority scorned this. One woman said, 'Wealth cannot exist without poverty. If we want to get rid of poverty, wealth also must be shown for what it is – injustice and exploitation.'

Towards Satkhira

The gradient west of Khulna descends gently towards the coast. A wide sky and landscapes of variegated green, here and there the brilliant corona of a crimson waterlily, bright yellow trumpets of creeper over the bleached rice-straw of house-roofs; a yellow bird flashes between the trees, soft green globes of coconut hang among the chattering palms, fluttering fans of bamboo. Everywhere jute sticks are drying on the verge. On raised platforms of land, vegetables – carrot-ferns, onions' tubular leaves, red-veined spinach, spiky leaves of garlic.

In Satkhira town, we stop at a building in a busy narrow street. A door of tinted plastic, a small room with three or four computers. This is Progoti Net, a small commercial business designed to generate income for cultural groups. Progoti Net does high-quality printing, laser-printing, colour-scanning, offers e-mail and access to the Internet. It gives courses in computer-training to local people.

The cultural group Progoti Samaj Unnayan Sangstha is supported by Proshika, which is experimenting in economic projects that will make cultural groups self-reliant. This project also offers employment and skills-training to local people. The investment was 300,000 taka, but it is a recent venture, and it is too early to judge its effectiveness. Designing economic survival models for cultural groups by Proshika takes a variety of forms: here, the experiment is high-tech, in Barisal it is forestry, in Khulna garments and hand-made goods. Abdur Rob does not want cultural groups to take loans and donations. 'We don't want to turn them into NGOs. They must find local support, use co-operative businesses to generate income. Cultural groups do not like to think of the market-place, but they have to find resources. Society is changing. There are no more rich patrons.'

A library has been set up in the name of the freedom fighters, which, its secretary says, is an anti-fundamentalist resource. One young man is collecting lore and stories of the ethnic communities in Satkhira and the nearby Sunderbans – the mangrove forests on the Bay of Bengal. Satkhira was an area of indigo-cultivation, forced on farmers by the British in the 1850s, to the neglect of their own food production. Here, labour was cheap, land could be requisitioned from farmers, and it was close to Calcutta. As farmers were unable to plant subsistence crops, their families starved. There were protests and uprisings, and in the 1860s many were killed.

The indigenous people are the Mund and Bono, jungle dwellers. 'Bono' means forest, and gives its name to Sunderban. The people worshipped a jungle goddess, Bonobibi, a deity of great antiquity, who was not ousted by Islam; many folksongs remain, and cultural events commemorate her. Only with the recent rise in fundamentalism and the incursions of the modern world is faith in her powers being destroyed. Every year a Bonobibi fair is held, where people offer gifts and request favours; a rare survival of a once universal animism.

This is a familiar story – the passing of the last vestiges of animism at the very moment when environmentalists are trying to rekindle a sense of awe and respect for all living things. Here was a practice, centred upon conservation of forests, rivers and earth. That the global market should be pushing this to extinction calls into question the sincerity of global pieties concerning environmental degradation.

The forests provided livelihood to fishing people, woodcutters and honey-collectors. The British ruined the culture by extracting revenue from non-cash societies, by the sombre art of making money from resources on which people had depended only for necessities.

The countryside is flat and wet; *pabla* trees – their hard wood is used for ploughs, household goods and construction – meet above our head. Suddenly we are at the end of a road, at right-angles to a riverbank. To the left, a rough stony road lined with wooden booths and shops; these back onto the turbid river. About half a kilometre away on the opposite bank, the olive-coloured fringe of the Sunderbans. The mangroves stand in the water, silent, primeval. In the foreground, the grey desolation of ruined prawn fields, former paddy-fields, destroyed by the brief profit-taking of prawn cultivation.

In the beginning, prawn ponds were profitable, and people were eager to make money, even though it was known from Thailand, the Philippines and elsewhere that the benefits of prawns are short-lived. Intensive prawn-farming proved a precarious business. Once they fail, the loss is total. The antibiotics and artificial feed pumped into the prawn fields cannot prevent all viruses from attacking the creatures, which then become deformed and unfit for consumption.

Around Satkhira natural prawns were cultivated for centuries. They remained in an untouched habitat, and were not the large profitable variety imported later. The rivers were rich in small prawns, so many poor people made a livelihood trawling for small shrimps and fish.

We came to a government rest-house beside a pond, the only source of fresh water in the neighbourhood. The rest-house is for use by officials from the Water Board. It shows no sign of having been recently occupied – a seeding of mouse-droppings, rusty piping in the bathroom, a trickle of brown water. The compound is set with newly-planted mahogany trees. It opens out on to the pond, where a few palms grow. Apart from mangroves, these are the only trees.

The desolation of prawns

Mr Asik-e-Elaki is waiting to tell his story. He had sixteen acres of paddy-land, but changed to prawn-farming.

> In 1995, we imported a fast-growing prawn from Thailand, because local prawns were scarce. We also had to import anti-biotics, pesticides and special feed. We had seen how Thailand and Malaysia were growing rich through prawns, so we decided to follow. But we did not think of the consequences. Once the salt water comes into your fields, it kills all the trees. Two years later, disease hit the prawns, and we lost money.

A stony embankment from the rest-house is surrounded by the grey mud paths and greenish water of abandoned prawn fields. On a spit of land in the middle of the river, a stretch of mangrove remains; everywhere else, the paradox of an aqueous aridity. We came to a concrete compound, with mud-floor sheds for packing the prawns, another shed for drying fish. In a third shed, the manager of this big prawn business lives and works.

This owner of this farm started in a small way in 1984 on 200 bighas of his own land. It was successful, so he leased 400 bighas from other farmers, paying 2,000 taka a bigha. He followed the Thai semi-intensive system. After recent losses, he has changed to semi-natural culture. Now he uses locally produced artificial feed and applies fertiliser with restraint. Intensive culture keeps hundreds of thousands of prawns in one small pond; semi-natural is restricted to a few thousand. The World Bank funded government banks giving loans in the so-called 'blue revolution' of aquaculture.

In the field we met Yusuf Ali, who was employed here from the beginning. He was dismissed after the failure of the intensive system, but was hired again after the change to 'semi-natural'. A shrewd man with a silvery beard and thin black hair, he wears an old shirt and blue *lunghi*. Grey mud has dried on his bare feet. He earns 1,800 taka a month, and does every job connected with prawns. If the water level falls, he adjusts it, if it overflows into neighbouring ponds, he drains it. He throws in new fry, maintains the embankments, keeps an eye on the health of the prawns, and guards them from thieves at night. There is a shortage of local prawn-larvae, so they buy from a hatchery in Chittagong. These produce small-fry ready for release into the ponds. The eggs are imported and only hatched in Bangladesh. Local breeds can supply no more than 20 per cent of the demand.

Yusuf estimates the present yield at one quarter of that under the intensive system. He is now very knowledgeable about all aspects of the business, and does work formerly carried out by several men.

He is landless. His father sold the family land during the famine of 1973. He lives 4 kilometres away. His four children all go to school. He does not want them to work in the prawn fields. He is here 24 hours a day, 18 of them on duty. 'This year there was only a small loss. Last year the loss was greater. In the early days, it was very profitable. Then the fish died from a viral infection – they change colour, their head is covered with spots, they fail to grow. In the good times, the owner invested in a fish factory. He sent his son to the USA for higher studies.' The prawns are washed, frozen and packaged, and then exported to Japan, America, Europe.

Yusuf Ali says that before the shrimps came all this was rice land – trees, plants, flowers, houses. In 1960, the government started environmental protection, because this is close to the Sunderbans. People came here to live. After 1983, they started to leave, as it became polluted.

Although his village is nearby, Mr Ali goes home only twice a month. He sleeps in the shed. Now – October – is the lean season. At peak times fifty or sixty people are employed; now only five or six remain. Four harvests between March and September have an overlapping cycle of three months. Mr Ali is now nursing the larvae in a small pond. In February he will transfer them to the big ponds, and in April the first crop will come. He does not eat prawns. 'They are so costly. In the market in Satkhira they are usually 450 taka a kilo (US$9); today they are 580 a kilo (US$11.50).' The traditional river-fishing community has been destroyed by prawns. 'They cannot make a living. The natural water-body has become saline, and in any case, the prawn-farmers prevented them from fishing in the river.'

On the grey embankment, the shadowless glare of October sun. Md. Manik Ghazi started shrimp culture in 1994. There were two years of good profits, then two years of heavy losses. He had 60 bighas of prawn fields. He started with high hopes, but now, he shrugs, only Allah knows. In the 1980s, he resisted prawn culture: he did not believe it could provide a lasting livelihood. In the end he joined them. Why?

Our houses and paddy-land were here. In the beginning we protected the sweet water against prawns, we protested at this change of our traditional life. Activists came to support us from outside. Then they went away, we could not stand alone. We were right to resist, but that is no use to us now. People should come back and start paddy again. It can be cleared – in the rain the water will become fresh again. I used to be a honey-collecter in the Sunderbans. I have fought Bengal tigers. I once rescued two men from a tiger. But the prawns have proved more deadly than tigers. The villages here all depended on the Sunderbans for fish, honey, wood.

The village of Pankhali is built of the same grey earth as the embankments; the dry mud walls are an emanation of the earth itself, rice-straw roofs, swept mud floors, smooth and cool; a few hardy trees in the yard, goats and chickens. But the green has gone from the landscape, a monochrome witness to the get-rich-quick and get-poor-quicker industry that has transformed it. People are bonded to a business that is destroying them.

Along the river, defiant patches of paddy remain. In the water, women and girls, wading to knee-depth, trawl long blue nylon nets behind them, looking for such small fish and shrimps as remain.

We came to a small shop, metal and wood, a shutter open to create shade for the wooden bench in front. Gazi Abul Basher Bulbashar, the owner, wears a T-shirt that says 'Great Man Lives For the Good of Society'. In front of his shop a wire mesh prevents birds from entering. The little shop supplies basic goods – scratched plastic jars of biscuits, cigarettes sold singly, bootlaces, lighters; plastic shopping-bags, bright yellow tennis balls, jars of *poori* (puffed rice), Love Candy; toothbrushes in transparent plastic, coloured hairbands, Lux soap, notebooks, mirrors, a stem of bananas. Mr Gazi owns 13 bighas of land. To the right of his shop, he has been cultivating prawns since 1985–86, and to the left only since 1994. It was profitable until three years ago. Since then there has been neither profit nor loss. 'This is the problem' – he shows a small pyramid-shaped mollusc:

This comes into the water, covers all the bottom, so the prawns cannot feed. It brings diseases also. May Allah help us all. Shrimps bring social problems – the very rich make a fortune in three or four years, then they do not care what happens. We have lost all our local produce, even fodder for the cattle is no longer available. Many human diseases have also come – gastric ulcers, dysentery, skin diseases. Cows do not give milk. There is only one pond now where the water is not salt.

Mr Gazi is unmarried in a family of nine – father, mother, four brothers, two sisters. He is a Kameel (in *madrasa* education, equivalent of an MA). He earns 70–75 taka a day in the shop. Other family members look after the prawns. Water salinity forces more people to give up paddy.

Ruined rural livelihoods

On our return to the guest-house, the farmers had prepared a meal. Others came with their stories. Krishna and Prafulla are paddy farmers, with 10 bighas and 3 bighas respectively. Their home is close to the shrimp-cultivation area. Two bighas of Krishna's land have been affected, and although Prafulla's is further off, he fears saline contamination will spread, as it has in many prawn-growing areas. 'It is not only the water that is spoiled. There is a shortage of fodder, the trees have died. Humans have been affected by diseases; cattle have died. We never wanted prawns in this area. We protested to local government when our land was damaged'. Local officials told the prawn farmers not to disturb the paddy, but it cannot be prevented. 'We organised and demonstrated against the prawns; we wrote to the district and central government. The government itself had acquired 500 acres for prawns, but when we protested, they stopped.' The unused land, embankments broken, lies quite useless.

'With the loss of traditional rice', says Krishna, 'we lost the fertility of the land, we lost sweet water, we lost the trees, the cattle. Birds no longer fly. All we have now to lose is our lives.' One of Krishna's sons is doing a BA degree. He hopes to work in government service, but his father says this is no consolation for the ruined tradition. I asked why so many young people no longer wanted to produce food. 'Educated people do not do this', they said. 'We were liberated, but we could not change our educational system. We should educate our children to produce rice, cattle, pulses, not to run after false gold of prawns.'

Three thin women sit at the table in front of us, poor, wraith-like, troubled. Mumtaz, Shajeeda and Fatima catch shrimps for the village market from the river. But since the river has been depleted for the prawn fields, their work is harder, the hours longer, the income smaller. They stand in water twelve hours a day. Before industrial prawn cultivation, they earned 100 taka a day. Prawns were plentiful. Now they are lucky to make 30. None of the women has land. Fatima's husband died 15 years ago. She is older than Mumtaz and Shajeeda, both of whom were abandoned by their husbands. Each has one child. To feed two people costs about 25 taka a day. Fatima stays on land belonging to her father; Mumtaz lives in a shelter on the roadside; Shajeeda lives on her grandfather's land. Fatima's daughter works with her; the others' children are too small to go into the river.

They spend the whole day in water, trailing the nets behind them. Over-fishing compels them to take even the small fry. No full-grown fish remain in this stretch of the river. Behind them, two girls, Jehanara and Anchara, hang their heads like dark flowers, arms delicate as young bamboo. They do not know their age, but appear 10 or 11. Even they remember earning 70 or 80 taka from prawn-catching in the river, but now they get 20–25 taka a day. They do not work every day, and Anchara goes to school. There is no other occupation for girls.

In the morning, they eat *pantha*, leftover rice diluted with water. At midday they eat hot rice with green leaves and dal, sometimes the same in the evening. Some days they eat rice with chilli and salt, the diet of the poorest of the poor. They may have a taste of fish once a week, a little salvaged from their pitiful day's catch. Never meat. Never fruit. Fatima used to earn well and saved money. She even gave some on loan, but it was never returned to her. If they or the children fall sick, they go to the fakir, who will say something from a religious book and give them *pani pora*, holy water. They do not know herbal medicine, and in any case all the herbs and plants have died.

The three women sit, backs bowed against the light. I cannot see their faces clearly, just the dark colours of their sarees. Their posture speaks of resignation, the choiceless acceptance of the poor.

Here, economic violence is made visible, brutal as a wound in their defenceless bodies. What a prolonged, profound torment it has been, to see the sustaining environment turn against them. What was benign has been made hostile by others. Also made tangible in their debilitated, wasting forms are the forces that drive people out of the rural economy. They will not be able to remain long at this work. They and their children will migrate to Khulna, find a house in a slum, become domestic servants. Here is the reality of 'economic change', 'urbanisation', all the neutral descriptions to protect the powerful against those driven to despair: the self-reliant robbed of function by somebody else's desire to get rich. Only when reduced to this level of need and hopelessness will they leave the home-place. Tomorrow's migrants, who will find insecure lodging in city slums, until moved on again by land-grabbers, *mastaans* in the pay of politicians and slum-lords. What they do not know is that they are at the start of an epic journey of continuous dispossession.They file out, a submissive frieze of defeat and servitude. Three young men take their place, Razak, 28, Gulam Mustafa, 18 and Adamali, who does not know his age, but looks about 15. All guard shrimp fields. Duty is continuous. Apart from a few hours' sleep, they watch over shrimps with a solicitude that few human beings receive; but human beings cannot command 580 taka a kilo in the market. In the season, for six or seven months, they have no day off. They earn 800 taka a month. They are fed by the owners, and eat diseased or deformed prawns. Razak is married. His home is half a kilometre from the prawn field, but he sees his family only twice a month. They are Muslim first, Bengali after.

As we went out into the dusk, the women were still wading in the river, a long blue net over their shoulder, trailing like some festive ceremonial train. Every few metres, they pause to see if they have trapped anything. Each has a stretch of 100 metres; when she reaches the limit, she turns and walks back. The tide has receded; as the water ebbs, a sparse green of wild rice is revealed in the muddy river-bed.

On the border

On the way back to Khulna we took a rocky byway through ancient stands of trees and small stone villages to the ruin of a Hindu temple, Jossushori Mandir. In the medieval Gohr period, this was the capital of Bengal, before it was overrun by Pathans and Moguls. Later, the Gohreshuri, the traditional lord of Ghor, came back to Satkhira with an army of supporters, took back the kingdom and erected the *mandir*.

Dating from the 16th or early 17th century, it is influenced by European church buildings on the sub-continent, with arcades and niches in the Portuguese style; and indeed, when the Gohreshuri returned, foreign mercenaries came too – Portuguese, Kukis and Pathans. They also built a church and a mosque, evidence of the religious pluralism of an older Bengal. The church has disappeared. The arcading and minarets of the temple reflect an eclectic mix of faiths. Part has now fallen down, but close to the main structure are the remains of a thick redbrick wall, with tiled pillars, in which a banyan tree has taken root. The traces of a gallery can be seen in the upper part of the wall, where court dignitaries assembled to listen to music; the brick is crumbling, and a vast raintree covers the ruin with its sombre canopy. That this deserted site should have preceded the swarming city of Calcutta as capital is a powerful reminder of the mutability of Bengal: not only the unpredictability of its invaders, its extraordinary ethnic mix, the interminable flux of land and water – everything in this country speaks of a capacity for metamorphosis.

Inside the temple, the priest guards the goddess among offerings of soft coconut, fruit, flowers, incense and an incongruous string of fairy-lights winking in the dark. Only thirty Hindu families remain here now. In an adjacent field, boys are playing football, splashing across its muddy surface, their shouts of exuberant life echoing off the ancient walls, the eternal triumphalism of the here-and-now over the past.

We are only 5 kilometres from the Indian border. It is late evening. We are to visit another cultural group. It is dark. There is mud on the path. There is a power failure. Again. We go into a brick building where candles provide the only light; a poor shabby place, where six or eight people are waiting. I immediately feel bad about my ill-humour, the more so since this is Semnagar, a place of vigorous fundamentalist activity, where the cultural groups and their celebration of Bengali heritage operate under constant threat. A young man plays the harmonium, another the *tabla*, while the singer tells of the longing for her native place of a young woman far from home. They perform and work simply for the love of it; to small audiences, for no reward, they live in fear of disruption and violence. Among the performers, a teacher, a student, a health worker, a small trader. It seems folk-tradition is upheld mainly by amateurs. It is a touching moment. They explain that the coming to power of the BJP in India has given a powerful impetus to the fundamentalist forces here: they are ground between the mill-wheels of two fundamentalisms.

The bomb blast

On the way to Dhaka, we stopped at the Jessore office of ADAB, the Association of Development Agencies in Bangladesh. Kamaruzzaman is its co-ordinator. Jessore was the site of a big bomb-blast in March 1999, aimed at a function organised by UDICHI, the cultural section of the now defunct Communist Party, and the best-known cultural organisation in Bangladesh. Ten people were killed. It is not clear whether the leadership of UDICHI was the target, or the foreign guests and performers, particularly those from India. Representatives had come from all over the world. UDICHI has outlived the political organisation that spawned it. Culture is the battleground. Here, this is no metaphor: it is a real war.

The bomb was placed in a field where an open-air performance was being held. It was midnight, and since the schedule was delayed, the foreign representatives were not on stage. Seven died on the spot, and three died later of their injuries; 150 others were injured, 30 seriously. Many lost an arm or a leg. No one claimed responsibility. Police and security forces are still working on it. Some *mastaans* were arrested, who said that the plot originated with the BNP. The aim was to make the country ungovernable and to precipitate elections. The BNP accused the Awami League of planting the bomb in order to discredit them. Proshika helped with rehabilitation of the survivors.

Local people were horrified by the carnage. 'They support the pro-people activities of UDICHI. Whatever the truth, there is no doubt extremists, fundamentalists and elements of the BNP are trying to destabilise the country, to create an outcry over law and order. Two fundamentalists were also arrested.' There are rumours that the Jessore police found training manuals that show links with the Taliban. 'If it is political opponents of the government, they are not thinking of the consequences of unleashing terrorism. If they make the country ungovernable, they will inherit the problems they have created.'

'The Left has been driven out of politics.' This is an extraordinary proposition. Mr Kamaruzzaman says that the last attempt to unite the Left was at the time when Sheikh Mujib formed the Bakshal Party 25 years ago. The Left has taken refuge in cultural organisation and NGOs.

I asked where hope was to come from in this bleak analysis. Mr

Kamaruzzaman said, 'Leftists in the Awami League, civil society and NGOs could create a Centrist alliance of Bangali nationalists which might reclaim decency for politics.' Why was Jessore the site of the atrocity in 1999 and not Dhaka?

They targeted Jessore, because this was the twelfth national conference, with many foreigners present. From this border town, miscreants can quickly cross to safety. The extremist arrested runs a smuggling syndicate. Those who planned it chose a smuggler with no ideological grounding, although he does have a political base. This gang also had good relations with the BNP local district committee. Hassan named a BNP leader in Jessore as behind the plot. This has divided the BNP. One group is now keeping quiet, but the supporters of the extremist named are raising their voices, holding processions, calling *hartals* to deny their involvement.

Some people hurt by the bomb were performers, some UDICHI personnel, but most were ordinary people in the audience – a ferrywala, a blacksmith, a tea-stall owner, a cigarette seller. The flower-sellers of Jessore went on strike in protest. Small businesses closed down and called a big gathering; small traders all over the country held demonstrations. After the bomb, we continued the programme for seven days to show we would not be deterred.

We went to the UDICHI office – an old zamindar building, another piece of elegant Raj decay. It had been the house of a prominent Muslim family, followers of Gandhi, who used to stay here on his tours of Bengal. UDICHI celebrates both traditional and modern popular Bengali culture. Shaheed Uzaman, District Secretary, says that after the blast, tens of thousands of people protested spontaneously.

The perpetrators defeated their own aims. Even the flower-sellers said they felt shame to sell flowers in a city where such evil things happen. The people know who did this. They know UDICHI and what it stands for, and they also know who our enemies are. The bombers may achieve a brief breakdown of law and order. The important thing now is the trial. Of course, the Court can also be corrupt. Those arrested told the police who are the patrons of this occurrence. The behaviour of those patrons is now bizarre – they are publishing criticisms of UDICHI and its activities in the papers. They are denouncing the supporters of Bangali culture. They talk of 'foreign support', but they don't mean the US or UK, they mean India – as though Bangali culture were an Indian plot.

We walked out to the spot where the bomb had been planted, under a banyan tree in the field close to the town hall; a space among decaying urban structures from the Raj – the rest-house that is now a godown, the ruined villas with their effloresence of mildew. 'After liberation,' says Shaheed Uzzaman, 'the first public meeting of free Bangladesh was held here in Jessore, as the leaders returned from India. The Pakistani army retreated through Jessore and Khulna. Now we are once more under attack from those same defeated forces.'

The poorest women

Before the ferry at Daulatdia, we stopped at an unpretentious yellow-painted bungalow surrounded by a wooden-pillared verandah. This is KKS, an NGO working with women of the nearby brothel township.

The town has been here more than a century. A steamer-station and railway-junction in British times, it was a loading point for jute, *hilsha* fish, *gur*, and a major crossing for travellers. Women came to service British military and civilians. Many working here now are the children of former sex-workers. Some are trafficked from the rural areas. Abandoned wives sometimes find refuge and livelihood here. The clients are truck- and bus-drivers, customs and police officers.

Fakir Abujjabbar, a former teacher, is director of KKS. A former freedom fighter, he donated some of his ancestral land for the building. Having always lived here, he felt for the women and children in the town with its 1,800 sex-workers. 'This was once forest, with little agriculture, and was always subject to river erosion and flooding.'

In this season the river is low; an indeterminate shore of mud, stretches of silty water, spits of land, provisional islands. A muddy crust glitters with silica as the sun dries out the river-bed. Because of the heavy erosion on both sides of the Padma, new bamboo huts have been built by NGOs for those whose homes have been washed away. On both sides, the river devours more earth every year. This has shifted the railway and steamer station several hundred metres from where they were in British times, when British soldiers, railway employees and revenue collectors used the women in the brothels.

93

Fakir Abujjabbar also works with some of the poorest women in the villages of those evicted by river erosion. On the other side of the river, the gravitational pull of Dhaka is felt, but here, it is a world away. The thin, malnourished bodies of the women themselves seem to have been half eroded by the river, by time, by want, by work. They are being trained to sew baby-clothes and bedsheets in the hope that this may earn them an extra 20 taka a day, enough to lift them and their children out of hunger – that other life-eroding river that sweeps through this country. Half the women in the room have been ousted by river erosion; four are abandoned, two widowed and six unmarried because their families cannot afford the minimum dowry of 5,000 taka. It costs 40 taka a day to feed three people; few can afford it. Their husbands are day-labourers on the ferry-*ghat*, loading and unloading, selling fruit, sweets, *bidis* (local cigarettes), water, snacks. They earn 50 taka a day. The women, haunted, shy, cover their faces with their sarees and speak in voices muted by the fabric. They are nothing like the self-confident women of Proshika, or even the sex-workers we met later.

Their children go to school in a building provided by Proshika. We met 250 of them: a crowded, sweltering tin hut with wooden shutters. They attend in three shifts. Many are working – carrying luggage, serving in hotels, selling water and bananas. The school was intended for the children of labourers on the *ghat*, but since there is no other primary school in the village, farmers and field labourers also send their children here. Each class contains over 80 children.

KKS runs a secondary school for children whose mothers are mainly sex-workers. They lead a life apart, although Fakir Abujjabbar has made strenuous efforts to unite villagers and sex-workers. 'Fundamentalists say, "Why do you educate their children?" We organised a meeting of mothers, sex-workers and villagers. The children have no prejudice – through them we have been able to establish understanding. We want to give girls the opportunity not to follow their mothers; many of course do. Many boys migrate out of shame as soon as they are old enough. Most villagers now accept the sex-workers, but there is pressure from fundamentalists to have the women evicted.'

Fakir Abujjabbar has opened a refuge for 25 girls aged 5–14, daughters of sex-workers. A new building, 200 metres from the road,

94

reached by a narrow causeway: a clean white-painted house, bunk beds in the sleeping quarters; a dining room; an enclosed metal verandah painted white and cinnamon. The names of the little girls – Lucky, Sweetie – evoke the occupation of their mothers. Parents pay 600 taka a month, and meet their children every four weeks. Most do not want their girls to follow them; but this is easier said than done.

The brothel town

We went to the little settlement given over entirely to sex. In view of public reticence on sexual matters in Bangladesh, this is a curious place. The houses have been recently rebuilt of tin. The late afternoon sun inflames the metal, so that even the appearance of the town takes on the lurid colour of shame. KKS has helped organise the women in a *muktisamiti*, offering classes on health care, general education and literacy. The women have become more assertive, ready to resist exploitation and abuse by local people, government, police and clients. *Mastaans* remain constant visitors, extorting money, although they have become less coercive. Parveen says, 'The worst problem is for older women who become sick, cannot work and are helpless.'

The township is a true monoculture: tin and sex. Narrow pathways between the houses open onto swept mud squares, where sarees blow in the wind, balloons of crimson and lime-green. Hens, ducks, cockerels with bronze and green feathers, red combs, saffron-coloured claws. A glimpse inside of beds covered with a bamboo mat, a curtain of coloured beads. The women are heavily made up, in accordance with expectations of symbolic abandon – rouge, shiny lipstick, heavy eye-shadow, bright colours, jewellery, loose black hair.

Parveen is a 'peer educator', a role she is pleased to assume since, at 40, her days as a sex-worker are finished. The interior of her house is painted eau de Nil. A jute sack on the floor encourages people to remove their shoes. There is a rusting metal cage with cooking utensils, a blue metal cupboard for valuables. Clothes hang on plastic hangers. A glass-fronted cupboard with glass trinkets given by admirers long ago, a couple of empty whisky bottles, Bell's and Teacher's. On the broad bed a thin mattress, a white and green cover, with bright crimson and gold pillows against a thick bolster. A pink mosquito net is tied by long tapes to nails in the wall.

Parveen is a big woman with an intelligent, handsome face. She

95

wants a different function from that open to former sex-workers, who become owners of brothels or domestic labour in them. Parveen says, 'Most clients do not consider us human beings. They use us and leave as fast as they can. We have no bargaining power, because there is no unity. 750 women are in the *samiti*, but over 1,000 have not joined.'

She sits cross-legged on the bed. The sun through the window-grille bronzes her face, her blue-black hair. She left her parents and came here 17 years ago. She was married, but her brutal husband – it was his fourth marriage – left her. Her child is being educated outside.

Parveen says, 'When I was abandoned, I tried to survive alone, I looked to people in the village for help. But men approached me illegally. I knew this place, and I thought I would feel better here. Relatives and guardians of women like the money they send, but do not want to know where it comes from.'

A sex-worker's story

Morjina sat listening. She is from a landless family, and after marriage, her husband demanded more dowry, which they could not give. He took a second wife. Morjina stayed with him for eight years and, though neglected, she tried to make herself agreeable to the new wife.

> I had a baby and when I was carrying another, I knew I could not live with him. I returned to my father's house. I worked as a domestic servant. In the village, young men molested me, older people harassed me. I could not exist there. One man promised to look after me, but he only used me. I left him and went to a woman who I thought would be kinder. But, sad for me, I was sold by her to a brothel in Shirazganj near Jamuna Bridge. That town was eroded by the river, so I came here. That was 1988.

Morjina wears a pale green saree and blue blouse, long gold-plated earrings. She has a broad melancholy face. 'My parents could not save me. I respect them, and the help I have given has provided them with prestige. I cannot tell them the truth. I say I am sewing in a garments factory.' Morjina says many clients promised to marry her but none did. 'If I told you my story it would be sad, a thousand pages long. Now I know it is hopeless. We have no future. How shall we live?'

Parveen's savings are now her only source of income. 'Clients do not come to me now. Beautiful young girls may earn 2,000 taka a day. Most women have no savings. Older women have no regular earnings. Boys promise the young ones marriage. They spend money on them, but in the end they do nothing. There is no profit in this life. No one supports sex-workers. The rich do not come here, only working men.'

Some older women invested prudently while they were working, and now own houses. Morjina says when you are young, you think life will go on. Only when health is lost, you know you have been living an illusion. Parveen has a regular check-up at the KKS clinic. 'If we have a sexually transmitted disease, we will be treated. Anything more serious, we go to hospital in Dhaka.'

Women manage the industry in the town, but real power lies with the 15 or 20 families who own the land. Everyone pays them in the end, even the house-owners. 'When there is a *hartal*, clients do not come, there is no transport. They lose their earnings, and when they return they cannot afford to pay us. There are worse things than sex – politics for instance, acid-throwing. Society is cruel. There is no justice.'

We came out of the town and drank tea on the edge of a field where boys were playing football. Another Morjina, a younger woman, spoke to us. 'I was betrayed by a rich man. He promised me everything, and then abandoned me. That is why I came here. This was my destiny'.

The wind clatters in the palms. The rusty railway line to Kustia and Jessore branches away at the Daulatdia junction. On an ornate grave by the roadside, a green shrub grows through a crack in the stone. A vast car-park, where Ashok Leyland and Bedford trucks are parked alongside Tata, Hino and Mitsubishi buses. Lights are coming on in the little town – women's services are in demand around the clock.

The traditional singer

The ferry is packed; lorries overloaded with cattle, bananas, paddy, bamboo. A violet sky like spilt wine in the river. On the passenger-deck, an old man sits cross-legged on a red plastic seat. He wears an old blue *lunghi*, a striped shirt ribbed with grime. He plays traditional Bengali songs for the entertainment of passengers. He holds a *dothara*, a wood and leather instrument with two metal strings which he plucks with a plectrum of buffalo-horn. He sings a Sufi devotional song by Lalon, an intense plaintive melody, which attracts a crowd.

The man's name is Gazi Sikader, a cultivator whose land was eaten by the river. He was taught to sing as a child by a local singer, simply 'for the love of music'. He sings another song by Lalon, poignant and profound, about the triumph of humanity over differences of religion, race and culture. People clap gently to the rhythm.

One of his sons is a labourer, one a rickshaw-puller, a third a construction worker. He himself earns 100 taka a day on the ferry. The attention of passengers is captured by half-remembered traditional airs; they pause – a living example of Bengali culture, sweet, authentic, but now without function, earning a few taka on the river. His family were once prosperous; he saw them degraded through industrial labour. They do not sing. There is bitterness in the dying music of Bengal.

On the road to Dhaka, an overturned truck, wheels spinning in the air. Further on, a bus has crashed into a cycle-van carrying three people. Their bodies are laid out on the grass: two poor women and a man, who will not reach their destination, their families, their children. Victims of development. Human sacrifice. A crowd gathers. The bus has a cobweb of cracked glass in its broad windscreen.

The zamindari system

DR FARUQUE:

My family were originally zamindars, but the system was reformed after Partition, and my father's land had gone. Memories of feudal culture lingered into my childhood. They left a bad taste – coercive tax collection, the use of force, the looking down upon others.

The system, set up in 1793, was called the Permanent Settlement. Before that, there were no permanent tax collectors, although taxes were collected by the government of the Emperor. The British created a form of privatisation: they gave the duty of collecting taxes to the zamindars. The zamindars had to pay a certain amount to the government; and if they could do that, they were granted it in perpetuity, unless the British cancelled it. Hence the term 'permanent settlement'. A zamindar was contracted to raise say, one lakh taka, and anything above that he kept. He had every incentive to raise two lakh or more, so he could keep half for himself. The theory was very nice. In fact, it was highly coercive. There was much sub-feudation: a zamindar would take an area for one lakh taka, and then divide it between 6 or 7 sub-contractors by district, and hierarchically. Some historians say they collected seven times more than the tax demanded by the British. You can imagine the brutalities that occurred.

This is how the British promoted a class, not of entrepreneurs, but of exploiters. The theory was that zamindars would invest and improve lands and agriculture. They didn't. They found it easier and less risky to extract rather than invest. Many zamindars lived in Calcutta, and encouraged the sub-feudation system, which made life miserable for the peasantry. Physical oppression, cultural domination, humiliation – all that goes with feudal culture. Those people developed an aversion to physical labour. They became the *bhadra lok* – the gentry – who did not soil their hands with labour but used the fruits of the labour of others, while the *choto lok,* who labour and create wealth, are denied the fruits of it. That psychic frame still permeates our society.

I struggled to reject all that. Being a non-conformist, I saw the ugliness and injustice of it. I never accepted without question anything I was told. I am a sceptic, but also an optimist. While rejecting bad ideas and practices, I am also aware of the possibilities of improvement, of creating a better society. If you are unwilling to accept, you will be in confrontation with received pieties and traditional ideas. That is why I was a rebel. This was not appreciated, particularly my position on religion. They said, 'Why do you have to argue with this?' 'Why must you quarrel with our society?' They said, 'We have improved so many things.' Yes, but they could be better still.

I wanted to understand why some societies are dynamic, capable of change, while others remain static. In Europe, at the time of the Renaissance, many people questioned everything, rejected ideas of religion and feudal society. You progress by logic, humanistic philosophy, scientific development and so on. You cannot develop if you accept injustices and values inherited thoughtlessly from the past.

The malignancy of the fatwa

Resisting the modernised feudal mentality and its alliance with contemporary fundamentalism is central in the work of Proshika.

This sometimes comes to open conflict. The most direct challenge came in Brahmanbaria, where fundamentalists declared *fatwa* against Dr Faruque, and threatened to kill him anywhere in Bangladesh.

I met Aksir Chowdhury, lawyer and human rights activist, who fled his native Brahmanbaria under similar threats. He was given refuge in the Bar Council Rest House, close to the High Court in Dhaka; a single room on the fourth floor, an austere cell-like place – a bed, a desk and a chair. He loathes the violence of fundamentalists. 'They don't attack drinking, gambling, money-lending, usury or prostitution – they attack NGOs, and Hindus. Money is sanctified when it is dedicated to Islam, no matter what indecency occurs in making it.'

Mr Chowdhury says,

> Before Partition, zamindars in Brahmanbaria were Hindus, the *ryots* (peasants) Muslim. Culturally, economically, Muslims were oppressed. After the war, Bangladesh had no chance to build society in the spirit of liberation. We changed violently in 1975; and when that ended, we were delivered to globalisation and big money. Some poor people became rich from smuggling or dishonest contracts. Money came from the Gulf for mosques and *madrasas*, and remittances from workers. An area that had been poor became rich suddenly. Those people became pious. This encouraged the fundamentalists, who saw who rehabilitated themselves through the illegally rich, who want to become respectable, to cleanse dirty money.
>
> Working at grass-roots level, I have no funds, no organisation. The fundamentalists know I am supported by NGOs, and assume I am atheist or a Christian. I was there when they threatened Dr Faruque. When I gave a statement to the press on what happened, their response was 'Catch him and hang him.' My family could no longer stay in our home. The authorities made no attempt to investigate. I informed the press, District Commissioner, police. No one responded.
>
> The alliance of dirty money with fundamentalism is very dangerous. The rich became wealthy without struggle, without earning, without education. Liberalisation and polluted capitalism swept away all restraint, and lawless capitalism joined with an unresolved feudalism.
>
> Bangali Muslims were peasants; and when they become rich,

they follow a path indicated by fundamentalists – delayed revenge against Hindus. People living high on remittances buy consumer goods, build houses. They do not know what to do with all their money. They may have a son in the US or the Gulf, but it is still a feudal sensibility. They have no commitment to society. The money is from Saudi or USA, relatives feel proud and spend conspicuously to show their new status. There is no democratic or progressive idea. A new generation is polluted by the corrupt origin of the parents' money. They have been English-medium educated, but it is mechanistic; tuitions, private lessons, rote learning. There is no cultural gap between the educated and the poor. Their empty education is the hinterland of fundamentalism. 'What car has your father bought?' is their concern. There is an alliance between sham piety and Western consumerism – the most malignant forces fighting our Bangali tradition are joined in their efforts to destroy us.

The meaning of secularism
This echoed a conversation I had with Dr Faruque in Koitta, where he insisted that to be secular does not mean to be anti-religion.

DR FARUQUE:

Secularism means only that religion is not allowed to interfere in public life, that it is not used to further the dominance of one section of the citizens over another, or to make laws that discriminate against women. That is secularism. But an individual is free to worship and to practise whatever she or he wants to.

There is no conflict between religion and materialism. People think fundamentalism is a reaction to consumerism, but I do not think so. In fact, religion promotes it. Where do religious leaders oppose the economically powerful? They act on their behalf. I asked a religious leader why he didn't issue a *fatwa* against dish antennae, which allow the propagation of anti-Islamic images and ideas. He said, 'I can't, because it would affect the rich.'

Consumerism is also promoted through the dowry-system, because dowry goods are radio, TV, motor-cycles; and dowry is negotiated through the religious process. So there is little conflict between materialism and fundamentalism. The oppressors of women have often been trained and promoted by the West – look at the consequences of Western support for fundamentalists in

Afghanistan and Pakistan. Nor do the oil-rich Gulf powers, which claim to be Islamic, show much restraint in self-indulgence in their palaces, cars and luxurious life.

I was influenced by Einstein's ideas on religion. He distinguishes three kinds. One he calls magical religion, where people are afraid of the forces of nature, and must appease them. The next stage is manipulative religion, with hierarchies of class and privilege. This is at the service of state power or privileged classes – religion for social control. The third is spiritual or cosmic religion: this meets the need of human beings for connectedness with nature and environment. This must be explored by the individual, without the mediation of a priest.

That is a basic human need; it may end up believing in a Creator or not, but it seeks the meaning of life. In that sense, I believe Buddhism is a more cosmic religion. It places responsibility upon deeds and actions rather than prayers. The good that comes is a result of your own good deeds. The sacrifice you make is not goats and cows but your ego. This demolition of ego brings you closer to Truth, although the Buddha does not say there is absolute Truth. He speaks of the Middle Path, between extremes: in the middle, you are closest to truth. That kind of religion cannot harm others. But magical religion, manipulative religion – these are harmful. Individuals must search for their own spiritual liberation, find that interconnectedness.

This is inhibited by consumerism. Consumerism is promotion par excellence of the individual ego for private profit. Everything is private. That is falsehood, especially in a globalised society – scores of millions of people interact, organise the economy. To say everything is personal is absurd, this concentration on the individual, isolated and atomised. The role of collective endeavour is eliminated. Marx pointed out this contradiction. Society has always ordered its productive activities jointly, collectively. It cannot be an individual thing. But the profit and accumulation are private. This is magnified by globalisation. And private profit translates into private consumption; in the political field, into individualism. Politics promotes this egotistic individualism, which is another falsehood. In my opinion, anything false will have to disappear. It will not disappear by itself. It is up to us now living in the world to change it. Actions – political, social, developmental – have to be taken. We should not despair. The world is as we have made it.

The destructiveness of the fundamentalists

As we drove towards Brahmanbaria, the mango trees along the roadside were in flower. The pale spindles of their inconspicuous blossoms filled the air with the sweet *mowghanda*, a scent of honey which anticipates the savour of the fruits to come.

A Proshika office was destroyed in December 1998. Mr Ali Azham Bhuiyan offered accommodation on the ground floor of his ancestral home. This is in a quiet compound, shaded by coconut palms, jack-fruit and mango trees. A peaceable place on a fine Saturday afternoon, the town somnolent beneath a tepid sun. There are two Hindu temples nearby, a school playground surrounded by an ochre weathered stone wall. Mr Bhuiyan lives with his family in the two upper storeys of the old zamindar's house.

Destruction of property was not the only problem of fundamentalist activity in Brahmanbaria. Here, we met Mr Giashuddin, from Proshika in Dhaka, who was sorting out the finances of the area. Mr Giashuddin is a retired banker, now working full time for Proshika. The violence of the past months also disrupted the finances and loans here.

Disturbances took place late in 1998, and when the fundamentalists started trouble, the work of all NGOs was halted, field workers were harassed, especially women. In November 1999, we filed a suit against them; the District Commissioner and Superintendent of Police, who had done nothing to stop the excesses of fundamentalists, were transferred. New senior personnel were appointed. They were more impartial, but even they did not seem to understand right from wrong. I convinced them that the fundamentalists were disrupting our lawful business. I said, 'There can be no progress or prosperity until women are working equally with men.' The fundamentalists want women to remain ignorant and illiterate. We were giving modern ideas, informing them of their rights. The new DC and SP understood this is in the interests of economic development, and they promised to see we could go about our work unhindered.

We have 1,100 primary groups here, which reach over one

lakh people. When the extremists made problems in 1998–99, our workers could not go to the villages. We lost contact with some groups. It was felt Proshika could not work here, which damaged our credibility. The programmes were interrupted. It will take a year to restore our work.

Proshika started here in 1982. Even after 17 years, our work was so easily disrupted. *Madrasa* students and teachers came with sticks and cocktails, our people were taken unawares. It became a question of government authority. This is also a border area with India – another stimulus to the spread of fundamentalism.

The Awami League politician
I went upstairs with Advocate Ali Azam Bhuiyan. His cool tiled drawing-room looks on to green tree-tops. He recalls the death of Sheikh Mujib.

After his death, the miscreants chose Mushtaq, a member of the Awami League High Command. He was part of the conspiracy. Although the plot involved only a handful of army people, the leaders of the League failed to forestall it. There was an internal clash because Mujib had given preference to freedom fighters.

Zia ur-Rahman was a freedom fighter no doubt. But he was ambitious, his real motives and feelings were obscure. When he came to power, he exploited majority Muslim sentiment. This town had been 60 per cent Hindu. Their departure opened the way to extremists. During the British time, the Hindus became wealthy, many were money-lenders; they took advantage of the chance for education. They became influential in government service, which the Muslims did not.

The Hindus were exploiters. Muslims feared with Independence they would be a permanent minority in India. That is why we were in favour of Pakistan. After Partition, Jinnah spoke in favour of secularism: 'From today we are all Pakistanis', he said, 'there is no difference between Hindu, Christian and Muslim.' But when Jinnah came here in 1948, he said Urdu alone must be the state language of Pakistan. A cultural revolt came when they said Bangla is the language of Hindus, not Muslims. Ayub Khan abrogated the Constitution and imposed martial law from 1958 until 1969. Then Yahya Khan came in, and held the election of

1970. He was confident the Muslim League would win most seats in West Pakistan, and enough in the East to ensure a majority. Of the 162 seats in East Pakistan, only two failed to go to the Awami League. In that election, I got 98,000 votes, and my nearest rival 5,000. Religious parties were routed. It was the best time of my life.

People suffered after liberation, but they still supported Mujib. I was close to him in 1948, when he was a student leader. He knew even the village-level members of the party. After 1975, the Awami League was banned for two years and re-formed in 1977.

Zia tried to poach me for the BNP. I would not. I have not changed. In our country, the anti-liberation forces shelter behind fundamentalism. Many mullahs are half-educated, they do not know their own religion, because in the hands of a true Muslim, the life, property and honour of other religious-minded people are safe. No true Muslim can kill, burn houses or dishonour others; this is not the teaching of our Prophet.

When Dr Faruque came, there was an anti-fundamentalist procession. Rumour-mongers spread stories that the police had killed four *maulvis* (religious leaders), and said we must go in numbers. Hundreds came from village *madrasas* and demanded a ban on NGOs. *Madrasas* were saying NGOs are anti-Islamic. They gave an ultimatum – all NGO offices must close and take down their signboards. Many did so. I would not take down the Proshika signboard. I have known some of the *maulvis* for 30 or 40 years. They called me, and I abused them by telephone. Of course they disavowed the mob they had created, saying these were miscreants and arsonists, nothing to do with them. They have now back-tracked, but say if anything is done contrary to Islam, they will set it right. They say they are not opposed to service for humanity, but they still don't want women to come out. We said women serve in government offices, why can they not do so here?'

The consciousness of the poor

Two Proshika group leaders told us their story. As we spoke, the lights failed repeatedly. Candles were lit. In the darkness, orange flames lit up from below the faces of people in the room; moths and mosquitoes wove their tangled skeins around the candle; shadows moved on the walls. Everything added to the sense of darkness and gloom.

Firoze Mir and Jehanara were both involved in the resistance. Firoze, now 70, has been organising since 1978. Jehanara joined Proshika in 1983. Firoze was organising before Proshika came.

> We knew that without unity, the poor would not survive. In our society, the rich dispense justice and are united. The poor quarrel and do not receive justice. We decided to create justice for ourselves. Proshika confirmed what we knew and we were happy to move with them. When I was young, we could not bargain for wages, we accepted whatever the landlords gave us. My parents gave little importance to education. My five sons and three daughters will all be educated. I was working in the agricultural field by the age of 10 or 11. After my father's death, our joint family separated, I got only a small piece of land. I had no alternative but to become a rickshaw-driver.
>
> I tried to form a trade union among rickshaw-drivers. A group of us bought 10 rickshaws. We became owner/drivers, so we should not pay daily rent to the owners. With Proshika, we started saving and formed a group to get credit. We also had training in leadership, and we deepened our understanding of social relations. We saved one lakh taka. We organised ourselves, but Proshika gave us education.

Jehanara is 40. Her father died when she was six months old, leaving five children.

> He was landless, and made a living as a vendor. After his death, we suffered hunger. My mother struggled. She worked as cleaner in a hospital, which provided a small income. I was married at 13. My husband was a textile worker, also landless. By the time I was 15, I was saving in the traditional way – every time I cooked rice, I saved a handful in a pot. After 15 days I would sell it, and save the cash. My husband's wages were low. Within three years, I had enough to fatten a cow for Eid-ul-Azah. With that money, I leased land as a sharecropper. I got three and a half maunds of rice as capital. I sold it and took another lease. When I had saved 15,000 taka, I bought a piece of land. I have five daughters and three sons. One boy has taken his degree; two boys and one girl have passed SSC.

I went to village school long enough to write my name and read the Koran. Proshika inspired me to join a group. I later organised many groups. I was educated by Proshika. That is why the fundamentalists attacked me. They tried to burn my house, and declared I could not stay here in my own society. They told my son to break my relationship with Proshika, or he would not be allowed in the mosque.

On 7 December 1998, *madrasa* students and teachers attacked and beat me. They hit me with *lathis* and threw stones. They tried to persuade my daughter's husband to divorce her. They threatened to burn his house if he refused. A group of women convinced him this was not Islamic behaviour. The whole group sat in the house. We collected stones: if anyone came to burn the house, we would cry out, and neighbours would throw stones at the tormentors. We put our loan books and registers in a safe place. The fundamentalists closed the school for a few days. Then it started again. They attacked, but could not prevent work from going on. The full programme is now restored.

Our group had benefited from credit for many years, returning the money and taking new loans. The fundamentalists tried to get group members not to return the money. Some listened to them.

When the fundamentalists heard that criminal cases had been filed against them, they feared arrest and punishment. They approached the people, saying if you do not disturb us we will not disturb you. Proshika suspended the cases, as long as they do not stop its work.

Jehanara now has two bighas of land. Her face softens as she tells the story of her eldest daughter. 'She is very beautiful; wherever she went, young men disturbed her. Even going to school was a risk; on the road she could not go unmolested. To avoid this I gave her in marriage. Now she is suffering. She became ill because she was married so young. I waited till my second daughter was 17. I want my children to have the education I never had. If the poor unite, they can make the government, since they are by far the majority.'

Firoze says that fundamentalism misuses religion for political purposes. 'Religion is honesty and honesty religion.' Jehanara says, 'To keep women in the house is not religion. This *fatwa* exploits poor women – *fatwas* are not issued against rich women. When people pray, they may do so as Muslim, Hindu, Christian, but when they are in the fields, do not men and women of all religions work together? They do not ask us our religion when they want the sweat and labour of our bodies.'

Firoze and Jehanara are able, intelligent people. Both had improved their lives before Proshika came to the area, although Proshika deepened and extended their emancipation. Without organisation, some people will always struggle against disadvantage and oppression. It is important not to claim too much for NGOs. They serve as focus for collective action. They don't make the people; they simply make them more confident in their work for social and economic advancement.

Memories of Liberation II

Later, I spoke by candlelight with Mr Harun, Commander of Brahmanbaria during the Liberation War.

> I was 17, not at all political. I knew that Bangalis were exploited. When the Pakistani army came here, they abused Bangali women. I recognised the truth in Mujib's speeches that we were exploited by West Pakistan.
>
> I was trained in the Pakistani Cadet Force. After the 1971 crackdown, our Bangali instructor gave us secret instruction in guerrilla warfare, because it was clear that we would have to fight Pakistan for our soil. About 30 or 40 of us decided to join the *Muktibahini* (liberation army). We withdrew to the Indian border, from where we made guerrilla attacks. Then in November we came into the front line. Three days and four nights of continuous fighting. Suddenly the enemy stopped replying to our fire. We thought they had vanished, but it was a Pakistani strategy to encourage the Indians to advance. Many were killed and injured. The Indians eventually overran the Pakistani position. This was the biggest defeat of the Pakistanis. Tens of thousands of people came from the villages, with armfuls of flowers, which they gave to the fighters; they wept tears of joy and relief.
>
> It was the most exciting moment of my life; never to be repeated. As we marched to Jagdishpur, we heard complaints against collaborators who had snatched girls for the enjoyment of Pakistani soldiers. They had seized property, stolen cattle, burned

houses. One man was accused constantly. He was called and judgment given by the army court. He was sentenced to dig his own grave and be buried alive. Many thousands came. The emotion against him was strong.

I thought after liberation it would be like the Garden of Eden. But the reality was crisis – food, clothing, shelter, everything was lacking. It was a bitter time. I had not fought for personal gain – I was happy to see our country and people free. But when I saw the condition they were in, how could I be happy?

After a few years, it was as though the Pakistani army had come again. We were ruled by a junta. Pakistani culture was imposed. Our big mistake was to release too many collaborators. We should not have done so. Most lived to continue their mischief. The defeat of collaboration on the soil of Bengal – that will be my life's achievement; the fundamentalists and the anti-liberation forces are more united than we. They are strong, but not a majority. The young are confused by two decades of anti-liberation people in power. Older people have grown weary and demoralised. I feel for the freedom fighters – 30 years on, many are unrecognised, their families beg; they have no health care, their children no education. If this government does not look after them, no more patriotic people will be born on this soil.

Meeting the fundamentalists

It was not easy to meet fundamentalists. They will not speak to foreigners or anyone associated with NGOs. We went through a chain of intermediaries – local administration, journalists and go-betweens. We waited and sat. An appointment was made and broken. At last, we were led to a small, decrepit printer's shop close to the mosque, with piles of violet and blue-stained metal letters, pressed into a wooden frame for printing. Two desks at the front of the shop, cob-webby frames hanging from the ceiling, a cracked concrete floor, ancient curling calendars on the wall; a cumbersome machine like an archaic mangle in the gloom at the back, ancient presses, piles of flimsy smudgy papers. A flickering strip-light illuminated the sombre interior.

After *namaz* (prayers), a group of men came out of the mosque; topi, white robes, beards. They gathered around the desk where I was sitting, twenty or thirty men, young and old, some voluble, others suspicious. The lights failed. Candles were brought. The scene was like a nineteenth-century painting, an allegory of Wisdom Conferring, or perhaps a secret conclave of revolutionaries. Somebody warns that Westerners cannot be trusted. We discuss 'brotherhood'. Sisters are not mentioned.

If we live according to the rules of Allah and his Prophet, we shall not face poverty or violence. We are not in the way of Islam, that is why our country is troubled. At the time of the Prophet, it was proved that society can run peacefully if it follows the philosophy and rules of Islam. If people heed Islam they will give up evil work. Religious education has been lost. The West neglects religion, yet it tells us how to behave. They rule over us because we are poor. But our mind does not accept their domination. They take advantage of weakness. The West degrades women. In the West, the family is being destroyed. There is no happiness in spite of their wealth.

The teachings of the Koran are universal, for all human beings. Islam gave us the concept of humanity and brotherhood. Islam does not hate other religions, it wants us to live with others. We are first human, then religious beings. To be a full human being you must accept Islam. We are working for an Islamic state. Those who teach secularism are our enemies, because they are enemies of religion. There is no model of an Islamic society in the world. We in Bangladesh have our warmth of heart. We are emotional. The people of the West are cold.

The greatest virtue of Islam is the fear of Allah.

One young man tried to convert me, urging me to recognise the truth that alone belongs to Islam; intense, earnest, passionate; in the candle-light, dust and a silvery spray from his words appear like a materialisation of faith.

The resurgence of communalism

DR FARUQUE:

Communalism governed the making of Pakistan. The British promoted communalism through the zamindari system. Hindu zamindars were established in Muslim areas, and Muslim zamindars in Hindu areas; so of course, hatred for the zamindars took on a communal aspect. This was the British divide-and-rule policy. The Muslims came to feel they had no future in India – wrongly in my view, but that was the psyche of the time. In 1905, the British had attempted to partition Bengal – they had to reverse it within a few years, because the Bangali sentiments of the people were too strong.

The Muslims of East Bengal saw that with Partition they would get their own foraging-ground. The Hindus made great strides in education under the British, but Muslims were slow to take advantage of modern education. The Muslim elite wanted to catch up with the Hindus, and they wanted an uncompetitive field, irrespective of the wishes of the peasantry or common people. That is why, later, the people of East Pakistan came to resent being part of Pakistan. British colonialism was replaced by Pakistani, which in some respects was worse. We had to suffer for these blunders, which led to the genocide of 1971. You cannot have a state based on religious identity.

I do not think those trying to revive Islam are interested in Islam at all. Religion is useful for political struggle: they are seeking dominance, not religion. If you are a religious person, you do what is right according to your faith; you follow the promptings of your spiritual relation with your Creator. When you stir up mass sentiment, you are up to some mischief. If religion offers you salvation in after life, why would you mobilise what is good for the afterlife in the here and now? To use what belongs in the spiritual sphere in the public, social sphere to permit dominance of one group over another, that is objectionable.

An individual may practise one religion or another or none – that is up to him or her. They may believe what they wish, as long as it does not encroach upon the freedom of others, claim to be holier than thou, dominate women or the poor because of some archaic transcendental values. I have no problem with religion, but when they try to do that, I have every problem. That is way to stop all progress, to bring down a society, to halt its natural course of development.

In the struggle between communalism and secularism, between religious bigotry and freedom of thought and movement, especially for women, I believe that secularism and freedom of thought are true; true, because they relate to solving the problems of living. Secularism is a force for halting conflict: conflict takes life, it doesn't promote life or give it space to flourish. Secularism creates the possibility of a non-conflictual world. And that is a requirement for life. The freedom of women is also a requirement for life. Women must be involved, their rights acknowledged; they must be agents in development. This is a requirement for life, and it is in that sense that I say truth is life.

4 ✿ Dhaka

The land

A Bangladeshi feminist
Shameema Akhter is a journalist and campaigner for women's rights.
She was studying at the time of the authoritarian Zia ur-Rahman.

The promises of 1971 had been stifled before they had a chance
to come to fulfilment. Even consciousness of our liberation war
was being snuffed out. The military regime took up where the
Pakistanis had left off.

There were street-posters saying 'Accept Gaulam Azam as a
Citizen of Bangladesh'. He was hated, because the Jama'at-e-Islami
had been against the freedom of Bangladesh. Gaulam Azam had
gone to Pakistan at the time of Independence. A small item
appeared in the papers, saying he had returned to Bangladesh
because his mother was ill. The military regime defined itself by
the welcome it gave him.

When we protested, classes were postponed *sine die*. After
1971, it was the best of times, the worst of times. Only the
Socialist bloc and Australia recognised Bangladesh. We had no
access to the West. The apparent calm of military rule concealed
the triumph of the anti-liberation forces. After socialism and
secularism were removed from the Constitution, money poured
in from the Gulf. Hoarders and corrupt entrepreneurs sprouted
from nowhere. A new class of nouveaux-riches sprang up, many
of whom got rich by selling off relief aid from abroad.

Since the return to a kind of democracy in 1991, the idea of a
socialist pluralist government has not existed. There has been a
little more space, that's all. The parties detest one another. They

have picked up political jargon, but there is no interpretation, no analysis, no thinking. They do not refer to the profounder issues, because of an intricate collusive relationship between the Awami League and the BNP – the class affinity of all ruling castes.

People have retreated to cultural self-presentation: to sing in public is for stardom and celebrity, not for values, an expression of identity. It is not real culture. We used to carry books of poetry in our bag, sit under a tree in our class-break and recite it; we listened to one another, were moved and excited. That has gone now. They go and listen to bands and pop singers. I don't condemn that, because it is at least a defeat for the fundamentalists. But culture has become a façade, a cocoon. It is called culture, but it is not cultural practice.

In the same way, 'democratic ideals' are taken for granted. They 'open up spaces'. But for what? Democracy has proved another illusion, another dream. It was given up. That is the Bangali tendency. Like before marriage – a man tries to please a woman, offers flowers, promises the earth, but once she is in his home, she is confined.

The Bangali sensibility is like that of women: we endure and endure and then finally, we burst out. We sustain every humiliation, say nothing, and suddenly there will be an upsurge of violence. All movements – against the British, against the Pakistanis – are characterised by patience and then a sudden eruption. People learn to live with pain. Loss, fatalism, it is inscribed in nature: drought and violent rain, then spring and the green come, hope, then cyclones, villages are wiped out. People move on, the dreams come up again. Endurance is the key – ebb and flow, tides, uncertainty. Erosion of the river, change in the landscape, water and earth shifting – there is no time for brooding, you have to get on with life. Natural calamities come and go – *bhavbad*, fatalism. Lalon's songs are not just about God and the afterlife, they also embrace the physical, the corporeal, nature. Bangali attitudes to religion were similar to that of the Buddhists, very personal. The fundamentalists are now changing this.

When people live with poverty and loss, they don't think much about it. That's the way it is. But it does mean you are susceptible to provocation. If someone says, 'Oh, what you are suffering is caused by this, you respond. The suppressed anger can be immediately ignited. It is like the Nor'westers, the dust and cloud and violent winds. Today it is calm; suddenly, it is the *kalbaishaki* storm.

The middle class likes culture, because it brings women and men together. But politically, there is a bamboo enclave for women. Cultural programmes admit women; but afterwards, men become themselves again. Bangali nationalism remains patriarchal with women. They go eagerly to a Ravi Shankar recital, they talk of 'modernisation', but when it comes to women, they return to their patriarchal roots. If a girl stays alone, she is 'Western'. Only when women who have been submissive rise up, they become powerful. Abandoned women who have to face reality become strong.

The emotions of Bangali people are real – love of the language, honouring freedom-fighters. The question is, how can this emotion be applied for social action, not just for symbolic 'cultural' activities?

The fundamentalist

In a modest monsoon-stained building close to a congested railway crossing in Moghbazar is an office of the Jama'at-e-Islami: a frugal interior, dingy curtains at the doors, metal grilles at the windows, gunmetal *almirahs* (cupboards), where I met Abdul Qader Mullah. He is a senior party member, who studied Physics and later became a teacher. Originally with the Leftist movement, he was instructed to do 'serious work'. He turned his attention to how Islamic morality might be introduced into Leftist ideology. This led him to study Islam in greater depth, and as a result, he embraced Islam totally. 'I seriously adopted Islam as though a newly converted Muslim. This was in 1966.

'Jama'at-e-Islami is an ideological party. It works democratically, renouncing all coercion and terrorism, to develop a moderate democratic electoral system. To that end, we promote our ideology through books, articles, symposia, seminars, personal contact.'

There is tension between this examplary democratic theory and what would happen if Jama'at gained a majority. Islam is a total system of life conduct. With what degree of severity this would be imposed in the event of electoral victory remains in shadow. It offers prescriptions for all humanity: a contradiction lost in the protestations of democratic commitment.

In the election, we shall spread our ideology, our plans for living standards of the people, human rights and other issues, and *Insh'allah*, we shall take part, in alliance with the BNP or alone.

Within the party, we have a uniquely democratic system which no other party follows. The internal workings, even the elections of the Ameer [spiritual leader], are all open to the members. Other parties are run by their President, and if there is anything he does not like, he overrrides internal democracy. No one in Jama'at is above the party. All decisions are exposed to criticism. We have a duty to obey our Ameer, Gaulam Azam, but if he does a wrong thing, any member may criticise. If a beggar asks him for alms and he turns him away, I have the right to criticise him. If a beggar asks, and you can give, you should, and if you cannot, you should say, 'Please forgive me, I have no money.' It is our duty to purify our leaders according to the Islamic way.

In our country, democracy is not there. The Prime Minister would never be where she is if she were not daughter of Sheikh Mujib. She has no political background. She is a housewife. Khaleda Zia, too, was never a political worker. If she were not widow of Zia, she would not be head of the party. The behaviour and mode of expression of these two women are not those of normal ladies. One is busy with revenge, the other with her husband's killing. Hasina thinks those entangled in her father's killing should be punished by any means. Women are emotional anyway, but how can these two be normal, think of the common people?

We cannot go back to the feelings of 20 years ago. History is important for learning and improving the future. We, in Jama'at, are free of this emotion. We work for an ideology which seeks to improve the social, judicial and economic system, even the political system.

What is written in the Koran is not practised by our leaders or by the common people. The ruling class prevents non-Muslim communities from understanding Islamic ideology. It was Bernard Shaw who said, 'When I go through the Koran, it offers the best ideology for the improvement of human society, but when I see the society of the Muslims, this is the worst.' If someone like Mohamad were dictator, he would remove all evils from the world, and people could live in heaven.

Sixty per cent of wealth of the world is in the hands of Muslims. Yet we have so many poor. More than 90 per cent of the world's homeless are Muslims – how will they say our religion, our ideology are the best? The Prophet says 'If a Muslim has everything and allows his neighbour to pass his night without food, that man is not a Muslim.' Whether the neighbour is Muslim or not is not important. Social inequality is against Islam. Those who have their money in USA, their children educated there, their dogs have meat while the man who lives under his building has not 100 grammes in a month. Most of our wealth has been captured by a few, spread through corruption, illegal business. When they go to the Baitul Mokarram Masjid on Friday, that is hypocrisy.

Unrest, tension, anxiety. I have diabetes and a heart condition. I had heart by-pass in Riyadh in 1999. This is a country of tension. If there is a procession, police will throw tear-gas, beat demonstrators, even old people. *Mastaans* and terrorists from the ruling party beat and shoot their enemies if they take out a procession. At 2 a.m. the police will come without a warrant, and the family have no right to know who has come to fetch their husbands and fathers or why they have come.

We offer discipline. To understand our philosophy requires minimum education. Most are uneducated, illiterate. Among the university educated, moral degradation is severe – hijackers, terrorists have graduation, master's degrees. Education could not mould their characters. The uneducated are not hypocrites like modern-educated people. It was your Milton who spoke of the harmonious development of mind, body and soul. Our education fails on every count except the body. Everything else has been sold to the Devil. All they think of is money from corruption, associating with political leaders to get contracts. Part of this is the price of colonial education: Macaulay said the colonial system should produce an Indian in appearance and colour, but that their tastes, attitudes and feelings should be Western.

I spent three months in UK. Peace of mind is absent, even though they have better food and clothing than our people. One morning, a pair is married, and by the evening, they have parted.

At 10 a.m. they say their relationship is fine; in the evening he comes from office and finds a letter saying, 'You are a good man no doubt, but I am going from your house and divorcing you from 4 p.m.' When a child is born, the mother's name is written as guardian, the father is unknown.

We are not totally Westernised. If we were, we'd at least have made roads and highways. But we haven't totally avoided it, because of our moral degradation. We are neither fully Islamic nor Western. Open sex, bad habits prevail among the upper classes. Openly, they will not say. They are ruining us and they know it. They believe in the right to enjoy any lady they like. They will not accept they are under the law.

I've highlighted the negative side of our society. There is a good side, especially among the youth. Many are seeking change for the good. Their numbers are increasing. Older people who have done serious mischief, ill-habits in front of their sons and daughters, now they are feeling, she is my daughter, he is my son, my prestige and honour have been degraded. I should tell society that is not the way to go. Young people say, 'I hate modernity and Western culture.' They wear full blouse and scarf, even though their mothers are modern, wearing sleeveless blouses. From upright families groups are coming towards morality, honesty, the ways recognised as good universal values.

If you go to a conference anywhere in the world and try to pass a resolution praising lies, no one will agree. We have increasing numbers of young from the university leading a pure Islamic life. They are going to *bustees* [slum hutments], helping, assisting doctors. In all Muslim countries, the rulers and common people are far apart. In Algeria, military rulers suppress Islamic values. In Egypt too. The people are Muslim, but cannot express their values.

You have to see the geopolitical context. India behaves as the enemy of Bangladesh, trying to destroy our independent development. Their products flood our market of 130 million. India never accepted the division of Pakistan. But in their dream of unity, my sovereignty is threatened. The RSS–BJP dream of uniting India, a united Mother India – they believe if their mother is divided, their worship will not be accepted by God. It is the duty of Hindus to unite India and all the Indian Ocean, Maldives, Andaman and Nicobar, Sri Lanka.

We have an alliance with BNP. We differ from them in 10–15 per cent of ideology. We are allied to them, because the Awami League manifesto is in favour of secularisation. They do not believe in total religion. Islam is a total code of life – education, welfare, social and economic life. The AL believes the relationship between man and God is private. BNP believes in Islamic values. They do not practise, but at least they pay lip-serivce. The philosophical guides of AL believe that Partition was wrong. The concept of a united India means Bangladesh is not viable, it should be a province of India; that would throw away our independence and sovereignty.

BNP is no doubt not committed to Islam, but is more so than the AL. If two persons are addicted to wines, and news comes that the mosque is being demolished by miscreants, one will say, 'I have no love for religion, let it burn, I do not care'. Another will say, 'I am a Muslim by faith, miscreants are demolishing the mosque, I cannot tolerate that'. He will throw away the bottle and fight. That is the difference between AL and BNP. BNP do not practise Islam, but they will not create barriers if people do. The AL is making barriers, saying religion is private, has nothing to do with social and economic systems.

Bangali and Islamic identity co-exist. Bangla was always the language of the common people, Sanskrit of the Brahmins, the upper class. When the Muslims came, those oppressed by Brahmins accepted Islam for salvation, and their language was Bangla. Hindi kings and rulers always used Sanskrit. Bangla was accepted and developed by Muslim rulers. Muslim rulers supported Bangali poets and writers.

The world is waiting for change. Most people do not know what will satisfy them. I believe Islam in the real sense, if it comes as a cultural force, a socio-economic system, it can fill the gap. There is a vacuum of ideology in the world. Capitalism is making money, nothing else. Democracy is not an ideology, it is a system to reach a goal, but not a goal itself. Wealth cannot give peace to anybody's life. Whether Islam can do, I do not know, but at least a moral revolution will come with Islam; all will be treated equally and equitably, and the suppressed will be given justice. In the whole world, the crimes of the upper classes are not treated seriously. Behind the curtain, they can do anything. In our country, businessmen, leaders, politicians do everything. They come to mosque on Friday, but the rest of their life is darkness.

Changing the meaning of development

DR FARUQUE:

By the mid-1970s, it was clear that a different development paradigm was needed. The one that existed then – and still does – was not serving the needs of the people. It did not alleviate poverty, but increased it. People were not considered actors in development, but objects. It was based on centralised authority, giving instructions, prescriptions: those following them would be 'developed'.

We had a pseudo-inclusive model, which sought to reconcile rich and poor. In Comilla in the late 1960s, Akhter Hamid Khan developed a model of village community, in the belief that the rich would help raise up the poor without discriminating against them. By the early 1970s it was clear that resources from the state and donors to these *samitis* (organisations) were monopolised by the rich. All the available economic development and education were appropriated by the rich peasants. Through greater surpluses they were buying up the land of marginal farmers, making them landless. Statistics showed increased landlessness occurred wherever agricultural growth took place using the miracle seeds and miracle chemicals.

Pseudo-community development went with the Green Revolution, which transferred profit from poor to rich. This became orthodoxy – economic growth would trickle down to the poor. Later evidence showed it trickled up. Women had no part in any of this development. The model also degraded the environment. In terms of benefit to the society it was negative, although to a section of the society – the already powerful – it was positive. The theory was, if you empower a small minority of the rich, they will look after the needs of the poor and disadvantaged. They didn't and they don't.

It wasn't a conspiracy, but it was based on assumptions that promoted vested interests. Ideas about technological development, economic growth are not totally wrong; but the idea that benefits will flow automatically to the poor, that is wrong.

We searched for an alternative, which we came to call Proshika.

The NGOs involved in relief and rehabilitation were by the mid-1970s, looking for long-term development. At first our model provoked hostility. It was heretical, impracticable. When we criticised the Comilla version, they said, 'You are breaking the harmony of the community.' To the idea of developing the poor separately, they said, 'Even if you get the poor to organise, they are illiterate, too ignorant. The poor cannot develop alone, they need the support of others, especially the well-off.' We believed the poor should become subjects of their own development. We felt the existing model didn't need people: its notion of development was to invest money, implement the technology, and the people will be developed. None of the evidence showed this to be true.

We chose experimental areas, and tried to organise poor people. We based our work not on our own ideas but on needs and priorities articulated by them. We should not go to a village with pre-packaged services, but to listen, work together, analyse why they are poor and see what assistance we can give. We had no prescription for what we were doing. In each group we identified a facilitator or change agent; we spotted a process, and encouraged those who had an important role in it, who wanted to do something, and make others share their vision. We looked to people who had been in the Liberation War, because they had energy, vision and courage; that vision had to be kept alive for the change we knew should come about.

The vision of liberation had been dashed, but many people working in the villages wanted to keep it alive. Proshika supported them. We called it human development. The ideas came partly from Paulo Freire in Brazil. His work of critical consciousness, raising awareness of the poor of injustice and exploitation was done in the *favelas* [shanty towns] of Brazil. We were enthused by his book *Pedagogy of the Oppressed*. We found brilliant ideas in Freire, but we had to develop our own form of organisation. I felt this, because in the famine area in North Bengal, I was acutely aware that people had no organisation or critical consciousness.

A number of elements came together. We got inspiration from the post-1968 movements in Europe, not in pedagogy or training, because we preferred that to be participatory, not instructive. Marxism is too dogmatic. We wanted dialogue, discussion, let people evolve the ideas, because it is our inheritance, tradition and

experience. We had abandoned one form of prescriptive develop-
mentalism, we were not going to throw ourselves into the arms of
Marxist revelation.

The participatory model started by asking people what they
needed to know. For most, that meant how poverty persists and
how it can be removed. People expressed their ideas without
feeling threatened, without having to fear they might not be *right*.
Right or wrong, we were not judgemental. This kind of training
process energised people. Their ideas mattered, the way they
interacted was important. It was not only the knowledge they
obtained, but the acceptance they gained.

There was concern that we would never reach consensus that
way. But we did. It was not in terms of knowledge inputs;
knowledge was made available but not as lectures; it was for the
people to take it, discuss and assess its relevance to their own lives.

The Bengali writer

Syed Shamsul Haq, one of the leading contemporary writers of
Bangladesh, is an adviser to Proshika. Whenever he came to the hotel,
the staff were impressed that I should be on easy terms with someone
whom they had seen only on TV, but whose work they knew well.

He is critical of those who support Bengali culture for nationalistic
reasons. This, he says, is against its profounder spirit.

> We talk of culture, but rarely understand what we mean by it. We
> thought after Independence we would be tapping the deeper
> resources of our heritage, but it didn't happen. By culture, people
> mean *going back*. They do not relate it to the present. They speak
> of rediscovering indigenous forms of theatre, but what they offer
> is pieces from the past; a spectacular show, but with no sense of
> direction. That means very little now. They have emptied of
> meaning the eclectic humanism – what should be our strongest
> point.
>
> If we stop producing plays for a year, would anyone notice? I
> doubt it. We refer to 'cultural resources' but we do not use them.
> We have done a lot of commemorating the Liberation War, all
> charged with high emotion, but superficial, without depth. When
> we speak of liberation, it should mean liberation, not only from
> the colonial power, but also from the oppression of women, from

social injustice, from the tyranny of the totalising culture of fundamentalism. We talk about our freedom, without seeing that
freedom can be destroyed by agents other than alien occupation.
The transformation we hoped for has yet to occur.

We are proud of our culture and literature. We take credit for
the lives laid down for the language on Ekushey February [1952 –
see pp. 232–6], but why is the skyline of Dhaka full of neon signs
in English? If there are two apartment blocks in Dhaka, and one
has a Bangla name and the other an English name – *Dakhiner
Hawa* or South Breeze – the English-named one will be sold first.
They will think the one with the Bangla name is inferior. We have
yet to assert and sustain a liberation which has so far been only
nominal.

In the city slums
Proshika also works in the urban slum areas. The closeness of city
communities is an advantage in organising people; but their insecurity,
the constant threat of eviction, poses other problems.

Mirpur 7 is very poor. This is a community of rural migrants to the
city – garment workers, domestic servants, rickshaw-drivers, cart-
pullers, construction workers, vendors, ferry-walas, handicraft
workers. The land is privately owned. Some owners have built houses
for rent, others sold small parcels of land for people to build their own
houses, yet others take rent for the land. The city caricatures village
society – extortion and physical coercion are added to oppressive labour.

In the slums, brown sugar (a heroin derivative), Phensidyl (cough-
syrup from India) and ganja are widely traded. People live in fear of
eviction. 'In Dhaka, construction workers have no homes, food-
producers cannot afford to eat and garment workers are ill-clad.'

House-rents are 500–600 taka a month (US$10–12). At festival
times, a 'tax' of 200 taka may be imposed, 100 for non-festival months.
Many slums are under unofficial occupation by private armies. A
Proshika group leader said,

> When we organise, the *mastaans* leave and go to where they can
> operate more easily. In some areas we cannot work. Patterns of
> social control change all the time. Middlemen arrange for illegal
> electricity connections, or water lines, and the people pay private
> interests for these amenities, not the government. In this way,

parallel administrations operate in the slums, a shadow system of pseudo-welfare, which is hard to break.

In spite of this, since 1990 Proshika has organised more than 1,000 primary groups in the slums. As well as income generation and human development, there are cultural and housing improvement pro-grammes. 'Proshika cannot help to build on land not owned by the residents, but we can help with sanitation. If people make a footpath or a water-line, and then are evicted, all that investment and effort are lost. In 1993, the government cleared an area where we lost a million taka invested in footpaths, electricity, water lines and tubewells.'

The insecurity that drives people from the rural areas is replayed even more brutally in the city. Government is a major contributor to this. In August 1999, 40,000 slum-dwellers were evicted all over Dhaka. Most had nowhere to go. Some remained on the footpaths, some were absorbed into other slums, some simply rebuilt nearby. The justification is that slums shelter criminals, drug-users, *mastaans*. Few government officials ever come near the slums. If they did, they would learn that the people are here for the sake of livelihood; and the work they do directly serves those who destroy their homes and incomes.

Many NGOs tried to persuade government to halt evictions until alternative sites could be found for those displaced. The Forum of the Urban Poor obtained a judgement in the High Court, which stated that government had the right to evict only if they found another site for the evicted. Proshika has proposed a plan for high-rise apart-ments, with 30-year loans to enable the people to become owners. Government expressed interest, but has offered no practical help.

The city landscape
Mirpur 7 is an extensive maze of bamboo and wood buildings, rusting tin and polythene, narrow paths that give access only to the houses behind, blind alleys and cul-de-sacs, where overhanging eaves of rusty tin threaten to cut your face as you pass by. Rough channels of dark waste-water meander wherever the ground dips a little; jagged stones, pebbles, pieces of glass pierce the earth. Everywhere people are returning from work; sticks glow scarlet in the breeze beneath cooking-fires, indolent ghosts of blue smoke drift through woven

bamboo or jute-sack walls. Ten thousand people live in this small area.

A misty red sunset bleeds over the city. Inkblot clouds subside and the small gash of a new moon slits the throat of the sky. Smudge-faced child collectors of *tokai* (waste) bring their small gatherings to the shop where the owner sits on a mound of junk, behind a pair of metal scales. Rubel, 12, tips up his jute sack: the metal socket of an electric light bulb, a green plastic sandal, some flex, broken glass, a few nails, the face of a clock, a broken plastic bowl, a tube of ointment, a length of rubber, and, most valuable of all, an iron hinge. Iqbal, 8, wearing only a pair of faded blue shorts, has even less. Iqbal's feet are cracked and hardened, his tiny face covered with dust. He earns 20–25 taka daily. The children offer up their broken lives in the same way they empty their sacks of broken goods. Iqbal's father is a cart-puller. He has two brothers and a sister, and they hope to be admitted into an 'orphanage'. He was born in the village in Madaripur. The family has no land, and came to Dhaka when Iqbal's mother died.

The rate paid for the waste is one and a half taka per kilo of plastic, 6 taka for iron, 3 for tin, one and a half for glass, 5 for wood. One boy has brought the skull and jawbone of a cow. This yields one and a half taka a kilo. Inside the godown is a large pile of dark-brown fluted bottles. These are Phensidyl; the sheer number suggests widespread use. Empty, they are worth 4 taka a kilo. Phensidyl is a cough syrup sold at 60 taka. Its morphine content makes it highly addictive.

Some men are playing cards on the dusty path. Md Salim is a cook. He learned cooking 'long ago from the Biharis'. (These are Muslims from India who came to East Pakistan at the time of Partition. They did not return to Pakistan after liberation, and are currently stateless. There are about 350,000 in Bangladesh, many in Mirpur 7). Salim and his companions work as a team, catering for marriage parties, festivals, birthdays. During the season, the work is well paid – 10,000 taka a month; but in the monsoon and during Ramadan they earn nothing. Salim and his neighbours were cheated of their land in Shariatpur 15 years ago by a rich man, a Member of Parliament. This is government land, so fear of eviction is constant. Salim has no affection for governments that rob the people in both village and city. Evicted from here in 1994 by the BNP Government, they returned 'because there was nowhere else to go'. Salim says this land has been allocated – sold – by government to private individuals. They will be shifted again.

Adverse international publicity after the evictions, and unity of the organised groups made the government hesitate before bulldozing the area. The fact that 80 per cent of the people here are – or maybe were – supporters of the Awami League does not inhibit the government. Why not? 'They do not care. They are not elected by the people. They are elected by money.'

The child workers

We went into a small tin hut, behind the main path. In it was a big wooden frame on which two children are doing embroidery. Nurjehan, 14, a girl of extraordinary beauty, large dark eyes, hair shining in the wan light from a single electric light bulb, is working at a *kamiz*; on a fawn background she embroiders a border of leaves and flowers in scarlet and gold. She places one delicate hand below the material; the other darts like a pale bird above and below the frame, deft elegant movements of unselfconscious grace. Nurjehan's brother, Joshim, 13, works with her. They have been working for five years, having learned through an informal apprenticeship to a neighbour.

The cloth comes from a local businessman, but they buy thread, sequins and buttons. The rate of pay depends on the complexity of the design. The two children work 12 hours a day. Nurjehan knows the work is beautiful, but she does not feel it to be so. She says, 'We have lost our feelings.' She takes gold thread from a reel and threads the needle. The work is seasonal, with nothing for three months after Eid. The room is claustrophobic: no windows, *chetai* walls, an uneven earth floor. The mosquitoes circle busily in the hot enclosed space.

The family are from Bikrampur, where they had neither land nor house. Both children were born in the village, but have been in Dhaka since they were small. Their mother is here, their father dead. A sister, Sorifa, leads a Proshika women's group. She lives next door with her husband, who does mosaic-work in buildings.

The strength of the women of the slums

Sorifa's house is tin, with a high ceiling.

The people here are under constant tension, in daily fear of removal. They have seen it once, how the bulldozers came and crushed their houses, how cruel it was. April 1993. We have seen so much suffering. When we first came, *mastaans* used to take young girls at their will, abused and raped them. We filed a case against them. They leave us alone since we organised. At one time, the local leaders also abused the girls. Now the leaders have changed, because we have the vote and they now know we will not tolerate their behaviour.

We have been here twelve years. We built our house, and with the help of Proshika, we raised our income, united against the slumlords. Our income is satisfactory now, but we lack security. The government has sold this land to people who are taking bank-loans to construct a multi-storey building. When we came, there was no electricity, no water. We have cleaned up the place, improved the land. This is why they now want it for their buildings. I do sewing, both by hand and by the machine which I bought with a loan from Proshika.

The neighbourhood is squalid, but Sorifa has achieved a modest comfort. There is a metal cupboard with a glass front, a big wooden bed. The sewing machine is near the window, clothes are drying on a string across the room; food hangs in bags from nails in the wall. A rusty fan creaks on the ceiling. There are aluminium vessels on a shelf. On the wall, pictures of the Taj Mahal and the Mosque at Mecca.

We had nothing when we came. Now I earn more than my husband. Here, finest export-quality sarees are made of *benaroshee* silk. No one knows where the beautiful things you see in the Sonargaon Hotel come from. Nor the beauty of our girls spoiled in making them. The poor are not the problem; they do not get the rewards of their labour.

In April 1993, the police surrounded the *bustee* before destroying it. Some people were sleeping, some working, some were sick. No one was spared. We lost everything. We were under the sun and rain with no shelter. Only Proshika gave emergency food. But even Proshika cannot fight the police, the military, government.

Mr Abdul Khaleque Howlader, leader of the *thana* committee, has a small shop on the edge of the slum – eggs in plastic crates, biscuits, rice; a wooden structure with lattice front, lighted only by a kerosene lamp. Mr Howlader is in late middle age. His wife, Sufia, is from

Barisal. He was chosen for her by her parents. She is chair of the Bhaggo Mohila Samiti, the Lucky Committee. She tells what a long journey her life has been, out of the seclusion and timidity of the old society. Suffering and hardship made her lose her fears, so she now dares to come out and speak in public. A frail figure in the pale lamplight, she is small and retiring; it is impossible to measure the effort of what, objectively, seems a small advance, but which, for her, has been an epic voyage of untold courage and tenacity.

The garment factories

Over the slum loom multi-storey buildings, ablaze with white neon. These are garment factories, palaces of glass and light. Six, eight, ten storeys stacked with women working at machines. Lights through the dusty glass, whiskery cobwebs, metal grilles, blue curtains flapping in the breeze from the ceiling-fans, the tender napes of young necks bowed over the work. The factories soar over the *chetai* and tin, the indigo slime that crawls between the huts, the vermilion splash of fires, the smoke and dust: here the reductive calculus of industrial necessity is as harsh as it is plain, in these unvisited places scheduled for demolition, where merchandise is fabricated in towers of luxury and the humanity that services it lives in the gutter.

The hazards of factory labour

In August 2000, twelve young garment workers, women and men, were burned to death in a factory fire. Their bodies were laid out on the damp pavements in the monsoon dawn. The fire broke out at 3.00 in the morning on the ground floor of the building, where the finished garments were stored. They were working all night to finish an urgent export order. The doors were locked, the emergency exits closed. This is usual practice, officially for security, but mainly to ensure that workers do not leave the workplace during nights of compulsory overtime.

The locking of the factory gates has a shocking resonance. Just as in the great epic of globalisation, workers are destined to remain locked in their countries of origin as a pool (or ocean) of cheap labour, so even within those countries, they must be incarcerated, as an instrument of industrial discipline, so that the delivery of merchandise shall not be delayed. The first action of the Dhaka authorities was to send two squads of police to the factory, including one from the Riot Control Division, to maintain law and order among distraught relatives unable to discover whether or not their loved ones had perished.

All the factories I visited in Dhaka were locked: a metal grille, closed and bound with a giant padlock. Each factory occupied one floor of a six- or seven-storey building. The stone stairwells and corridors were crammed with garments ready for dispatch to Complices near Paris, K-Mart, Walmart and other Western companies. In some places, work had been interrupted by a power-cut. Exhausted workers lay on the backless benches where they sit for 12 or 14 hours a day, or rested their heads on the silent Juki or Brother machines. Great swathes of material – vivid blue, scarlet or black lay across the floor. Management were unperturbed by the stoppage: the workers would simply make up the lost time at night.

On another occasion, I went with a trade union, which had organised a protest of about 50 or 60 workers who had received no salary for three months. Mostly young country girls, they marched to the Press Club in Dhaka, a procession of slender young women outnumbered by police with bellies bulging over their belts. The (male) organisers stopped for a meeting at the kerbside. They harangued the small crowd for an hour, as though addressing a revolutionary multitude in 1920s Leningrad. The heat was intense. The words floated over the heads of the young women, who fidgeted and looked away. They then marched back to the trade union headquarters.

Who are the poor?

In Bangladesh, who are the poor? The answer is not obvious. The poor are not a static entity, waiting to be 'lifted' out of poverty. People are becoming impoverished all the time, while others are emerging, sometimes briefly, from poverty. Some become poorer, others less poor. During the cycle of life, children are impoverished before they earn. Loss of land and livelihood occur constantly; river erosion, flood and drought, industrialised agriculture are agents of loss; eviction of urban slum-dwellers imposes new forms of insecurity. On the other hand, a government job, work in the Gulf, employment in a garment factory means a change in fortune. New forms of poverty emerge out of loss of self-reliance and the growth of market-dependency. Loans from moneylenders at a time of illness become a lifelong debt; dowry payment may force the sale of land, a cow, a tin house. Prosperous farmers become marginal, marginal farmers become rickshaw-drivers. A loan from an NGO may bring freedom from moneylenders. Middlemen take a farmer's profit; a slumlord burns down a community for possession of land; politicians hire musclemen to extort money from those living on the edge of survival. Poverty and subsistence, self-reliance and misery constantly change places.

The evictions of women

Not long ago, when Dhaka was still a provincial capital, Mohammad-pur was on the edge of the city, where cows and goats wandered freely on agricultural land. Now it is the site of a heart hospital, local authority offices, apartments. Its future does not lie in ragged huts of bamboo and tin, in which live some of the poorest women in the city.

A Proshika group called Shoikhat – Seashore – was formed a year ago. Today is the first day of a literacy class. A hut of woven bamboo with holes in the wall; a cramped crowded place, for 25 women who have suffered every imaginable kind of eviction – by nature, by government, by husbands, by poverty, by landlords. It seems their destiny to be perpetually moved on in a world which grudges them even the narrow space required for their spare bodies. Some in their 40s, ravaged by insecurity, exhausted by struggle, eroded like the landscapes which can no longer sustain them. Most are maidservants or home-workers; their husbands mainly rickshaw-pullers. They are from Faridpur, Bhola, Barisal, landless, reluctant migrants, who thought they had found asylum in the city, only to find that even from this secret, shabby place they must move again. 'We are still living, that is as much as can be said.' Many were evicted from other slums; some went elsewhere in 1993, and then returned after subsequent eviction. Here are new kinds of nomadic urban poverty, a wandering of perpetual outcasts.

Now they have organised, an effort from beyond despair. 'We have nothing to lose from resistance,' one older woman said, 'since we have lost everything without resisting.' This land belongs to the Water and Power Development Board. In August 1999, they were due to be removed by the government clearance of slums. Karima says, 'On that day, government declared by microphone that within 24 hours you must leave.' Thousands of police came. Twenty thousand slum people blocked the road. 'We marched to the local government office, to police headquarters, and we sent a memorandum to the PM. A writ petition was filed in the High Court by NGOs on our behalf. The court decided that the government could evict us if they gave land for rehabilitation.' There has been no response from the government, who may try to evade the Court order. 'We are waiting for their move.'

'That isn't all', says Amina, 'here, there are drugs, police arrests without evidence. They arrest the innocent with the guilty. There is no peace. With land, life in the rural areas is far better. The government has no plans to send us anywhere. They just want us to disappear.'

One man was arrested just before we arrived. There was no evidence he had done anything wrong. Arbitrary arrest helps the police to augment their meagre salary. 'It is police hostage-taking, kidnapping the poor. The government talks of law and order. The disorder is within the law.'

The Gulshan slum

Korail is a large slum area of Mohakhali, only 200 metres behind the main road that leads to the middle-class suburb of Gulshan. A stony alleyway between two high-rise buildings leads across a causeway of 150 metres between two stagnant glassy ponds to a large expanse of dusty trodden earth, surrounded by huts of tin, bamboo, polythene, palm-leaves and industrial debris. Channels of waste water create crooked furrows in the land. A large open space in the centre of the slum appears to have been set aside as a market or meeting-ground. In fact, it is disputed land, claimed by private individuals in litigation with the government. Today, the square is crowded with men, women and children. Flags fly, and a loudspeaker on a bamboo pole calls the people to a meeting to resist threatened demolition of their homes.

Mr Adbul Mannan, who came from Barisal ten years ago, explains: '17,000 families – about 80,000 people – live here. I live with my brother, sister, wife and two children. I sell vegetables, my wife is a domestic worker in Gulshan. We built our own house. When we came, this was a dirty place, marshy, mosquito-infested. The people have improved the land; now it is desirable; and those who desire it want us to move.'

After popular resistance last August, the government changed its approach. Abdul Mannan says, 'A letter came into our hands from the Senior Assistant Secretary in the Housing Department, telling that the government wants to create an Information Technology Village here, so the residents must move. The letter was not sent to us, of course. It was a proposal from the Ministry of Science and Technology to the Housing Department, suggesting the area should be vacated as soon as possible. It reached us from a sympathiser in the department.'

The All-Dhaka Slum Co-Ordinating Committee of the Urban Poor was asked to help. Dr Kamal, a barrister, who had been involved in drawing up the 1972 Constitution of Bangladesh, filed the writ petition in the High Court in December 1999. The High Court judgement encouraged the slumdwellers to believe they would be given alternative sites. The letter from the Ministry of Science and Technology seems to be a ruse to evict them by other means. They fear that one morning police will come with bulldozers, burning and breaking their homes.

Habibur Rahman has been in Korail for eight years. Landless, he left his village in Noakhali 40 years ago, moving from slum to slum. A former construction worker, he worked on many big city buildings, but never had a secure place to live. Now ageing, he irons and presses clothes in middle-class colonies. Before coming here, he lived in a railway slum, but was evicted by the State Railway Company. He made his four-roomed house here for his family with the help of a Proshika loan.

Mrs Anwara Begum left Noakhali 18 years ago. In 1988, a year of severe flooding, she joined a union of the urban poor. They organised resistance when the government's objective became clear in August 1999.

> The poor are united against their plans. They want to send us back to the villages. This shows the ignorance of the rich. We left the villages because we lost our ancestral land. There was no proper record of land ownership. My family owned four acres, which was claimed by an outsider. My grandfather went to court many times, but judgement was given against him. We are not the problem in the city. We are all working – garments, rickshaws, domestic labour. If all the poor people go back to the villages, how will the city run?

I sell sarees, and my husband has a small business. For our children we want education and a roof over their heads. Basic human rights. The government knows but does not care. The opposition are also against the poor. We have Dr Kamal, Proshika, other NGOs on our side. They are doing government's work in health care and education, but instead of thanking them, government sees them also as its enemies. Last time, we voted for the Awami League, because this was the leading party of the Liberation War. Bangabandhu lost his life for the poor. We thought, surely his daughter will help us. They come when there is an election, then they shake our hands and go away.

A crowd of children has gathered; born in Barisal, Comilla, Kustia, their fathers are rickshaw-drivers, their mothers maidservants. Between 6 and 11, they can already tell an epic story of loss, poverty, migration; childhood shadowed by a foreknowledge of a lifetime of dispossession. I asked one child what his father did. The other children shouted in chorus 'mastaan'. He is a member of a gang used by the political parties to extort money. The little boy hides in shame.

The causeway is lined with vendors of tomatoes, aubergines, spinach. Some have only a few black bananas to sell, mildewed oranges, individual grapes, a speckled papaya. Homecomers carry the tools of their labour – basket, spade, sickle, trowel, hammers, unsold goods. They walk slowly, exhausted after a long day's work. As children run to meet their parents, tired faces are transformed: daily reunions of joy in the peril of city slums. Industrial accidents, injuries, loss of labour, violence – much can prevent the daily return, while unpaid wages mean a day without food. Relieved to have come through another day, fathers pick up the children, balance them on tired shoulders; mothers scan their faces for signs of sickness. They cling to one another, flesh against flesh, the only security. In the dusk, fires are burning, ready for what is sometimes the only meal of the day, little celebratory bonfires of survival, festivals of being together; before an unquiet sleep, the certainty of another day's insecurity.

Memories of Liberation III

ABDUR ROB:

>   After the war, I wanted ours to be the happiest country in the world, with democracy and plenty. We fought for emancipation

of the people, and we thought this would now happen. By 1972–3, I saw many in the Awami League grow rich, even some who had fought with us. Law and order was bad. The bias of the leaders towards the rich was a shock – this was what we had been fighting against.

I had to work against the Awami League government. I joined the banned Party of the Have-Nots, working inside the army. Very strict rules had to be observed. Party members did not know each other. I worked with army people. In the air force, the party people didn't know me, I didn't know them. In October 1974, they got information that someone in the air force was working with the army. They were all looking for me. One man arrested in the air force had my address in his diary. The intelligence branch started watching me.

My contact, was arrested. I think Intelligence got the information from him. I was arrested on 6 October 1974. On 2 January 1975, Shiraz Shikder, our leader, was also arrested. I was in an army cell, segregated, no reading material, not permitted to speak. I was mentally and physically tortured. They didn't get anything out of me. Shikder was brought before Sheikh Mujib and killed that same night.

After his death, they ceased to interrogate me so rigorously. I was still in an army cell – one room, one light, no one else present. I saw only the interrogator. The sentry even had to take me to the toilet. In May 1975, the military trial of 36 air force people began. There were nine charges against me – anti-state, anti-government activities. They said I had been to India, met extremist leaders, we had a blueprint to take power by a coup.

When the judgement came I was released because they could prove nothing. Six were found guilty and sentenced to short prison terms. I was acquitted, but they used the Special Powers Act to blacklist me from all Defence departments and to discharge me with no benefits. I came out after 7 years' service in the air force with no money. I had married in 1972; we had a child. My wife was studying at university.

It was bad for me. I did not rejoin the party, which had split. I ceased all activities and went back to my village to start some small business to keep the family. My father, impoverished, died in 1973. I joined a friend as business partner. We bought raw jute in North Bengal, and sold it to the mills in Chittagong. Whenever I went to the mills, the buyer, the manager, the accountant wanted a bribe. I could not live like that. I left. If it was not ethical, I was not happy. I went back to my village to think what I could do independently.

In 1977, Proshika workers came to the village where I was working with young village people. They talked to me about their idea of development, and I told them of Shikder's ideas – farmers' and workers' co-operatives, organisation of poor people, together with his version of Marxism. They said I should meet Dr Faruque Ahmed and work with them. I placed little importance on this. I said, 'You are getting paid by this organisation, how can you be working for the people?' A month later he came again and asked me to help organise the poor. I agreed. I suggested they should invite poor people to a meeting. They sent word to Faruque – Rob is an efficient organiser. He asked me to meet him.

We had a long discussion. He convinced me to join with Proshika. I started in a rural area in 1977. I then expanded into North Bengal, which we could scarcely reach, because communications were very bad. I got a new department in 1992 – Organisation-Building and People's Theatre. In 1997, this became the People's Cultural Programme Department – the cultural programme expanded in response to the growth of fundamentalist cultural organisations. The struggle in Bangladesh is increasingly in the cultural arena. We support a network of independent grassroots cultural groups. Our main agenda is to work against the fundamentalists through women's development, democracy, human rights. It is also our mission to save Bangali folk culture, strengthen its traditional forms.

This new departure also marks the limits of Left politics. We Leftists had been arrogant and short-sighted. In 1973, our party decided to call Victory Day a Black Day, because we maintained we had not achieved full victory. This was true, but tactically foolish. In December 1973, the government had to cancel all ceremonies because we had boasted of our strength in the army, and air force. We sent thousands of letters to army and air force personnel, saying if they took part in the march-past they would be killed. Of course, 1971 failed to give us the emancipation we sought, but our intransigence was very wrong. We were not constructive. So many factions on the Left, so many leaders – how could a worker get an answer to simple questions? Everyone was quoting Lenin, Marx, Mao, with a different objective. Activists became frustrated – they started fighting, and then killing each other. They lost leadership of their groups or parties and turned into dacoits. In our party, there was no leader after Shikder. His successor could not save the party. It still exists, but they torture, hijack and still raise the slogan. It stands for nothing now.

I never supported the murder of Sheikh Mujib. I respected him. I saw no hope in such a killing. I knew from the history of China, that we should help the nationalists first. Capitalism should come, then you fight for equal distribution and organise, both grassroots and cadres. You should have a long-term plan – after 20 years come to power with the people. Go along with the nationalist policy, change things later. Power without experience – that is what happened to the Awami League. I was upset more by the jail killings than I was by the death of Mujib, because it was instigated by Mushtaq, who was a US agent inside the Awami League. People knew he was pro-US, but then so was Mujib, although Mujib didn't sell himself to them.

Mujib was never really a threat to the US. He was a victim of global politics at the time: USSR and India were in favour of our liberation, China and the USA were not. The US distrusted him, and when he made a one-party state at the prompting of the USSR, they would not tolerate it; especially since he insisted on selling jute to Cuba. He was no socialist. He was a liberal, forced by global politics into positions he would have preferred to avoid. The US could have saved him, but they used Mushtaq to get Zia ur-Rahman. That was their victory.

Many former Leftists became rich. Some are dacoits and crooks. Many young men and women of that time abandoned their studies to fight for the excitement of liberation. Many who joined the Left lost their livelihood, lost their lives, lost everything, victims of the time.

After 30 years, we have still failed to achieve a national consensus. We were under military rule for 15 years. Our political institutions are not democratic, so how can we expect democratic rule from the political parties? There is no secular education policy. We face globalisation, which is modern imperialism, and fundamentalism, which is furthered by globalisation. We have to fight internally for democracy and externally against those two monsters. We work with the ordinary people and civil society, in the hope of a better future.

5 ❦ North-West

The journey north
We made a 400-kilometre jeep journey to Dinajpur in North Bengal;
a twelve-hour drive, much of it in the dark, under vaulted raintrees,
with moths, bugs and pale-winged insects crashing on to the
windscreen. The petrol-pump pagodas are the most elegant structures
on the highway; icons of modernity, mobility and the future, they are
constructed like spare, elegant temples.

The countryside is full of people. Children hungrily watch goats
feed. A lonely girl of 8 with three cows, stick in hand, ragged and
barefoot. A woman is transplanting paddy at sunset: her reflection in
the water creates a perfect circle with her body, so clear that it seems
her drowned twin is pushing up the green plumes of rice. The fields
are transparent, holding the darkening sky in their shallow bowls. We
crossed Bangabandhu Bridge, a major engineering work in the country,
a triumphal stride on concrete legs across the vast Jamuna. The silver
thighs of the river are covered with a bright pubescence of wild green
rice. Carts carry long olive arcs of bamboo, cauliflowers of creamy
foam encased in a silver-green furl of leaf. *Shimul* trees form an
architecture of bone. A woman kicks up drying rice with a bronze
foot, and the chaff winks as it flies away in the sunlight.

Everywhere, soil fertility is squandered on brick kilns: chimneys
scribble enigmatic messages on the sky in plumes of white, pink or
grey smoke. Everyone is working, in the curious paradox of the
energetic inertia of Bangladesh, the desperate struggle of individuals
surviving in an unchanging order. A woman is bowed under the tiered

lotus of a headload of bananas; two men push a long-handled cart, bodies spangled with sweat. A little boy sells water at the bus-stand from a bucket, a plastic beaker attached by string; men with the shiny blades of their tools glinting in the sunset; children with bamboo fish-traps, taking their daily catch to market; the smell of the garlic harvest, papery skins winnowed by the breeze; girls bent beneath a knot of firewood. Buses, their roofs crowded with passengers, create tableaux of rural servitude, faces turned to metal by the dying sun; beggars at ferry-crossings, hands locked in gestures of supplication.

On the way, we stopped at roadside tea-stalls, took meals in country restaurants full of truck-drivers and labourers: a metal grille at the front, a stove where a black kettle simmers; inside, the owner sits on a high stool at the cash-desk; tables with plastic tops, wooden benches; concrete floor covered with cigarette butts, dusty bare foot-prints; at the back, a cracked sink for washing hands. Men in *lunghis* scoop up the last of rice and dal, using their hands in ways that make mine look like blunt instruments. Everywhere I was watched by other eaters: would I eat the food? How would I eat it? Would I leave any? It was as if they might read in my behaviour some clue to my purpose here.

The villages of Bangladesh

The villages of Bangladesh are beautiful – houses of clay, *chetai* (bamboo) or tin, the shade of spreading trees, beaten mud floors, clay *chullas* (stoves), fragrant fodder and grasses, courtyards with hens and ducks, a cow tethered to a pole, the squeaking of the pump-handle. But as soon as a village becomes a town, it is curiously squalid; as though towns are an aberration, more temporary than villages, even though villages are made of the most impermanent materials. Villages are of local and renewable construction, while towns accumulate industrial debris. There is always a bus-stand on the edge of town, ramshackle vehicles parked on waste ground, rubbish on unpaved streets, plastic bags and industrial garbage, roughly built wood and tin stores, a tangle of telephone and electricity wires overhead, crude hutments beside the polluted pond, with their toilets – a circle of jute wound around bamboo sticks, human waste trickling down the banks into the water; uneven surfaces, potholes and overflowing drains; thin dogs sniffing piles of rotting vegetable matter; outsize black crows, sleek rats. Towns are symbols of the collapse of an ancient agrarian culture, the destination of the defeated; towns give grudging shelter to an injured, wasting peasantry; towns represent loss of land, therefore of meaning.

The poorest part of Bangladesh

We reached the Proshika office at Domar, a small town near Dinajpur. Here, most men wear *lunghis* – a sign of poverty, for they cannot afford trousers. This is the poorest part of Banglaesh.

Salauddin, our driver, loves long journeys. He is in control. He takes a break when he is hungry, chooses the places where we will eat. He hates days waiting around, but relishes distant destinations. He lives in Dhaka, half a day's drive from his family near Chatpur. When he is working, his concentration does not falter, which is as well, because on the drive north, we came across four major accidents and several minor ones. A truck carrying passengers had swerved off the road and landed upside down in a ditch; a bus had collided with a truck and was on its side. Bodies covered in blood are laid out on the verge. Other drivers, undeterred by these spectacles, continue to overtake vehicles, which are themselves overtaking a bus or truck, although oncoming traffic on the road ahead is quite invisible. The enormous death-toll on the roads is part of the martyrdom of present-day Bangladesh, victims of a development where the rich freely import vehicles but the infrastructure to carry them is absent.

A cultural evening

After our twelve-hour journey we were given tea and biscuits and told we had arrived 'just in time to enjoy a cultural evening'. It was about nine p.m. We had to drive a further 20 kilometres to get there. It was mid-February. The night was cold. It was an open-air performance.

We bypassed a broken bridge over a river, where concrete girders had collapsed – no doubt the result of another corrupt contract. We arrived at about 9.30. The play had started, an epic about the language struggle, the resistance to the imposition of Urdu upon Bengali-speakers in the early 1950s. In the play, Pakistani military authorities instruct local elites to give orders only in Urdu. They cannot do it. The poor do not understand. It was funny and bitter.

A strange evening: shreds of mist dance like ghosts over the paddy fields; a large wasting moon filling the hollows with liquid; a blue landscape, water glinting like metal in the cold light. In the village square, an improvised stage and *shamiana* (tent) had been erected. Children sit in front of the wooden stage in a wide semi-circle, enthralled by the spectacle, attentive, rapt. As the younger ones grow sleepy, older sisters and brothers draw them into the protective chamber of their arms. Many wear balaclava helmets, bonnets, scarves. The women sit behind, and men stand at the back, shawls around their shoulders, the red blot of a cigarette below their white eyes. Kerosene lamps hanging from the bamboo frame of the stage are blown out by the breeze. Their bleaching light swings to and fro. At 10.30, an interval, and the cast sing *Amar Bangla Bhasha* – My Bangali Tongue. We congratulated the performers, who gave us sweet, strong tea. We left, although the programme showed no sign of flagging.

I was so cold, I could neither eat nor sleep. By eleven o'clock an evening meal was ready. I made an excuse, no longer caring whether this was a rejection of Bengali hospitality. Beneath the quilt and the mosquito net, I couldn't stop shivering. I got up, dressed, and got under the quilt again. I slept for a couple of hours around dawn.

Morning in the countryside
At seven o'clock I went out, relieved by warming sunlight, eager to walk off the stiffness of the previous day. In the town, small shops were just opening, a bus-stand was busy with the inexplicable arrivals and departures of the countryside. Children on their way to school said, 'Good morning, what is your name?' then collapsed in giggles at their own daring. A pond of water-hyacinths, a bridge, where some men were smoking sociably in the morning sun.

They say the minimum daily wage in Domar is the equivalent of three and a half kilos of rice; even of the lowest quality, that suggests 35–40 taka. In practice, wages are lower. In the lean season, people still offer their labour for two meals a day. Some take a loan, and sign a document which commits them to working the whole year to pay off the advance – a form of bonded labour. This is dying, because people can now migrate to Dhaka by means of Bangabandhu Bridge. Earlier, the journey involved a long diagonal crossing of the turbulent Jamuna.

Agriculture here is now a capital-intensive occupation. Increased amounts of fertiliser and pesticides are required by high-yielding varieties of seed. This has changed the method of production, although the workers have not changed: older psychic structures confront a capitalist system of agriculture. They are a hybridised people, neither peasants nor industrial workers, like the hybrid seeds that have taken over their land: a hybridised society with hybridised values.

The people in popular culture

In Domar, we met a cultural group made up from Proshika primary groups. They had just celebrated Language Day. Their next big event is *Pahila Baishakh*, the Bengali New Year. As in all the cultural groups, men and women mix freely. They say that the privilege of the rich blinds them to the intelligence of the poor. That the members of this group have not lost their roots through education is a poignant comment, both on education and on rootedness. Many have witnessed tragedy and loss; heroic lives.

Sumitra Rani has one child; her husband died nine years ago. She has been in a Proshika group for ten years. A loan for a social forestry project yielded enough to buy two cows. Milk provides 15–20 taka daily – half of what is needed for survival, and barely enough merely to feed herself and her little girl. She says, 'We are still living.' In spite of a penurious existence, Sumitra finds time to sing and perform. She says, 'We sing because it is our dream to change society. We have nothing else to change the world – only our conviction and energies.'

Ranjita left school at 9 to be married. Her husband waited until she was of age, but left her shortly afterwards. Society does not allow her to marry again. This brief sketch poses unaskable questions; although most child brides are not subjected to sexual relations before puberty, many men are impatient for them to grow up, and take them before they are psychologically ready. Ranjita is caretaker of a social forestry project, earning 800 taka a month. She lives with her family. She is 19.

Arjuna lost her husband twenty-seven days ago. He was a member of the Jagpa Political Party (allied to the fundamentalist Jama'at), and went to Dhaka for a meeting. He died on the train coming home. He had two wives; with Arjuna, two girls, 10 and 11. They have no homestead, but live on land belonging to a local school. The teachers allow them to stay under the verandah. They survive with difficulty. Arjuna is husking rice with a machine that replaced the old *dekhi*. She earns 500–600 taka a month and spends 20 taka a day on food.

Farida joined a group ten years ago. She left school at 10 for marriage. Her family were very poor. Later, her younger siblings could continue their education. She has one son and three daughters. Her husband is a gardener, on the muster-roll, not permanently employed. Farida works with a tree-nursery project in her group, earning 600 taka a month. She joined the cultural group 'because of the oppression of women. I feel the injustice done to women, and all I can do is tell others about it. Fundamentalists, landlords, money-lenders do not like men and women to work together, but the people we perform for appreciate it.'

Shila has been in a group eleven years. She has two girls and one boy. Her husband is a labourer, earning 30–40 taka daily, but has work only five months of the year. Shila is rice-husking, with a loan from her group, and this allows her to send the children to school. She can also feed them more adequately. Proshika has made her con-scious. What she said was, 'Before then, I was awake, but my mind was sleeping.'

Meena has been with a Proshika group for four years. Her husband died of TB eight years ago. She has three children, and one bigha of land. Her 12-year-old son works the land, and she helps him. This provides three months' food security. The rest of the time, Meena is a day labourer. If the farmer gives one meal, her wage is 15 taka daily; if no meal, 20 taka. Men are paid 35–40 taka, although men and women do the same work. She says, 'This puzzled me. People used to say, "Oh, women get less." Now we say, "Why do women get less?" We do not accept it in our hearts, even though we have to accept it in life.'

Shatendra's family is more prosperous. They live as a joint family, with 14 bighas of land. This makes them middle-class farmers. He has been married two years, with one boy. The family is self-reliant throughout the year, and can sell 40–60 maunds of paddy each year.

Govinder is 22, a flute-player. He was attracted to the melodious-ness of the flute as a child, and has played since he was 10. This is his passion.

Othik Birman has three boys, two married, one studying in Class X. His group was formed almost twenty years ago. Then, Othik had 2 bighas of land. The group took a loan for a nursery project. North Bengal was badly deforested, so much of Proshika's effort has gone into planting in this region. After that, Othik had a rice-husking business. With the money he saved, he now has 20 bighas of land.

Cultural groups attract Hindus and Muslims, men and women, the well-off and the poor. Many women who have suffered join such groups, often impelled by a sense of personal injustice. This requires great courage in poor rural areas, to defy convention, resist the strictures of fundamentalists. In this group, the men are better-off than the women, and they are motivated by less immediately personal factors. The outcome is the same devotion to an inclusive humanism, but women are moved by a more direct sense of injustice.

How do they find the time to sing, act, rehearse and perform?

> Time is different here. Work is what you do to earn a livelihood. Families are usually extensive, and in this lies our only wealth. They help look after children, they share our burdens and sorrows, and this leaves time to sing and celebrate. This is the purpose of life. Even if you are poor, why make yourself poorer by not laughing or singing?

The poor often speak with a visceral, scarcely conscious profundity – not what they have learned, but what they know; a knowing of the heart.

Vision and action
DR FARUQUE:

> Having a vision is one thing, but translating it into action was a challenge. Empowerment of the poor is a fine phrase, but how to achieve it in economic, social and political terms? Strategies for action were required if the poor were to be organised separately from the non-poor, and women separately from men. Social analysis has to be part of it – human development, leadership skills, ability to communicate, understanding the mechanics of injustice and poverty.
>
> Then it came to social programmes – enabling the poor to claim resources, organising movements around access to land, redistribution of *khas* [government-owned] land. Economic empowerment too. The poor did not get credit from banks. The only source of credit was moneylenders, who charged outrageous rates of interest. We developed our micro-credit system, although at the time the word was unknown. Environmental action was also

urgent. Trees had been cut down for commercial reasons. People organised to prevent further devastation, and to plant more trees. We set up extensive nurseries, so plants were readily available. We encouraged them to plant trees in their homestead, on the side of the road, on fallow land, the margins of any field; to replant in government reforested areas, make contracts with the government, so they would get a share of the trees later – crops, branches; and to prevent surviving natural forest cover from being cut.

We also promoted ecological agriculture. Farmers saw production going down. In spite of increased agrochemical inputs, the land was deteriorating, the soil less fertile; they were getting fewer fish from the water-bodies. Our version of ecological agriculture did not use chemicals, but organic matter mostly from their own land. Not just cowdung, which is in short supply in Bangladesh: nature offers huge biomass production. Organic matter can be produced from within the farm. You don't need fertiliser, even organic fertiliser, from outside.

The cultural department also flourished. We opened this complex at Koitta in 1980 with an international theatre conference. People came from Latin America, Africa. We had a great theatrical innovation. Everyone else was taking middle-class theatre to villages and slums, and leaving by the next train. We said that is not satisfactory. Capacity for theatre must be in the village. They should pick up issues in the village, dramatise them, use their own dialect, their own symbols. That theatre will not go by the next train, it will act out issues of injustice, exploitation, oppression of women in front of local people. They will then know what action to take. The theatre then is not just an entertainment, but a form of initiatory action. The poor themselves are the actors. Capacity of the poor is there, you have only to support them with training and ideas. We showed village performers to international theatre groups. Of course, some middle-class theatre also supports the grass-root people. But there was no faith that poor villagers themselves could perform.

There is a long Bangali tradition of travelling theatre coming to a community, peforming and going. But people said, 'Villagers need a script, a book, a standard Bangla to be spoken.' We said none of this. You don't need a book. The book is the story in the village, not fairy tales, people's actual lives. It can be dramatised so that it speaks to the people. There are many forms, *jatra* or *jari* – two poets debating with each other or *shari*, or *poothi*, a recitation. All are familiar in the villages. Let them use whatever forms, or combination of forms – a bit of the *jatra*, *shari*, *poothi* …. The new element in these old forms is the capacity of the poor to do it. It was not thought the poor could do such things – a theatre troupe of the poor and for the poor.

We doubted whether women would come, but they did. Now there are about 500 troupes, men and women performing regularly. That is how theatre should be, part entertainment, part social action, developing awareness and acting on it. There are many examples of theatre leading to social action – people collectively reclaim land that has been taken by cheating, a moneylender will be chased from the village, all as a direct consequence of the play. We use theatre to help the poor gain access to resources, to claim services from government authorities; to get better treatment from hospitals, vaccines for their children, family planning services, the *khas* land due to them.

A feudal area

From Domar towards Debiganj we passed paddy fields on the margin of the Kartua river. The soil is sandy; this tributary of the Brahmaputra floods every year, and deposits sand over a wide area. In this region, 85 per cent of people are landless, and land ownership is concentrated in the hands of a few families. Social change has been slow around Debiganj. There is no tradition of migration. Small farmers sold their land to feudal families for short-term survival. People were isolated from high-earning areas by the Jamuna. Since the bridge was built, produce – wheat, rice, eggs, groundnuts – commands a higher price, which has undercut the monopoly of feudal families. As a result, these have also taken advantage of improved communications by large-scale farming of cattle and poultry.

The trading sector here is in the hands of dealers from elsewhere – grocery, cloth, food. The literacy rate is low, many of the literate are outsiders. There is exploitative in-migration, the reverse of the poor going out for livelihood: here the rich come in for extractive purposes.

The district of Panchaghar is tranquil in spring sunshine, the rice-fields green beside a pale sandy river-bed flecked with silver: yet the gap between rich and poor is wider than anywhere else in the country.

In the fields, mending the embankments of the paddy fields, two 16-year-olds. They are preparing the ground for the *aman* (rain-fed) crop. Nizam was at school until he was 12, Moznu left at 9, because he didn't like to study and wanted to be outdoors. The families of each own 14 or 15 bighas, are well-to-do farmers. The boys are barefoot, their knees covered with dry mud, feet still wet; mud has also gloved their hands and splashed their faces. They are sturdy, healthy, smiling. Both wear *lunghis* tied up at the waist; they exude a self-confident contentment. I asked why their parents did not let them stay at school. Their smiles widen at the ignorance of the question – their sense of well-being and freedom is palpable. In their free time, they do *adda* (gossip), watch TV, go the cinema, meet friends at the village tea-stall, roam the countryside, catch birds and fish. They are totally secure. Their future lies before them – marriage, children, land – open as the plains of North Bengal with their perpetual harvests. Why would they look elsewhere for livelihood? What would education teach them that they do not already know? They do not express this in words. They do not reflect on their lives, but merely live them, heedless as the wild flowers and birds with which they share their landscape.

The network of NGOs

In the town of Thakurgaon, we went to the Human Welfare Development Organisation (HWDO). Proshika supports sympathetic NGOs all over the country, creating networks around thirteen major issues that Proshika has identified as crucial. Particular NGOs are designated as leaders on each issue. The HWDO's role is in the empowerment of women. (In Rajshahi, the leading NGO deals with *khas* land; in Khulna, preservation of the Sunderbans is the key issue; in Jessore, child abuse and the traffic in women and children.) This programme involves over 500 NGOs. Rabiul Azam, director of HWDO, says,

> We want NGOs to support and reinforce each other, especially small ones that do not have much money. We reach women who have been inaccessible through *pardah*, illiteracy and conservative social practices. Our work is against the two great curses of dowry and fundamentalism.

Culture is our lifeline in the struggle between religion and fundamentalism. We try to change the values of the common people, and for this, popular theatre and song are more effective than processions and slogans, much more so than pamphlets and books. In Bangladesh, our culture is being broken and degraded. In this area, we are poor and backward, no industry, no employment sector, no modern agriculture. The rich landlords, the people in the cities think only of conserving their privileges. The towns take resources from the villages, the people in the villages buy everything from the towns.

Around Thakurgaon, the minimum wage, the value of three and half kilos of rice, is not implemented. Here, radical peasant movements were defeated in the 1940s and 1950s. Town people own land in the villages, but all the profit goes to the urban areas. Absentee landlords invest in business with money from the land. With the money from feudal wealth, the feudal mentality also migrates to the towns, and the poor in the industrial sector are treated with the same disregard and contempt they knew in the village. Servants, garment workers, rickshaw-drivers are looked upon in the same way as rural day labourers: to be used at the convenience of the rich, and then expected to disappear when their services are no longer required.

People here work to pay off debt. They may have to labour for one month or ten years, depending on what they owe. If people need money for medicine or other emergencies, they mortgage their labour, and work for a trifling sum. Sometimes they sell their crop in advance. The contract with the moneylender is made three months before harvest; they may pay up to 1,000 per cent interest. NGO credit systems are undermining this abusive system, but they do not reach some places, and many poor people do not know of this alternative.

Up to the 1980s, people worked for food, but this has stopped in Thakurgaon. There are more modern forms of bondage now – trafficking in women and children. Agents promise parents jobs in garments or domestic service. They are trafficked to Calcutta or Delhi. There is also a trade in body-parts. As old feudal abuses vanish, new capitalist versions appear.

Women as battleground

Shamim Ara Begum is one of the few women in North Bengal to head an NGO, Polli Sree (Village Beauty) in Dinajpur. This group has articulated issues previously not discussed in this poor region.

Marriages are now registered. That is a step forward. We draw attention to cases typical of injustice to women. An 18-year-old was killed by her husband because the family refused more dowry. The police did nothing. We got the people to demonstrate for his arrest. Without that, he might well have gone unpunished. He is now on trial.

Women and girls are trafficked from here over the Indian border which is nearby. We rescued one girl. The community fined the agent who abducted her 5,000 taka. Divorce here is easy – men can divorce their wives by *talak* [the traditional triple hand-clap mode of divorce]. Fundamentalists say if he divorces her, he should marry her to another man, although that was abolished by reforms in 1962. Extremists want to enforce strict Islamic law. We work to transform the lives of women: if we do that, the whole fabric of tradition unravels. Women are a battleground in Bangladesh – they will decide whether we change or stagnate. Women are the site of the most ferocious struggle between secularism and the fundamentalists.

There was a notorious case five years ago. Yasmin, a 14-year-old, was abducted and killed by the police. A junior officer and two constables were accused. It took two years to bring the case to court. The BNP government of the day tried to cover up police involvement. The Home Minister expressed his confidence in them. People protested, and the police shot four people. Civil society organised a mass demonstration – government institutions must know that the people will not accept this abandonment of their duties.

Poverty often preserves harmful tradition, but becoming wealthy is not necessarily an agent of change. For instance, the newly rich often support the fundamentalists, particularly if they have made money dishonestly, and wish to make up for it by religious observance. This makes them more conservative. Families with money are under pressure to give more dowry. The demand will be for a motor-bike and TV as well as new furniture and household goods.

Some damaging aspects of tradition are made worse by wealth: men who have worked in Saudi Arabia bring with their money a reinforcement of patriarchy.

Memories of feudalism

We met a member of an old landowning family, although Mr Mirza Anwar ul Islam is scarcely typical. He is a former Communist, Vice-President of UDICHI, and Secretary of Dinajpur Cultural Organisation. He lives in a quiet road, a house covered by the vivid flowers of an orange-coloured creeper. There is a portrait of a local peasant leader on the wall. Mr Mirza has not renounced his radical views, although the world which shaped them has altered beyond recognition. This lends many older Leftists a sense of melancholy, which mimics that of *bhadralok* in an earlier generation – people stranded by changed values which they neither accept nor fully comprehend.

The zamindars were violently anti-Left. Peasant movements grew in this area where share-cropping is common. They paid for the inputs and received two-thirds of the crop, but they were worse off than those who share–cropped on a fifty-fifty basis. There was a strong Leftist tradition here. The movement was crushed in 1946 by the British Government and the Muslim League. The Left can no longer get into the hearts of the people. They don't feel we are on their side. They vote for their enemies.

Big feudal landholdings were in theory dissolved in 1954. No one was supposed to hold more than 100 bighas. Ways round it were found. Feudals transferred land to the names of relatives so government could not get it. They kept land by stealth and continued to benefit. Members of government were all from feudal families – why would they be enthusiastic about enforcement? Now the rich take loans from banks for industrial development, but build apartments with the money. They sell these at great profit and send the money abroad. They have no intention of repaying the loan. But if a farmer takes a loan from a bank and cannot pay back, he will be arrested, his property and house, his tin roof and cows will be taken.

My family came originally from Arabia or Persia. We were zamindars. We collected revenue and gave out our land to *jotdars* [small landowners] who, in turn, leased it to sharecroppers. It was taken by government in 1954. The zamindari system was abolished, and the land occupied by the cultivators. But there was considerable leakage in the laws. Feudals contracted with officials and MPs to transfer the land to the names of daughters or servants. Later, they bought it back from their servant, who had no idea what he was doing by signing a document.

Our family did not do that. We lost most of ours. Big farmers still give it to sharecroppers, as they always have. Those who actually cultivate are the losers. If I have 100 bighas, I give it to a sharecropper. I get 250 maunds of paddy, he gets 250 maunds. He works all the year, he has to buy bullocks, the whole family work. He can do no other job. He takes a loan from a moneylender to buy the bullocks, which must be repaid after harvest. He gets only 50 maunds of the crop, because the rest goes in interest. Then he must take another loan just to survive.

If government were serious, they would take land from those who hold it illegally, and distribute it to the farmers. If they did so, the level of cultivation would rise, and the problem of food production be solved.

Here, the peasant movements pressured the government to enact reforms. The government appeared to give way to popular feeling, but they were not sincere. The owners and zamindars *were* the government, and evaded the law. Many feudals lost nothing. Hindu landowners sold to Muslims, a few distributed to the landless. Some idealists sacrificed their land for the sake of the country. My father was a servant of the Raj. He felt he was doing a moral thing for the people. He surrendered his land and derived satisfaction from that.

After abolition, we had some difficulty. We gave what remained on contract. My older brother got a government job. We went to university. Before, that was not the ambition of landed families; but now, everybody wants education, since government service is the chief occupation and source of livelihood.

I have been in business, but politics was my main activity. I have one brother in America, one in London. My daughter is married, my son is in Dhaka Commercial College. In our village, my cousin looks after the land, and passes the money on to us. I have some scattered land – 70 or 80 bighas, 20 near Dinajpur, leased to a sharecropper.

I am Bangali, proud of it. The present feudals have neither ideology nor commitment to the country. They are busy doing politics to save their property – Awami League, BNP or Jama'at. Some, like our family, who have commitment, become poorer by the day, and come no closer to our political goal.

Mr Mirza has an air of rueful dejection: his family gave up privilege, but failed to see the poor benefit from it. Their sacrifice forfeited their advantages but did not improve society.

At the time of the legislation, most of our relatives opposed us. We felt that the time of that system had passed. We thought the farmers will come up; we will come down, but we'll live together without rancour. It did not succeed. I thought, if we can establish a system where need will be answered, all will get food, whether or not I get rich. It was not achieved. People are in politics to maintain privilege. The people no longer believe us. They still depend upon the rich. The Left are unable to motivate the poor. I still believe in Bangali culture and nationality.

This is the last refuge of the Left: economic goals abandoned, a more circuitous route is now followed to reach people by social and cultural pathways. The hope is that popular cultural organisation will lead to democratisation. This will make the people demand economic and social change, which the rich will be unable to resist.

A modern farmer
In Dinajpur, I met Manower ul Islam, a 'modern' farmer, successful in terms of industrialised agriculture. Although he knows that the increase in production through chemical fertiliser, pesticides and high-yielding seeds is now reaching its limits, he does not question the paradigm he embraced so enthusiastically. His commitment remains; but he knows the long term will not sustain the high profits.

My ancestors lived on the Indian side of the border. My father and grandfather lived in Dinajpur, because my father worked in the Collectorate here. My forefathers were zamindars on the Indian side. At Partition, they exchanged land with Hindus. It was all done amicably, legally. For every acre we took here, they took one there.

I cultivate 15 acres of my own and 60 acres belonging to my relatives. Part of it is given to sharecroppers. I provide water, they provide fertiliser and pesticide. Most landowners stay in town; they never go to see their land. They do not care whether it is cultivated or not.

Some landowners hold thousands of bighas of land in their own, their relatives' or *benami* (false) names. But they do not cultivate. They give it on contract or for sharecropping. The zamindars lost interest out of laziness; they failed to raise their children properly. Society changes, the world moves on; they remained as they were. They cannot survive like that. Thirty years ago, the children of landowners never went out of Dinajpur. They had no need of education. Now NGOs have made the people aware of their rights. The feudals have to change.

I am a commercial farmer. I was in Dhaka, but as an only son, I thought it proper to return, which I did in 1983. My wife was appointed in a government college. I couldn't sit idle, so I invested in agricultural machinery – power-tiller, a shallow machine-pump to extract groundwater. I took loans from the agricultural banks, quickly repaid. I grow paddy, dry season and rainfed. All 60 acres are contiguous, in one command area. I go each morning and come back in the evening. I use outside labour for transplanting and harvesting. Ten workers per bigha are required if there is no calamity. Two months' labour is needed for both transplanting and harvesting. I have five permanent workers – one operates the machines and is in charge of procurement, the others are supervisors. Two guards watch the machinery and godown at night. After harvest marginal farmers have to sell immediately to repay loans. We do not have that compulsion.

Labourers in North Bengal are a bit lazy. They kill time. If not supervised, they spend three hours chatting, smoking, eating. In East Bangladesh, they are more dynamic. At harvest-time, labourers work day and night for 50 taka with breakfast. Women start later, at 7.30. Women are better at transplanting. They work slowly, but well.

I have been working for 15 years. Other landowners say, 'All day you are going, what are you doing there?' For zamindars, not to go to the land is prestige. Their managers pilfer and steal – still they do not go. All our seeds are HYV [high-yield variety] hybrids.

Many traditional paddies are extinct. We left the old varieties, because the yield was one-quarter of the HYVs.

Fertiliser, pesticide, herbicide now cost 3,500 taka a bigha in the *boro* [dry] season. Farmers cheat the paddy-plants by giving less nutrients than they require. These are old lands; the soil is degraded. More fertiliser is needed now. This is now a time of diminishing returns, and profit is in decline. I can test the soil for deficiencies, and make these good, but it is more costly each year. In the future, who can say how much pesticide and fertiliser will be required? Pests are many: stem-borer, *majra, poka, badami, ghasporim* – like locusts, they can wipe out a whole crop in 24 hours. There are other problems: maintaining machinery. We cannot find good mechanics. We have seen good times. How long it will last we cannot say. Future days will not be as they have been. There are 18 different elements necessary for paddy – all are available in cow-dung; in oil-cake too, but that is now very costly.

MR ROB:
Bangladesh had all it needed from traditional fertiliser – cowdung and compost. This was our culture. It was lost through the Green Revolution. HYV were promoted by Western seed companies, the financial institutions and development experts.

MR ANOWER:
It still is our culture. We abandoned it because of population growth. Only 35 per cent of the landmass of Bangladesh is arable. I got a quick return, and profit increased until 1990. I have no other business. I worry for the future of my three girls who are still at school. Land is the greatest security for children. But if they are too secure, they will not strive – that is what happened to the zamindars.

I support democracy, but belong to no party. If Bangladesh is to be on the map of the world, political attitudes must change. Strikes, partisan politics are destroying us. There should be a national consciousness to love Bangladesh first. The *hartal* should not be an instrument of politics. I am Bangladeshi first, then Bangali, then Muslim.

The nature of science and the science of nature

DR FARUQUE:

Going back to nature, learning from it is a very sound idea. But to deny progress to science is another kind of orthodoxy. To think all answers lie in our traditional culture and practice – that is another fundamentalism. It misses the truth. In traditional practices, there are good things but there are also damaging superstitions. In Bangladesh, it was said that diarrhoea was caused by exposure to evil spirits. To drink water would make it worse. As you know, this is wrong, but this belief is still responsible for the death of thousands of infants. It has been weakened by the spread of oral rehydration therapy. This use of modern science is wholly positive. To believe that traditional practice can learn nothing from the modern world is wrong.

Nor is it correct to think modern science can learn nothing from traditional practice. The right principle is to pick and choose. You take from both what is acceptable in the social and cultural context, and also what is appropriate to the level of development. You have to select from both knowledge-systems and combine them. This is not difficult, it becomes natural.

In Proshika's ecological agriculture, we have taken good traditional methods and excluded those which do not make good ecological sense. For example, green manure was a traditional fertiliser, but the use of chemicals wiped it out. We are trying to reintroduce it. But it was also traditional to burn the straw in the field. That was bad, because it killed off not only insects, but also microbes useful for the plant. That we didn't take. Again, we chose some modern techniques and concepts of ecological science, such as biodiversity, to stabilise the farming system, and to make the income-flow regular. With just one crop, say only potato, you are vulnerable to pest-attack and vulnerable to the market, because it is all harvested at the same time, and the market-manipulators take advantage. That is traditional. But if you plant potato, rice, dal, pulses and vegetables, harvest times vary, so you have a regular income, not too much of one crop at a time. Potato disease will not wipe out pulses and vice versa; rice pest will not attack vegetables. You become stable, economically and environmentally.

JS:

Did that not exist in traditional practice instinctively?

DR FARUQUE:

Possibly, but this is part of the design of a farming system, a concept not visible in the agriculture of the past. We were using *neem* [a naturally occurring pesticide] to kill off pests. We discontinued it, because ecological science makes it unnecessary. If you restore the ecological balance in the soil and in crop diversity, the pest–predator ratio will be such that these pests will be controlled. If pests are balanced, they do not affect productivity of the field; even biological pesticides will not be needed.

We are also using modern testing methods to compare ecological and conventional systems, to determine the health of the soil, the productivity of the land, the food value of the crop. We use modern scientific tools, with a UK-based researcher in the Natural Resource Institute, the Soil Research Department of Dhaka University, and the International Rice Research Institute [IRRI] in the Philippines. They have found that ecologically maintained soil is far better than chemically treated soil. The quality of food is higher, with more micro-nutrients and vitamins; productivity of the soil is increasing, while in chemically treated soil it is declining. We use very sophisticated scientific testing. There is no quarrel between science proper and traditional practice which has elements of good science.

JS :

How can you tell in advance whether modern scientific practice is going astray? Everyone believed in the Green Revolution – how do you know if the next scientific 'miracle' will work?

DR FARUQUE:

Science has been – and still is to some extent – a one-dimensional science – chemistry, physics, that's it. Only in fairy-tales do miracles happen, not science. The Green Revolution took no account of other branches of science. No use was made of ecological or environmental science, sociology, anthropology – important branches of science were missing. If the collective vision of multi-dimensional science had been used during experiments and field-testing, it could have been foreseen.

Genetically modified food [GMF] and hybrid seeds are examples of science going astray. You have to ask what additional benefit genetically modified food will bring to natural systems of food production known to be good? If you have no food, maybe there could be an argument for it. But if you want a better rounded, a more red tomato – for that you need GMF? The premise is wrong. And the premise of the hybrid seed is also wrong from the farmer's perspective. A hybrid seed is also genetically modified, and cannot be reproduced by farmers. It leads to total dependence on the seed-company. It creates monopoly. So even if it is scientifically credible, technologically possible, the social application produces a wrong outcome. If you can see its consequences are not good, or if you have doubt, you shouldn't use it. If there is a one per cent possibility of harm, it should not be used.

We do not use hybrid seeds in our farming, but we do use high-yielding varieties. High-yielding varieties are developed by combining traditional varieties and selecting seeds which have high-yielding potential; so these are crossed in a marriage of traditional seeds, which can be reproduced by farmers. If they could not be, we would not use them, because to enhance the autonomy of farmers is one of the ecological principles. They should not be dependent on seed companies far away in the USA.

The proponents of GM foods use arguments we heard at the time of the Green Revolution 25 years ago. The question of availability of food does not lie in growth of production. A country may produce a lot of food, while half the country starves. Look at India – godowns and silos stacked with foodgrains and yet millions of hungry people. It is not food production or supply at the root of hunger, but distribution. Governments speak of national food security, but not of food security at the family or individual level. These are two separate things. The intervening factor between them is justice – economic, social and political justice. That is where it goes wrong. If there is justice, you can feed the world without going in for genetically modified food. That is for making money. The population argument is another red herring. That is a modern superstition. You see, people are never the problem, not even in a country where there is a huge population.

The resources of Bangladesh are sufficient to feed twice our population. We have agricultural land twice that of Japan, and the same population. Our growing seasons are three, not one as in Japan – you can say six times more land. So we are not land-poor. Secondly, after Canada, we have the world's largest fresh-water resources. We are not using even ten per cent of it. The third, and, I think, the most important, the human resource. If you see them as a problem, it becomes a problem, but they are a vast resource of energy, which can be tapped through human development. And of course, gas and oil – I don't consider those to be so big; but with other resources, we could feed twice our population with no problem.

We experimented here by forming a household – we call it 'smallholder sustainable livelihood.' We have a five-member family with less than an acre, three bighas, and we show they can have not only survival food, but a surplus. The homestead comprises two cows, four goats, 25 chickens and a vegetable garden, with two bee-hives; then 50 decimals of land (that is, one and a half bighas) for ecological farming. After meeting the family needs for food, there is about 10,000 taka-worth of surplus. This is not the most fertile land. If it isn't fertile, you make it fertile by ecological means. In Bangladesh, you don't need acres and acres. A combination of some staple crop, livestock, bee-farming and vegetables – the income flow is staggered, paced, not all coming at once. That stream is very important. If rural people do not get a steady income, they are vulnerable to manipulation. You can design it so they can escape this, with 50 decimals (half an acre), a farmstead of 6 decimals and a capital investment of 50,000 taka (US $1,000) to buy cows, goats and chickens. That is all you need. You can create household food security and have a surplus also.

This breaks the idea that we are a land-poor country, that the poor cannot be brought out of poverty because of population, that there is no land to distribute. We say, give one acre, half an acre, that's all you need. Land can be distributed. Land reform is feasible. Buy land from those who are landed. Our land reform says above a certain ceiling land will be confiscated, but it is never done. We say, 'Don't confiscate it, pay for it, and give it to the landless. Recover the cost over 15–20 years.' To do that in Bangladesh would cost two billion dollars. The World Bank is ready to give 10 billion for a flood action plan. I said to them in a recent meeting, 'why not give this loan to the government?' It is not the best way to do land reform, but it is politically possible, without social tension. The landless will pay back, because we have experimented with half an acre of land and seen the income potential. I keep on with these ideas, but they have not been taken yet.

They say land reform is impossible in Bangladesh, because there is not enough for two or three acres per family. You don't need so much. The other requirement is to help with credit. Half an acre without this diversity will not do. We have done the work – based not on one year but over five years. Each year yielded a profit. There may be a bad year as in 1998. You have to store some of the surplus for a bad season. This increases the income – that is always stressed – but it also frees people from the market and from exploitation. This isn't shown in any development indicators – pride and dignity, the emancipation of women. We are a biomass country, the managers of biomass are women. Ecological agriculture is the practice of managing biomass for agriculture. Women have an instinctive understanding. These benefits must be calculated in any initiative: how far does it increase the power of people, their dignity, freedom and capacity to participate?'

A monument to Bengali pluralism

Leaving Dinajpur, we stopped at Kantujir Mandir, a splendid Hindu temple begun in 1722 and finished 30 years later. It stands on a square platform, ornamental arcading at the doors, and covered in terracotta carvings, long continuous friezes of intricate portraiture – an exuberant and eclectic mixture of Hindu deities, Mogul emperors, animals, gods, soldiers and mythical creatures. These miniature terracotta panels are to be found all over Bengal. Here, there are camels and elephants, images of the life of Krishna: his birth in the jail of Kongshoraj, given by his mother to a servant, growing up among the milksellers, a Kongshoraj henchman trying to kill him, crossing the river with *gopis* (milkmaids). There are images of Shiva, Kali and Durga, Rama and Sita, the fight of Ram and Ravanna next to panels of Babar and Akhbar; there are players of instruments, celebrations of harvest. It seethes with life. How profane it must seem to fundamentalists: it looks defiantly on to the plains of North Bengal, hot winds over the ripening paddy: a reproach, in these ample spaces, to the narrowing of the horizons of tolerance. A fair is held in December, but fewer people come each year.

The building is slightly rounded, surmounted by a tiered dome and a crenellation of green bronze shields. It is in a dusty courtyard, worn grass, a fawn-coloured dust; a *shazna* tree is coming into flower – its whitish-green clusters sweep the clear blue sky like the brush of an obsessive household cleaner. Tea is unavailable, because the tea-sellers are playing cards – the tea-glasses, black kettle and jars of biscuits remain undisturbed.

Outside, a causeway divides the low-lying wheatfields and expanses of sugar-cane. Dust blows over the deforested plain. A couple of hundred metres on, three *shimul* trees, in vibrant red flower on bare grey branches. They shield a stepped *rashpuja*, to where the idol is taken from the temple at the time of the annual festival.

The tribal area

We drove on to Panchbibi, where we were to spend the night in a Proshika office. In the centre, a language monument, where garlands of flowers and foliage tied to the metal structure on Ekushey February hang now, sere and brittle. Panchbibi is a forlorn-looking town, dim in the late evening, a resplendent moon the principal source of light.

The area around Panchbibi has a high proportion of Adivasis – as tribal people are known – thirteen or fourteen ethnic groups, of which the Shantals are the best known. Traditionally, the Adivasis lived in kinship villages apart from Muslims and Hindus. Many have converted to Christianity. By far the biggest building in the locality is the Seventh-Day Adventists' campus on the edge of town; blazing with a white phosphorescence, like something dropped out of the sky, the object of a strange cargo-cult. There are about forty thousand ethnic people in the district, twenty-five–thirty thousand in Panchbibi *thana*. Most are landless day labourers. Much of the traditional culture has been lost. The Shantals were among the first Adivasis to rise against the British, and they were brutally repressed.

Late in the evening, we went to a community centre in a nearby village. The little shops were closed against the cold February night; slivers of light through wood and *chetai*. The few walkers on the road were muffled in shawls. The community centre is a substantial new building, constructed by government, a belated compensatory gesture for the injuries the Adivasis have endured for centuries. The auditorium is full: young men in front, women behind them, muted-colour sarees framing large eyes, hollow cheeks, angular bodies. They are the poorest in the country on every count: landlessness, dropping out from school, poor health, child labour, mortality, anaemic mothers, low income and low body weight. Yet when the songs begin and the music plays, they overcome exhaustion, their eyes shine with pride that some of their culture has survived confiscation of land, destruction of forest, environmental ruin and every impoverishment that prejudice and power can impose.

They performed Bengali, Shantal and Sadri songs. The Adivasi dances are sinuous, exuberant and sexy, the easy, joyful body movements exhilarating; no wonder the British colonial authorities hated it, the fundamentalists are affronted, the Adventists think it obscene! They asked me to say a few words in Bangla after the performance, in which I expressed delight at the beauty of their culture and its transmisssion to a new generation. The courage and tenacity of people in the face of suffering, their stoicism and forgivingness put to shame power and wealth. They could not understand the tears in my eyes. This was, after all, a celebration.

The tribal leader
Dr Dinesh Chandra Sarkar is the only graduate from the area, a doctor living in Panchbibi. To many of the young people, he is a symbol of hope, a model of what they might achieve. He is a Malo, his language Sadri. A key figure in organising the cultural group, he has pieced together the vestiges of a culture close to extinction.

> Ours is the only organisation working for indigenous people We have a pre-school programme to transform Sadri-speaking children into Bangla speakers. There is no other schooling. It is tragic they have to lose the principal element of their culture – language – as soon as they have acquired it. We live under a colonial culture, as we did with the British. We are a minority among minorities; our most urgent work is health and economic uplift. Now the government support us, although many officials in the bureaucracy undermine their efforts, saying such programmes are impossible; we, the Adivasis, are not ready for it. We have a school building and some desks, but no salaries for the teachers,

no help for students going to higher education. Teachers give voluntary service. Proshika supports seven schools.

There is no written form of Sadri, so we cannot give instruction in it. Our education came from the family, our knowledge from the forest; but the forests have been destroyed. The Shantals have a proud history. We rose against the British in the late nineteenth century. People say we should not say such things, or foreign donors will stop giving.

We said to government, 'We have been exploited too long. We want our language, our culture, our feelings for the environment to survive. The government says it recognises our claims, but the machinery does not exist to protect our way of life. A new generation is coming up who are not ashamed of our culture, as many elders were taught to be.

Before 1947 religious Hindu leaders converted people. Certain Hindu gods – Kali and Loki (Lakshmi) are recognised in our tradition. Some follow Hindu custom and burn the dead, but we bury. Recent converts to Christianity weaken and dilute our cultural identity. We were always exploited by landlords and educated people. They buy land, call it three bighas when it is two acres, transfer the land and cheat us. If people come from outside, we will follow them – that is why many people listen to the missionaries, the Seventh-Day Adventists.

In 1999, I was seized by a dacoit who took my motor-cycle and tried to shoot me. The Administration was least bothered. Only when people went in numbers, the police listened. Three thousand people went to headquarters. Dacoits are organised by fundamentalists, who are busy here. We have to call our people together to show solidarity. The MP is from the BNP, in alliance with the Jama'at, the anti-liberation forces.

In 1994, we wanted to attend an international meeting of indigenous peoples. We asked the BNP government for help. Their response was, 'We have no indigenous people in Bangladesh.' Their attitude was the same as that of the British or the Pakistanis: they deny our existence.

The Adivasis are victims of both Islamic and Christian fundamentalism.

The churches tell the Adivasis to follow Jesus, saying they will go to heaven if they convert. Because of poverty, if they are given financial help, they accept. Christians are not concerned with the spiritual enrichment of the Adivasis. They want to stop traditional worship, but they are also struggling against Islam. Muslims, on the other hand, exploit us in the secular realm, socially and economically. They do not exploit us spiritually.

We have our own spiritual tradition. Some customs come from before the time of Muslims or Christians. The most widespread worship is the *dala puja* of the *korai* tree branch – one of the most magnificent trees of our jungles, with its canopy of dense foliage. It is a symbol of peace and victory for the Adivasis. In the month of *Ashina,* on the tenth of the lunar month, we perform *dala puja.* During our marriage ceremony, the bride is joined with a tree, while we do *puja* to the river, to ensure the fertility of male and female. We collect earth in a basket and plant wild seeds, and if by the tenth day of the month they have begun to sprout, we know the worship has been successful.

When a woman is pregnant, she must not go to uninhabited places, for fear a *bhoot* or spirit may enter into her unborn child. Bamboo forests and big trees are specially dangerous, as are stretches of water and graveyards – all the places spirits are known to dwell.

At birth, all the women from the maternal side are present. No male may enter the room. In a corner, they keep an old broom, or a tree-branch with three twigs, to sweep away evil. Our women bring fire in a pot to the new mother, and a leaf, a *behrinda patta* to press upon her abdomen. The heat from this protects her against fever or infection. They tie the umbilicus with silk or cotton thread and seal it with oil.

When menstruation begins, the mother secretly offers rice to beggars. It used to be possible for a Shantal boy who saw a girl he wanted to marry to seize her by force. Later, he would take her to his village, where a ceremony took place. The Urao, Munda and Malo people make a more settled marriage. The guardians of the young people visit each other's family, the close relatives make a proposal. They don't do it directly. They speak in symbols, and will say, 'I have seen you have a good fruit in your garden. We could take it to my house if you agree.'

People believe disease is caused by outside evil. I was treating one child with fever. The father-in-law said, 'this is brought by some outside influence'. They treat it by *montor* [mantra], challenging the evil to cast it out. If they speak bravely, reciting some formula or poem, the evil will flee. [Mr Rob once had fever as a child. His grandmother took him to the junction of three roads, lit a wood fire and jumped across it reciting verses. Some of the practices described by Adivasis are also part of mainstream Bengali folk-culture.]

At death, the body is kept outside the house. The household break pots and vessels. They provide new white clothes for the dead, and build a bamboo roof over the body. If a husband dies, the widow breaks her bangles and takes off her jewellery. During the period of mourning, no rich food may be taken, no meat or fish.

In our culture, there is equality between men and women. Musical instruments are played by men, but women dance freely, and both dance together. Women work harder. Men have become addicted to alcohol. Our lives were broken with the destruction of the forests. Men have been more disturbed than women, because women transmit values, they pass on life and the spirit. That is why they convert more readily to outside religions. Men are less active spiritually. They take drink, they look for consolations. Men cannot express sorrow, grief or loss to others. When we lived in the forest, our men were brave, they had a function, life had meaning. Loss of the meaning of life – this is what colonial oppression does. When a man has lost his land he drinks; he thinks, 'I am finished'. Women have a stronger instinct to survive.

A woman's life

In the Proshika office at Panchbibi, I had noticed a young girl of about 10, shy but always smiling. This was the daughter of Jehanara Begum, who works as a cook. We sat one afternoon while she told her story.

Jehanara was born two kilometres from Panchbibi, the second of four sisters. Her father is still alive, her mother dead. The family has no land. Jehanara had no schooling, and was married at 12. She had a child soon after. Jehanara's husband drank, and he beat her. Three years later, he divorced her. She returned to her father's house and worked as a domestic servant, going home at night. After two and half years, she married again, this time to a man also addicted, as she wryly says, this time to polygamy, since she later discovered she was the third wife. 'He was play-acting. My parents had visited his father's house. They knew he was already married. They did not tell me. We were so poor, they wanted me to be settled. So they didn't listen to his father's warning.'

When Jehanara went to her husband's house, she found the two previous wives. 'I was angry and would not stay there. Neighbours, relatives, parents – everybody persuaded me to stay. They told me it was God's decision if my husband is a polygamist. I listened to them. I was 22 at my second marriage. My daughter from the first marriage is herself married now. This girl, Shiril, is from the second one.'

Jehanara's second husband owned some land. 'I stayed there eight years. He cultivated the land and crops, and his wives worked in the fields – labouring wives. He just wanted labourers, but didn't want to pay them. Then he got married again.' The irony is not lost on Jehanara that the name of the town, Panchbibi, means 'Five Wives'. After his marriage to Jehanara, her husband became poorer, and she was sent to labour for another family in Panchbibi.

> I thought, 'should I stay with a man who has four wives?' I was given shelter by this family, and also part-time work in Proshika. My daughter also worked: from the age of 6 she was sweeping the floor, washing vessels and dishes. She was not paid money, but was given her food there.
>
> I was not divorced by my husband. I left him. I sleep in my sister's house. I work for Proshika, for 1,050 taka monthly and food. My husband tried to bring me back to his house. I would not. I have now saved 10,000 taka. I will buy a piece of land, build a homestead. He sometimes comes to meet me and his daughter. Shiril is now 10.

Jehanara is a small woman; she wears a bronze-coloured saree, a lilac blouse; in her nose, a silver floral stud. As she speaks, she holds her daughter close to her. Shiril says of her father, 'He does not love me. My mother loves me first, then my uncle, then Proshika.' Shiril is in Class V. Her mother does not want her to be a servant. Many people have an eye for virgin girls, marry them and leave them. Jehanara is determined that Shiril will not marry as she did. 'Poor families think a growing girl should not stay where she might make a relationship with a boy or man. A girl should be made "respectable" by marriage, even if the husband abuses her and abandons her afterwards.'

In my bag I had a packet of coloured felt-tip pens. Shiril was delighted with them; her mother's eyes moistened at her daughter's pleasure at this small gift. She says the understanding her own suffering has given her will be devoted to the protection of her daughter.

The Buddhist past

On the road to Bogra, we stopped at Paharpur, the remains of a Buddhist monastery from the time of the second Pali emperor, Dharampal, 770–810 CE. It was once the most extensive Buddhist monastery south of the Himalayas. In the adjacent museum, a bronze Buddha from the eighth century, a sandstone Krishna, a Vishnu in black basalt, statues from the sixth century. North Bengal was invaded by the Vayala armies in the eighth century and by the Turkish Sultanate in the twelfth century. The temple was abandoned in the thirteenth. The Islam of the Sultanate Muslims was open and tolerant, receptive to other influences. They lived beside Hindus and Buddhists. During the Turkish period, Bengali culture developed and grew; education and literature flourished. The Sultanate was defeated by the Mogul Babar in 1557.

The most significant feature of the site is a steep grassy stupa by the traces of an ancient staircase. Fragments of carved terracotta walls remain on the slope. From the top, the misty paddyfields of North Bengal. Scores of school and college excursion buses are parked close to the monument. Boys are playing loud Bengali and Hindi music on a cassette machine. They drink Coca Cola, throw the empty cartons on the grass. The flowerbeds are planted with dahlias, marigolds, asters, salvias – a reminder of an old colonial practice of making the Bengal winter resemble an English summer; already the flowers are fading, and will soon be replaced by the more dramatic flowering trees which perform an annual effacement of these transplants as effortlessly as a longer season has buried the Buddhist past at Paharpur.

It is harvest-time in this potato-growing area. On the highway to Bogra, in the fields, on carts, in trucks, mounds of purple potatoes bruise the earth. Workers dig in the fields with hoes, mattocks and blades, careful not to cut the skins; men, women and children with jute sacks bulging with potatoes, bamboo baskets on their heads. As evening draws on, a procession of people carrying potatoes in plastic bags, bamboo bowls, wicker baskets – wages are measured in potatoes.

Lean times

We passed through Shibganj, where Abdur Rob started a branch of Proshika in 1980. There was no office.

> Meetings took place under a tree, in a school, in a borrowed room. Workers were volunteers who often went five or ten kilometres on foot to meetings. Taking a rickshaw was a luxury. All were enthusiastic young people. For a year I slept on the floor of my room in Bogra. We started organising the poor twenty years ago. Later, we tried to set up a people's organisation, using the experience of this area as an inspiration – not just as primary groups, but politically. We never followed it through properly.

> Later, as the economic programme expanded, new workers came in, we found it hard to train them politically. We achieved much, but grass-roots organisation is not satisfactory. We have millions of taka to operate, we have skills and personnel, primary groups function well, but the broader organisation is wanting. The time and effort given to loans and credit were never devoted to organisation-building. No doubt it is important to make people self-reliant, but in Bangladesh, where elites are well organised, it is vital the poor should be also, especially agricultural labourers, who cannot bargain for their rights.

Behind the failings of NGOs lies a profounder story of loss. The destruction of Left ideology has repercussions far beyond the end of Communism. The belief of the Left in the people was an enabling myth, the certainty that history was on the side of 'progress'. Without that, Proshika is trying to make people 'conscious' without faith, creating organisation without conviction, development without the empowering psychological support essential for change. This is why many new recruits to Proshika see a job, not a transforming vision: a career, little different from government service. All this is a distant consequence of globalisation, the so-called end of ideology which is no such thing, for it means the victory of one ideology over others.

Memories of Liberation IV

We reached Bogra after dark, driving through the choked streets to the house of Mr Bhattacharya; a once-secluded building in a little frequented byway, now engulfed by the city. We sat in the upstairs room of the old Raj building, a tiled floor, a plain room with an ancient poster on the wall, advertising 'Swami Vivekanand, the Hindoo Monk of India'. Mr Battacharya is mild-mannered man, historian and linguist, one of the many humane and learned Bengalis I was to meet. Born in 1939, he has clear childhood memories of the Raj.

I was a boy when the British left, and I grew to maturity under Pakistani rule. This made me want to fight in the Liberation War. I trained in guerrilla warfare in India, and returned to Bogra with the Indian army in 1971. The Pakistani army surrendered here on 12 December 1971. I was a teacher. Of a contingent of two hundred, nearly all were former students of mine. Of seventeen graves of freedom fighters, all but one were my students. This road where I live is named after two of them. I had to kill people who had collaborated with the Pakistanis.

The anti-liberation forces are stronger now than they have been at any time since the war. The Muslims hate India, and they see Hindus as the enemy. They will make an alliance with the most fervid fundamentalists because of their loathing of Hindus. Fundamentalists say that to be a good Muslim you must be fundamentalist. The Nazis in Germany said what the fundamentalists are saying now, both in India and in Bangladesh, and indeed in Pakistan also: just as Hitler said Aryans are the master race, Muslims say only Islam holds truth.

I do not believe they will win over the young, who are being separated both from religion and fundamentalism. But the secularism which appeals to them is not the humanism of our traditional Bangali culture. My former students want to associate with the West, Western ideas. They have a desperate desire to leave the country, to get out of Bangladesh. This is partly because of a lack of opportunities, social injustice, stagnation. Ownership of land is in few hands – a small number of families run thousands of hectares, while a growing majority are landless. People are selling their few bighas to big landholders for the sake of the education of their children. They are then left with nothing, and the children have no work anyway. Middle-class boys finish up with a nominal education, no skills, no expertise. Many with the highest degrees know nothing. Many cannot write a simple sentence, either in Bangla or English.

When the Moguls ruled, when Burmese pirates invaded, when the Mahrattas [a warrior caste for Maharashtra] came, when the British took over, they looted and robbed Bengal. This sense of loss seems to have entered our soul. Only in 1971, for a short time, Bangabandhu inspired our youth. When the famine came, this was associated with Sheikh Mujib, who could not control the country. The military took power and tried to persuade the people that India was the enemy. If this country cannot be Pakistan, let it at least be Islam. They tried to invalidate Bangali identity. The people are illiterate – the Government says we have 36 per cent literacy, but that includes those who know only the alphabet.

People are credulous. They believe what educated people tell them. If a well-dressed man says 'Give me your eldest daughter in marriage, here is 200 taka', they will give, and she will go into prostitution. Girls are smuggled to India to the sex trade – Kolkata, Mumbai, even Lahore. Children roam the streets like stray dogs.

The Leftists lost, although their leaders were the best people. My eldest brother was a Communist. He joined the party as a student in Rajshahi; a good man, learned and generous. He suffered in jail for 15 years under the Pakistanis. There, he associated with the finest of his generation. My next brother was arrested in Class XII, taken to Rajshahi jail, where he lost an eye during the jail killing in 1950. Our best people. Originally they were in the Awami League. Bangabandhu was not a Leftist; he was an agitator, but not a radical. In 1952 I led a procession of school students in favour of the language movement.

A history lesson

We went next day with Mr Bhattacharya to Mahasthangarh, a few miles from Bogra. Formerly Punaranagar, it is the site of a vast Mauryan city of the eleventh to the third centuries BCE. The ruins cover several square kilometres. If this were Europe, it would be a major heritage site. It is settled by peasants, farms and homesteads; at every step you crunch fragments of ancient pottery underfoot.

169

Mr Bhattacharya recognises positive elements in the legacy of the Raj.

> The British did not come to Bengal out of love for the land, but they performed many unwitting services for us. They wrote Bangla grammar and established Bangla College at Kolkata. Before that, there was only oral transmission of the language. On the other hand, they did great damage. In the famine of 1876, twelve million people died; the British did nothing. They learned the art of starving their subject peoples to death in Ireland. The British and the zamindars were attacked; food was looted and distributed by Maznushah, a great Bangali hero criminalised by the colonial authorities. He hid out in Mahasthangarh. He was killed in battle against the British on the Bhutan border, about seventy kilometres from here. This was also the site of the Shantal revolution of 1885–86 – the Adivasis resisted British efforts to tax their forests, and were brutally persecuted as a result. The British simply cleared the forests, destroyed their land. Two-thirds of their produce was taken in punitive tax. Shantal resistance continued until 1901, when their leaders were hanged.

> There was always powerful resistance to invaders in North Bengal. The Moguls were driven out three times in the 17th century. Resistance is of great antiquity – the Pali kings were removed by peasant revolts in the eighth century: the rulers abandoned Mahasthangarh, because they could not defend themselves against their own people.

> After Partition, zamindars held high office. My grandfather was a *jotdar*, a small landowner. My father became an advocate. Our lands were forfeited when the government introduced the Land Ceiling Act in 1954. My father refused compensation because we were Leftists.

Mahasthangarh was a great walled city. It is now reduced to the foundations of the citadel; skeletons of ceremonial gates and towers remain. An astonishing spectacle – a city, founded by the Maurya king, Ashoka, occupied by the Guptas and Pali emperors, occupied mainly by poor people unconsciously living among the stones. An ancient *khudar patta*, Stone of God, part of a triumphal arch, lies where it fell, it seems, beneath a banyan tree, its lotus-shaped carvings almost effaced; people still sacrifice milk here: this makes their wishes come true.

People cultivate the land as they do in the neighbouring plains – green pumpkins with yellow flowers and coarse leaves; patches of paddy and vegetables. Rough dwellings in the shadow of former palatial halls, where creepers and bamboos have taken root. The Kartua river protected the city on three sides; it was displaced and silted up by an earthquake in the 1830s, and is now only a shallow stream. The river was created at the marriage of Siva and Parvati: when the priest poured water on to their hands, it cascaded to form the Kartua.

Much of the site has not been excavated, although a joint French–Bangladeshi initiative has opened up one area. Originally the central fort covered four square miles. It was abandoned after the Kaibotto revolution, which was put down by an alliance of eighteen kings. Bhim was the Kaibotto leader who defeated Mohipal, the Pali king. Rampal, grandson of the king, finally killed the Kaibotto leader. Hiuen Tsang, the Chinese traveller, left an account of the wonders of Mahasthangarh in the seventh century CE.

One entrance still stands: rounded watchtowers, bricks at right angles bound with lime and sugar-cane juice, the foundations of halls and courtyards clearly marked in the grass. Within the fort, there is a tomb of a Muslim saint, Hazrat Shah Sufi Sultan Bhilki. Local people know he came from the Gulf of Arabia riding on a dolphin. Apart from this, no one here knew anything more of the history of Mahasthangarh.

Cultural continuity

Here was a rare insight into cultural continuity. Close to the former armoury of the fort, there are metal workshops. At the roadside along the base of the walls, workers sell the objects they make, mostly knives, sickles, axes, spades used for agriculture: *hashim*, a traditional sickle found all over Bangladesh, *kural* for tree-cutting, *nirani* for weeding, *dao*, an axe for cutting bamboo and hardwoods, a smaller *hobal* for twigs, nuts and bark. But the style of the spear-shaped knife-blades gives the clearest indication of a craft transmitted through time. The young men with their artefacts spread on lengths of jute in the bazaar are unwitting bearers of a military tradition of great antiquity, unconsciously perpetuating a craft of distant and (to them also) unknown origins. Here is the most vital element in the successful transmission of cultures. It is unaware of itself, spread through time, delicate and fragile, yet the most tenacious form of human continuity. The skills of fingers which have learned through observation and practice without formal teaching, without need for innovation or change. It depends for its survival on its *functional necessity*.

Mr Bhattacharya says,

> The daughter of the last Hindu king committed suicide for fear of being raped when the Muslims took the region. She drowned herself in the Kartua. Since then, Hindus have come in pilgrimage every twelve years. The Muslim saint, Hazrat Shah, defeated the Hindus. It is said (in a story which, in one form or another, is widespread in South Asia) that he came and asked the Hindu king for a small piece of land, 5 feet by 3 feet, to say *namaz* [prayers] five times a day. The king refused, ordering his men to expel him from the court. The saint went to the jungle, spread his carpet and began to say his prayers. The king sent troops to remove him. As they did so, the carpet became bigger and bigger, covering more and more land. When the king's men attacked the saint, from nowhere soldiers with swords appeared, crying 'Allah u Akbar', and the king's men were defeated.

Education and tradition

We went to Proshika at Shibganj, a peaceful enclosure, where winter flowers are fading as the days grow warmer. Here we met Mr Billal, one of many whose life has been transformed. An elegant man in middle age, he speaks with a dignity and self-confidence that belie his impoverished origins. NGOs work most successfully with able people whose poverty denied them formal education.

The Western educational system separates capable individuals from their communities. This does not happen here. The educated poor remain in their villages, and provide leadership and inspiration. The fate of their children is another matter: the next generation may be severed from their roots to become part of the new middle class.

Mr Billal has been a member of a primary and cultural group for 13 years. 'The village elite respect the poor only when they organise collectively to gain access to resources. People like us never got loans from banks or institutions.' Mr Billal buys paddy, boils and dries it, then sends it to be husked ready for market. 'Here, people eat rice that has been boiled. The taste and texture of boiled rice are different.' Mr Billal owns one bigha of land, but is a sharecropper on 8–10 bighas, on the lease-system: he pays a fixed sum to the owner for the full value of the produce. He now has year-round food security. His children are educated. They are no longer poor.

> When I was a child, we were hungry. Often there was no work. I worked on a vegetable stall in the market. My father had four bighas of land, but he sold it for food in the famine time after the war. I worked as a cattle boy, and transplanting and cutting rice. I loved traditional songs, work-songs, songs of harvest. This is how I got involved in the cultural programme. We no longer use the old stories, but we use old forms to discuss current village issues. Traditional stories cannot motivate people today, but we use familiar forms to convey modern messages. There are many songs and stories about Shukladevi, daughter of the last Hindu king who sacrificed her life by jumping in the Kartua. We might adapt one of these to speak of a recent case of a girl who has committed suicide in the village because of the cruelty of a husband or a dowry demand.

This use of traditional forms to promote modern ideas illustrates the tension between activism and culture. When the content is removed and the modern message has been conveyed, what will be the fate of the old form? Culture expresses the values of the stories and songs it encodes. Will the diversion of old forms to bear new messages in the long run undermine the Bengali culture they are trying to preserve? This question was always avoided.

Mr Billal is first Bangali, then Bangladeshi, then Muslim. His father preferred to sell his land for food rather than go to the money-lender, even though the outcome was the same – loss of control over their lives. Neighbours bought their land, and never paid the full value. Mr Billal says, 'This ate into his heart, because the land was always there to reproach him for allowing it to fall into the hands of others.' Mr Billal wants his children to go into higher study. He hopes that they will get 'a real education, so they will do something for society'. He knows this is not the real purpose of modern education, which is designed rather to enable individuals to do something for themselves. The context in which education takes place is as important as the content. 'This is why Proshika insists on social awareness: it is in permanent struggle with a society which promotes other forms of consciousness.'

Village women: change and continuity

We paused at Vasu Bihar, site of a seventh-century Buddhist monastery which accommodated several hundred students. The position of the small individual cells can be traced in brick foundations among the grass, which is a mosaic of *ghasphal* (tiny wild flowers), little purple cockades, yellow bells and green pincushions. The site of the temple and refectory are clearly marked. The wind comes over the rice-fields, ripples the grass, blows through the ruins; a reminder that nothing perishes so easily as wisdom, nothing is effaced as rapidly as experience. We were near the spot where Khudi Ram was caught by the British in 1898. With another 17-year-old, Prafulla Chakri, he threw two bombs at British officers. The first missed, and Prafulla killed himself. Khudi Ram was tried and hanged.

Bihar village is two kilometres off the main road. We sat in an open space, surrounded on all sides by brick and clay houses, outside a house with a grey earthen arch leading from the courtyard. In the compound, a jackfruit tree with flaking bark, and built into the earth a zinc stove for boiling paddy. A pump, around which aluminium vessels are being cleaned with grit; they wink and gleam in the sun. A creeper grows over the roof of an outhouse; some cows placidly chew dry straw. The wind blows papery leaves around a mound of fire-wood. Ornamental markings on the wall suggest a recent celebration. The yard is fragrant, dusty, peaceful. Speckled grey hens, black and gold cockerels forage for spilt grain.

Khairun Begum is 35. She was born here, and moved only a short distance on marriage. Her husband, formerly a day-labourer, now buys rice in the market and boils it on the stove. It is then dried in the sun and husked, ready for sale. He makes 30 taka a maund. This area is fertile and yields three times a year. The rice is boiled for 20 minutes in the big metal vat, and laid out to dry in the road. Khairun Begum used to cut grass for goats and cows. Now she stays at home to help process the paddy. She has been in a Proshika primary group for four years. Since then, income has risen, they no longer go hungry, and can even save. The new house is made of mud with a tin roof; formerly it was *chetai* with rice-straw. They now have 1.5 bighas of land. All of the 16 women in Khairun Begum's group took a loan to buy land, a rickshaw, a cow for milking.

As we sit in the mild sunshine, her husband arrives on his cycle, carrying five maunds of paddy, balanced precariously in bulky jute sacks. He has driven nine kilometres and is bathed in sweat. The paddy is soaked overnight before the fire is prepared beneath the stove.

Three women in the group boil paddy. Two widows used loans to apprentice their children in metal workshops. Some have leased land as sharecroppers. The women have improved their lives economically, but the biggest change has been social.

'Ten years ago, we could not talk with men who were not husbands, fathers or brothers. We could not discuss with each other. We were insulted by the rich, not honoured as men and women, because we were poor. We are more free in every way, no longer so dependent on husbands. At first, they were suspicious of why we wanted to do this.'

Zorina, Khaleda, Aproja, Rohima are sitting with Khairun Begum. Others come and go. Of the sixteen women, most had no schooling. Now all the girls study. 'We cannot go back to the suffering of before. We don't want to give our daughters in early marriage.' The five women present were married at 12, 16, 12, 8 and 13 respectively. They say they now know of the damage to young girls from early marriage – lost health, early pregnancy, shock from early experience of sex. In spite of this, two women have married their own daughters at 12 and 13. Both fell sick when they became pregnant soon after, suffering from anaemia. The mothers knew this from their own experience. Why did they repeat what was so harmful to themselves?

There is a silence. Women's greatest fear for their daughters is that they will become *noshto*, spoiled before marriage, by being molested or abused, or by making a relationship with a boy. This ruins the chance of a good marriage. Marriage is the safest place for a girl; through it social shame is spared, *no matter what damage is done to her*. She may be beaten or divorced by her husband. There is an almost pathological social fear in the rural areas of the sexuality of girls. The best thing is to put them securely behind the bars of marriage. One woman says sagely, 'One spot of cow's urine will spoil a pot of milk.' That is, the purity of girls is paramount. Whatever the women know from education and experience, social custom and practice still take precedence.

The struggle of the landless

We went on towards Pabna, missing the turning in the dark. We found our way along a narrow causeway, bumpy and unlit, with deep water on both sides. It was nine o'clock when we reached our destination of Bishnopur, where Samata is based. Samata works with landless people, and is Proshika's leading partner in the network for the distribution of *khas* land to the landless. Proshika gives resources, training and legal aid.

Khas land is unused government land, designated for redistribution to the poor under land reform in the Pakistani time. In 1976, a group of young people called the landless together in a collective effort to recover lands, records of which had been falsified by the privileged rich who had taken possession of them. This landless group became Samata.

A crowd in the building had come to see a play about landless people taking over *khas* land usurped by the rich. All the performers are landless. They act with rare feeling, since this drama is the story of their lives for the past twenty years. The struggle of Samata on behalf of the landless has often been violent.

The landless increased in Bangladesh from 31 per cent of the population in 1971 to about 67 per cent now. Most *khas* land – estimated at 130,000 acres – has been occupied by 'landlords'. Eighty per cent of the people of Bangladesh work in agriculture, but they own only 5 per cent of the country's resources.

Samata has identified 11,994 acres of *khas* land in its working area, and has distributed 1,705 acres at Ghugudah Bheel in Pabna district. The movement has spread nationally, and more than forty NGOs are now working in eleven districts in North Bengal.

In the morning, I walked in the surrounding villages; mud causeways and embankments, plantains, palms, small gardens and homesteads. I met Mr Hassan Ali, who took me to his compound to see how his life has been transformed. His house is now built of tin; a year ago, it was still clay. As a result of the redistribution of *khas* land, he owns 3 bighas. The status of the whole village has risen. He had just bought provisions for his small shop beside the lake, where he sells soap, cigarettes and biscuits. He is a member of the central committee of the organisation of the landless. Mr Ali has a fringe of white beard, intelligent eyes; hands and feet weather- and water-stained from years of annual migration in search of work in distant fields.

'Divide and rule' – the strategy of the rich
People involved for years in the struggle come together with workers of Samata to tell the story. It is a narrative of the heroic endurance of poor people, whose struggles often go unrecorded in the wider world. Sekander Ali, chair of the Landless Welfare Society, tells the history of Ghugudah Bheel.

The water-body provided fish protein for the poor. It became *khas* land when the zamindari system was abolished in 1954. At the time of the Green Revolution, the government dug a canal, the water was drained and this provided 3,000 bighas of agricultural land. This was taken by former zamindars and their agents, some local, some from outside. They drew up papers, and registered the land in their names at the Revenue Office.

The outsiders quarrelled with the local rich. The local elite promised land to the landless if they worked with them: they would be given as much land as they could clear of scrub and bushes. The poor were used to help the elite get possession. When the land was cleared, the outsiders returned with *mastaans*. The landless resisted. In the fight, an influential outsider was killed. By that time, those who had led the landless had completed the paperwork in the Land Office. The land was already in their names.

When the rich started to cultivate land cleared by the poor, a new struggle broke out between the local elite and the landless. The poor knew they had been cheated. They had given money to record the land in our names. Those who had them had sold houses, cattle, ornaments under the promise that the land would be ours.

Sekander Ali gave 3,000 taka, and received a false document. 'When we tried to take possession of the land that should have been ours, we realised we had been abused by the rich. I had supported them, but I changed my views and joined the other landless people. We tried to work the land, but with no legal ownership we had to withdraw. The rich started selling it off to urban people. The upper and middle class united, but the landless could not show the same solidarity.'

Before they organised, the people had known hunger and want. They were day labourers or fished for a livelihood. Many migrated seasonally. 'It was a tragic life.' Hassan Ali migrated every year to Rajshahi, where he worked, sometimes for no money, especially at harvest time. In the harvest-field he was paid in food three times a day, plus 3 or 5 taka. That was the early 1970s. Momina, of the Women's Group in Bishnopur, says women were paid 500 grams or 1 kilo of rice of lowest quality per day. Women, widows and abandoned wives who worked in rich households were fed once or twice a day, although they did all the cooking, washing, cleaning, rice-processing. Young girls and married women did not come out of the house.

Hassan Ali says that after the Liberation War their hopes had been raised that they would get justice or higher wages; they got neither.

Mr Sarowar Alam, former freedom fighter, was a founder member of Samata. He says that when the local elite cheated the people, those who could afford to pay money to the rich were not landless. They hoped to benefit from the alienation of *khas* land from the poor. The truly landless were powerless, scratching a living as best they could. 'From the early 60s to the mid-70s, the struggles were not between landless and the rich. These were quarrels between factions of the rich, who sought allies among the poor, the criminal and desperate, and used them to fight each other. They were not the poorest.'

Mr Sikander was originally a fisherman, who lost his fishing grounds when the Bheel was drained. That was why he joined the elite. It is true that he never got the land promised, but at first he was not part of the struggle of the very poor. Mr Sikander admits this; he changed sides when he saw he had been cheated.

The strategy of the poor

Mr Sarowar says landlessness is a continuous process, by natural forces, such as river erosion, and by alienation of land by the powerful. After liberation, marginal farmers lost their land through debt, poverty, dowry, or by being cheated. With the disruption of war and the return of refugees, the personnel of the Land Settlement Office were susceptible to bribes and corruption.

If I am a Settlement Officer, I am invited to a rich man's house, I eat his fried chicken, of course I am biased in his favour. I'll transfer your land to a big landowner; I'll fake leases, issue false papers. I'll say to a rich man, 'I'll give you land if you give me money. I'll give false papers to the poor.' The poor buy the papers, thinking this entitles them to land. Or I'll sell the same land to four or five people, and they will fight over it. The recording of land is a major problem. People have experience of agriculture, but none of landownership. They are vulnerable to cheats and land-grabbers.

Between 1976 and 1981, Samata identified the problems, found leaders among the landless. We investigated why the State Acquisition and Tenancy Land Act, enacted in 1972 after Independence, had not been implemented. We found out who had taken over *khas* land instead of the poor. The rights of the poor were restated in the Land Reform Ordinance of 1984 and in the Guidelines for Redistribution of 1987, under Ershad. We mobilised thousands of people in demonstrations, claiming what the Sheikh Mujib, Zia and Ershad governments had all reaffirmed. Some poor people occupied land; that was when the conflict with land-grabbers began. We identified 2,800 bighas as *khas* land.

We took over 75 bighas. We verified that the documents of those occupying it were false. The landless subsequently took all 2,800 bighas we had identified. We vacated 200 bighas which the rich were occupying legally.

The rich filed false cases against the landless and Samata workers. Everyone in this room was accused – murder, rape, dacoity, theft, burning, looting, robbery – heinous crimes in a place where violence was unknown. A rich landowner murdered his own partyman and accused the landless. Many cases were dismissed, but in one false murder case seven were jailed. A Jatiya Party leader pressured the judge who condemned them to seven years. Two hundred and two people were jailed, injured by police torture, including many women. The villages where people lived all their lives were closed to them; men became fugitives in their own land. This was 1986–7. The rich bribed politicians, courts, police. They wanted to break the organisation and scatter the people. They wanted the landless to surrender all claims.

The worst torture stopped after 1991. Many cases are out-standing, but the atmosphere has been more relaxed since 1996. The Awami League government started to distribute land. Earlier governments, whatever their rhetoric, made no effort. Even so, many people in government have relations with the wealthy here, there is pressure to drag their feet, do nothing. But there has been some progress.

In 1984–5 we took 221 acres; in 1986–7, 250 acres; in 1994–5, 300 acres, all of which is occupied by poor people who now have the titles to it.

Most of the formerly landless now have three bighas. Local land-owners are still trying to oust them, but because of Samata and members of the local government elected from among the landless, there is stalemate. The people have been strengthened by the struggle. Their role now is to serve as inspiration to other landless and impoverished people.

The story of Ghugudah Bheel is well known all over Bangladesh. It has had significant consequences. Few rich landowners or land-grabbers live in the area, and their social power is now in decline. As a result, some have acquired land in Dhaka. Their stranglehold over the people has been weakened, but it may be that their field of operations has widened to the urban areas.

Women's status has been enhanced; gender equality is one of the informing principles of Samata. Momina says, 'During the cases against our husbands and brothers, the men fled. Women stayed on the land, to work, face the insults of the hirelings and *mastaans* of the rich. In June 1985, when we occupied the largest tract of land, twenty thousand landless people faced two thousand armed *mastaans*. It was a hand-to-hand battle. That day, women nursed the wounded, carried weapons, provided water and food. We helped families of those who were jailed; many were in jail for months. There can never be peace between rich and poor.'

'Land is more important than money', asserts Sabura Khatun. 'Land is life. Land is security.' 'Land is freedom', says Hassan Ali. He knows this, remembering with bitterness the annual migration to Rajshahi with his wife. While he laboured in the fields, she was a domestic worker. For both it was a degrading time. 'Now I have ownership of a small piece of land, I have peace of mind, freedom and confidence.'

Sarowar Alam says that even the government does not know how much *khas* land exists in the country. If anyone goes to possess land, she or he will find many others also laying claim to it. Corruption and confusion have made a mess of things. The only certainty is that the proportion of landless is rising. A new legal system of recording ownership is needed, with a systemic programme of land reform. The biggest obstacle to this are government officials.

Mr Sarowar says that the aims of Samata are to establish land ownership and redistribution of *khas* land to the landless, a review of land use and land law, and management and agricultural reform. 'This will transform Bangladesh. Without reform, no one should be surprised to see increasing violence, unrest, civil war between rich and poor. The NGO culture of credit is not useful, unless it is allied to structural reform, so that it becomes an instrument for creating a good life.'

Samata has developed links with like-minded organisations at local, national and international levels. According to 1995 statistics, there are 121,000 hectares of *khas* land under government control and 405,000 hectares of 'unused land' under the Forest Department, Railways and other ministries; 7,000 markets throughout the country are under the jurisdiction of the Ministry of Land, and 400,000 hectares of 'excess land' accumulated through land-reform ceilings. Many waterbodies are also common resources upon which the poor have a claim. Members of Samata have been elected to local administrations. In 1997, 43 of 53 candidates from the landless poor were successful.

Water – a common resource
DR FARUQUE:
  In Bangladesh, the landless may not have access – at least in the near future – to land. But what about water? Water has not been privatised. It is a common property resource. How can that be made available to the poor? Our idea – which came from the people themselves – is that in the 1970s, when tubewell and pumpwell irrigation were introduced, the rich monopolised it, became water-lords. Poor people said, 'How can we gain access to the water?'
  We collaborated with a British academic, Dr Geoff Wood, an adviser to the Agriculture Ministry, who was working on the socialisation of agricultural resources. We told him of the people's need. It all came together – a social scientist, people on

the ground and a new phenomenon in Bangladesh – tubewell irrigation. With him we devised an action research programme. How can the poor use this common resource to improve their economic and social position? The poor would make a contract with landed farmers in a particular command area to sell water to them, for cash or a quarter of the crop.

We wanted to see if farmers would make an agreement with the landless, and if the landless would have confidence to manage the technology. We were testing our assumption, that it would achieve distributive justice and improve the income-flow of the poor.

It worked. The farmers accepted the landless as water-sellers. This was because big landlords, from whom they usually took water, are more powerful than they are, and they could not protest at any wrong-doing on their part. They found it better to take water from the landless, who are neutral. They own no land in the command area, so they will not take more for *their* land than they give the farmer. They were also more efficient: since they had a share in the crop, the higher the productivity, the greater their share. We were surprised. There was little conflict, even from the big landowners.

Why was this? Our research showed that the landholding of big landlords is not all in one place. They may have 500 acres, but in bits and pieces. A landlord cannot set up tubewells in such scattered sites. If someone else provides water close to one of his pieces of land, he is happy. In Bangladesh land fragmentation is supposed to be a problem. In this case, it worked in our favour. We found landless and women's groups competent in the irrigation programme, both in technology and management. With a little training, they did it beautifully. The income rise was tremendous. It proved you can increase the control of the poor over a common resource.

It is now a big programme in Proshika and other NGOs. There was no defeat of one side in order for the other to gain. It isn't always like that. But there are occasions where a benefit going to the poor does not necessarily mean a loss for the rich. We use the model in other branches of agriculture. Cattle are used for traction. There is a shortage of traction-power. We helped landless groups to buy power-tillers, which they hire to farmers for a fee. Provision of some services in agriculture can be given by the poor, in exchange for which they get a share of the crop.

In some contracts they get money, in others a quarter of the produce. This is how we promote access to resources, and to resource-management by the poor. Of course, all this is in the absence of thoroughgoing land reform. We are not giving up land reform, but in the meantime, we must find other forms of participation.

The fate of the handloom weavers

From Pabna we passed through Shahjatpur, centre of the handloom weavers; small factories, sheds crammed with looms, some with one or two looms open to the air. A road off the highway leads to Parkola, an extended village on rocky earth, at different levels, shaded by palms, bamboo and jackfruit; scattered houses, small factories, open sheds, neither urban nor rural – like early industrialism in Britain, with factories built close to available water-power, often in the countryside.

People here have been weaving from antiquity. Their story echoes that of handloom weavers in Britain in the early industrial era, as their capacity to earn an independent living was eroded. They were starved out of their trade, forced to send their children into mills and factories. Here, declining work for handlooms, competition from power-looms and mills have cut into the traditional, semi-domestic craft.

Sufia has been a handloom worker for 25 years. She now has three looms operating, but three years ago she had ten: she sold when her husband fell sick. A loom costs 5–6,000 taka. In her shed, the looms stand idle – a tin roof, open metal-grille walls on a concrete base. Sufia made good quality sarees, and for each she got 500–600. Her market has been ruined by cloth from India. She has three boys, three girls. Her husband and one boy work at looms in a small factory, each earning 500 taka a week for a 12-hour day. Sufia acquired her looms by saving and loans. Her father had been a weaving labourer but owned no loom. She became very skilled, proud of what she produced. Now she processes thread with the traditional *charkha*, rolling it ready for the looms, for 100 taka a week. Her own income has declined; only the work of her children saves her from falling into poverty.

Md Sonaulla is in his 40s. He works in the house of a loom-owner. The owner sends thread to his home, where his wife and children work with a *charkha*. Md Sunavilla earns 70 taka daily, a decline from 100 four years ago; the family members who roll thread earn 12 taka a day. He weaves high-quality cloth for sarees, working from sunrise to sunset with his two oldest sons. One of these is married with a family of his own. He does not like to think of the future.

This area was badly affected by floods in 1998. Proshika provided drinking water and medicines. The water here is contaminated by arsenic, which has affected much of the drinking water in Bangladesh, leading to serious illness, skin lesions, and as yet unmonitored side-effects of slow poisoning. Although arsenic occurs naturally, it becomes more concentrated as the water table falls. This disaster by stealth threatens to be one of the worst catastrophes the country has known.

We climbed a slope to a higher part of the village. A factory is perched on a promontory in a bamboo-grove; bamboo frame, tin roof, walls open to the air. The twenty looms are close together in two rows. The owner, Izzat Ali, is now losing money. The market price for his cloth is too low. Indian cloth is undercutting even the local market.

There are twenty employees and two overseers. About half the looms are working. One man is making cloth for sarees patterned with silver. He pulls the silver thread by hand; the rest of the cinnamon-coloured material is woven with the shuttle, which he moves by operating a wooden treadle and pulling on a rope. The wooden looms are crudely made; many have been clumsily repaired, but all are functioning. The work is highly skilled, and requires constant vigilance; any break in the thread is repaired by hand. The work is slow and laborious.

The workers do a twelve or fourteen-hour day for 70 taka. Izzat Ali owes 60,000 taka. If the price falls further, he will have to close. He cannot get money from the bank, which will not lend for such unreliable concerns. The debt is not owed directly to moneylenders: he gets thread for the cloth from a dealer who gives credit on commission. He has to pay back in the last month of the Bengali year (March/April). He must also pay the interest on the credit, and if he cannot do so, he must sell something of value. He bought the factory seven years ago, and makes 10 taka profit for every two pieces of cloth. Twenty pieces are made daily – 200 taka profit. There are seven people in his family; his wife, mother and four children. He says, 'I use

Bangladeshi thread, because I am a patriot', although the reward for doing so is slender.

Over the tin roof of the factory purple flowers of a creeper are in radiant bloom. It is a surreal sight and sound – the clatter of looms through the trees and bamboo, the grey earth and stagnant ponds green with algae and coloured cotton-dust – a melancholy beauty, the pervasive sadness of uneconomic and declining labour.

The weavers' champion

In Dhaka I met Bibi Russell, designer and vigorous defender of the handloom weavers, whose craft has made a unique contribution to Bengali art and tradition. She has a studio and office in Motijheel, the commercial centre of Dhaka. Her passionate commitment makes her a one-woman global ambassador for weavers. She smokes incessantly, talking animatedly. She wears a dramatic blue and green saree, hand-loom cloth, which cost 145 taka – itself the most eloquent tribute to the beauty of the work of people she wants to rescue from the demoralisation we saw in Shahjatpur.

I work in the villages, I live in a village, I am inspired by the villages where 80 per cent of our people live. I work solely in the handloom sector. I am a designer, I have a degree from the London School of Fashion, I had a fellowship at the Textile Institute in London; I came back to Bangladesh six years ago, designing for handloom fabrics. There is a lack of textile designers, and that is my second subject. As a designer, I need fabric. I use traditional design, but if I'm doing a collection for London or Madrid, I use my expertise in colour and style for the particular market. I'm not aiming at Bangladeshi expatriates. Bangladesh can compete in the world market. I must be familiar with the colours of the skin, the climate, the colours people can wear.

I stayed in the village two years before I showed my collection. From the villages I get confidence, both in myself and in the weavers. This has been my dream. It has taken twenty years to make it come true; and those who made it happen are the weavers who also realised their own dreams. I love my life and work. Financially it is not rewarding, since I work with some of the lowest-paid people in Bangladesh. I made my career in Europe. I took my time, and now I am giving my time back to those who inspired me. Today, if I am able to show at the British Fashion Collection, it is because of the village people.

Culture and creativity will eliminate poverty. Think of 1971. Why was the War of Liberation fought? To keep our culture, reclaim our history. The history of Bengal is the history of textiles. The museums of the world hold our wonderful muslins, our handloom work. If the weavers suffer, it is because Bangladesh is not using its human resources properly. The two great sources of livelihood in the countryside are agriculture and handloom-weaving. The craft is dying in Bangladesh, only NGOs try to revive it. The people need a proper education, to learn to revalue what is wonderful in our past. How many children are familiar with our crafts? In all the big libraries of the world, our motifs have been written about, admired, copied. I could spend my life reviving these – if the government of the country does not realise, at least Proshika, Grameen and BRAC [the two largest NGOs in Bangladesh] should give scholarships to help recover and celebrate our rich heritage.

When I went to Europe I learned the music, art and literature of those countries. I could do so because I knew my own culture. I was not selling flowers in the street. When you know your own culture, you can appreciate that of others. In Bangladesh we do not know our culture.

I went to a Bangla-medium school. Now people with money send their children to English-medium schools. It isn't bad to learn English, to go to discos, enjoy yourselves, but it is if you forget your own culture. No problem with junk culture, as long as you know it is junk. Not knowing there is anything else – that is dangerous. If you lose your roots and come adrift from your culture, then your culture is threatened.

Bangladesh made history out of its muslin, so sheer and beautiful the whole world wanted it. I cannot revive even 20 per cent of them – they were not recorded in any books. In the 1851 Great Exhibition at the Crystal Palace, muslin was a sensation. In 1998, in the Natural History Museum in South Kensington, I exhibited my design – traditional garments, the *lunghi* and *gamcha*, the varied and versatile uses for these wonderful articles. I got great coverage in the British press. But I cannot revive the whole village economy alone. My work shows to the world positive images of Bangladesh to draw attention to the splendour of our country, its art, culture and music.

I have been promoting Fashion for Development. People in the fashion industry think it is about expensive things. My saree cost three dollars. Fashion is also culture. You have to know how to wear it. Village women who have not eaten for two days still cover themselves gracefully. Fashion doesn't mean items costing five hundred dollars.

My slogan is linked to development – food, shelter and clothing are basic needs, and we should give due recognition to the third of these, not because we are sorry for poor people who make the garments, but because they make beautiful things. They can compete with the world if their confidence is restored, if they have the technology – not technology that drives the world faster and faster, hi-fis, computers; that will leave behind 80 per cent of the people.

I was in Shahjatpur ten days ago. I am going to Rajshahi, where silk-making goes back to the thirteenth century. If we made silk then, why not now? I don't need academic knowledge, I want to know how the fabric was made, how it is made. In Rangpur, Dinajpur, names synonymous with poverty now, there is no handloom industry left. You can learn it only from old people. I am collecting the styles and techniques stored in village memories; to help the craft survive is my passion. The 1971 war was fought by weavers and wearers of *lunghi* and *gamcha*.

If no one appreciates you, you lose confidence in yourself. Confidence in the local has to be restored. Handloom – the two hands, two feet, two eyes, it is a rhythm, a dance. I do not want computer-generated design, I want the intelligence and creativity of the people. The children must learn, so the next generation is educated. Weavers who can read will bring heightened skills to their work. I'm against child labour, but not against children learning the creative miracles of our past. They will have the advantage of going to school, they will learn marketing and how to sell their products.

When a weaver leaves the loom, he or she does so out of desperation. They are not rickshaw-drivers, labourers, farmers. This is why I tried to make people in the villages understand. They said to me at first, 'You will come and then you will go away again. Who will continue?' I said, 'No, I'll come back.' They know now that I'll always return.

I am not threatened by fundamentalists. In the villages we have some beautiful mosques. I love Islamic architecture. When I go to the villages, if I wear a saree, I always wear a sleeveless blouse. I smoke in the village. I even smoke in NGO meetings. You can do *namaz* five times a day, as long as you don't interfere with me. When they abuse or torture women, then I get angry. If they won't let her go outside, it is they who are acting against Islam not the woman. I find much to admire in the Islamic tradition.

The village economy today, where is it? All the funds, where do they go? Poor people need to be earning, they need the pride that comes from earning a living. I don't own any enterprise. I buy some fabrics from Proshika. There should be scholarships so people understand colours, blending and dyes. People in the village do not know what potential treasures they have. Ever since I was small, I was always in villages, exposed to traditional artists, musicians, artisans. Whenever I speak about villages I talk of their creativity, not their misery and injustice. Behind me are a million weavers. UNESCO gave me special envoy status for my work on behalf of the weavers.

I came back because I was ready to return. I have kids, I was married and divorced. I lived in Italy. People thought, 'when she comes back, she'll open a shop in Gulshan or Banani'. Others thought I came back because I couldn't make it over there. They find returning under any other circumstances inconceivable. I was successful abroad. I came back to the grass roots for the sake of the weavers. They say, 'She's been away all this time, and she didn't even bring a TV or a car.'

The garments industry? All we are doing is tailoring, not design. The garments industry buys only foreign fashions. They don't get fabrics from here. Everything from outside. I have begged them to take my designs. It all confirms the view that Bangladesh is fit only to make up other people's fabrics. It is a repeat of history – stop making beautiful muslins and import Manchester goods. The garments industry is here only for cheap labour. They say we cannot produce the fabric. It is a lie. I show nothing I cannot produce here.

6 ❀ South-East

The provincial town at night

We arrived in Comilla at 11.30 at night. The lightless town had closed down, apart from a few rickshaw-drivers on the dark road. The hotel reception was locked: a grille held together by an outsize padlock. On faded plush sofas two young men were asleep. We rattled the bars to rouse them, and the grille parted. The rooms were also padlocked, high-ceilinged chambers with dirty cord carpets, covered in trampled cigarette ends, some of which had burned holes in the fabric. A dim wall-light, no ventilation, a suffocating smell of dust and insecticide to which mosquitoes had acquired immunity. A grime-penetrated towel on a tarnished silver rail; a residue of dried suds inside the plastic bucket. A drinking-glass stained with grey water spots stood on a dressing table; a mirror so faded it looked like a doorway to another room. The strip lighting sang, flakes of whitewash drizzled down.

Next day, I spoke to the young men on reception; one 20, the other 21, both were from large village families owning 2 or 3 bighas of land. They sat behind the formica-topped counter, a picture of Sheikh Mujib above them. Even in the daytime they sleep, head resting on arms folded on the counter, full of dreams, longing for places they have never visited, from which guests occasionally come. 'Show me some foreign money', they asked. 'Take me to your country. Let me be your cook. I will drive your car.' They smile. They know these are not even real requests.

We took breakfast in a spacious eating-house just outside Comilla. These luxurious buildings are set back from the road: a sweeping drive, gardens blazing with scarlet dahlias, salvias and marigolds. A dining area extensive and empty, with employees clustered around immaculate tables set for some not really expected banquet. Lavish and functionless, these places are perhaps a means of laundering black money. It is rumoured that this one is owned by a government official. Money from smuggling, trafficking, fraudulent bank-loans, extortion, corruption has to pass through the cleansing ritual of legitimate business. What better metamorphosis than to reappear in the world in the smiling guise of an inn in a garden of exotic flowers?

The crest of the Hill Tracts soon appears; bare flanks, rockfalls and jagged serrations bite into the misty blue. We reached Mirsarai, 60 kilometres from Chittagong. It was March, the time of the SSC exams. Outside every school building were crowds of friends, siblings, guardians, parents, servants of examinees, holding the railings as though visiting the unjustly jailed. The importance with which exams are invested is unimaginable in the West. Relatives cosset and spoil the entrants for weeks beforehand, see to their well-being, terrified of failure or worse, since some even take their own lives under pressure. This is a true rite of passage, not so much into adulthood, as into the next circle of hope of those aspiring to a career, government service, higher education, a green card, a passage outside, into a wider world.

The women in a conservative area

In the Proshika office women come and go. Most wear the black *burkha* which covers the body, with a narrow aperture for the eyes. Rani Begum says her husband sold the last portion of land to go to Abu Dhabi; there is a tradition of recruitment from here. The sale brought enough to pay an agent for a job. He sends home 60,000 taka a year (US$1,200). Khaleda's husband returned after two years with a good sum, but is now working in a jute mill. He lost it all through gambling. Now he earns 2,500 taka a month. He still gambles, so she returned to her father's house. She is 23. Her group is called Melody of the Universe.

Monjuranee is Hindu. Her husband is a river fisherman, and his earnings are irregular. He is also a sharecropper, on the basis of two-thirds profit, but he pays for all the inputs. They have three children. Although Hindu, she put on the *burkha* after marriage at 13. She dislikes it. It is hot and unhealthy. 'If the head of the family compels us to wear it, we must do so. It is uncomfortable, but we have no choice.'

The other women were married at 12 and 14. 'We do not want early marriage for our daughters, we do not want them to wear *burkha*.' But everything depends upon husbands or fathers. 'The *burkha* is a prison. We are captives.' Most women had no schooling, or only a little in the *madrasa*. All expect to give dowry – the 'demand' – at marriage. 'If you don't answer the demand, there will be no marriage.' Shoorjehan's brother took nothing when he married. He went to college after the *madrasa*, got a degree, and is now a teacher. 'What is the demand?' 'Cash-money, a TV, a cycle, a wristwatch, ornaments. Sometimes the family asks for more. If you can't give, trouble begins – beating and quarrels.' All know of women who have committed suicide.

'A job in Abu Dhabi costs 120,000 taka. This is paid to an agent. Sometimes agents take the money and disappear. There are many cheats, not only in Mirsarai. Cheats are running our country.'

The women say they have made progress, in spite of the conservatism of the area.

Earlier, we could not sing in public. Now we take part in dramas, we mix and discuss together. Of course, children work together in the fields, gathering firewood, weeding, cutting rice, looking after animals. They play together. But when they grow up, boys and girls are separated. Women suffer many indignities. There was a case of acid-throwing here last year. One man killed a young girl, because her father had arranged a marriage for her and this man wanted her for his nephew. Girls go to garment factories in Chittagong and Dhaka. Some go to be maids. We always fear for their safety. Will they be properly treated, looked after? Will they return?

Aklima, 19, is wearing an orange saree. She is to be married shortly, and will wear the *burkha*. 'It is the custom. We do not like it. It is like going into the dark.' Marriage thus becomes an intimation of death.

The road to Chittagong

Approaching Chittagong, the traffic was more congested, the narrow road blocked on both sides, especially where it passed through small towns. With traffic density, pollution increases; dust, fumes, smoke, carbon monoxide – everything stagnates in the still, sunny air. Rickshaw-drivers wear small linen masks over the nose and mouth, curiously erotic, a mixture of bandit and brain-surgeon; others wear a *gamcha* over the face. A woman, skinny and gaunt, spits a long jet of blood-red betel-juice through stained teeth: a consumptive vampire. A gleaming white palace bears the logo Glaxo-Wellcome. Here drugs are produced to cure the sicknesses and accidents caused by cars and industrial vehicles imported for roads that cannot contain them: the ugly circularity of a development that damages only to be 'healed' by further damage; the pollution and disregard for life and limb created by multinationals and 'cured' by the products of yet another.

In Chittagong, we were met by a teacher, a member of Bodhan, the leading group in Proshika's cultural network. Bodhan is dedicated to conserving and enhancing Bengali culture. It runs a school, teaching drama, folk-themes, dance, dialogue, story-telling, ballad-singing, recitation, choral work and song; a rich storehouse of tradition; but more significantly, a resource in the struggle against fundamentalism.

Much funding for the resistance to fundamentalism comes from the West. This predisposes the recipients to leniency towards Western dominance, compared with their revulsion against Islamic fundamentalism. I asked many people whether the greater danger to Bengali culture in the long run would come from the fundamentalists of profit or the prophets of fundamentalism. The answer is not obvious.

We went with Nazma of Bodhan to her house in the centre of Chittagong, an area of small cycle-rickshaw workshops, where vehicles or parts of vehicles are sold and repaired; scores of concrete cells, each stacked with one piece of what will be assembled into rickshaws: an astonishing division of labour in these elegant, apparently simple structures – wooden hoops for the folding frame of the hood, hinges, painted plastic panels behind the hood, painted metal at the base, silver arcs of mudguards, wheels, axles, festoons of chains, pedals, spokes, the shell of bodywork. The drivers themselves are only the most conspicuous part of an intensive and extensive labour in which millions of Bangladeshis find a livelihood.

A social occasion

Nazma's house is in a small courtyard, surprisingly tranquil so close to the clamour of the streets; two or three trees and a cement wall are enough to block the sound of the traffic and create an island of calm.

Nazma recited a poem by Tagore. It is called 'Africa'. It is about slavery, and the shame which falls upon all humanity for this outrage. The poem celebrates the beauty and harmony of the traditional cultures of Africa, which were broken by the Europeans who, in the name of civilisation, tracked down the people like beasts to work as slaves under distant foreign skies.

Nazma recites the long poem in her beautiful Bangla, the sweet sensuousness of the language articulated with passion and clarity. This is itself another art-form, between music and poetry, where the voice itself is a different instrument from that heard in song or speech. It would be unthinkable in Western society to recite a poem to strangers.

Nazma says,

> Recitation is important in our culture. In ancient Bengal, our forefathers recited from religious books, and the only other material – stories, fables and myths – was transmitted orally. Then, this was not formed as a 'culture', it was a practical means of carrying forward our sense of identity. Our group is motivated by the desire to share, to preserve our inheritance of poetry, literature and song.
>
> All our work is against fundamentalism, because this is contrary to our Bangali tradition. We emphasize poems and songs in favour of humanity. Fundamentalist activity is higher in Chittagong than elsewhere. They have created many problems for us. They break up our auditorium, sometimes cause a disturbance during our programmes, break the chairs, throw bombs. Yet every month we give our performances. At our school we teach traditional Bangali arts. On Language Day the fundamentalists forbid the placing of flowers on the memorial of the Shaheed Minar. They say this is *puja*, a Hindu custom, and Muslims may not do it.

Nazma has a law degree and works in a solicitors' practice in Chittagong.

As I gain confidence, I am gaining independence. My family think they are giving me independence, but this is not a gift in anyone's pocket or bag – it must be worked for. Women think they have to be submissive and quiet. They are captives. Most caged women in Bangladesh do not even know they are in a cage. They do not have the chance to be themselves. Not only those in *burkha* – they are obviously trapped, but so are many rich and middle-class women in sarees, jewels and gold. They see wealth as privilege. Young women in college are looking for a husband, a home, security. Who will give them security if they cannot secure it for themselves? Security is not something external like a guard at the gate of your compound. A woman gets married, she goes eagerly to her husband's house as if towards her future, taking jewels, money, goods. When she gets there, she may be killed because she didn't bring enough for the family. Where is her security? The demand for dowry is increasing, because consciousness is affected by TV, satellite dishes; they want more and more. Parents are selling their children for goods. The worst of tradition is reinforced by commercialism. Dowry and consumerism is a marriage of what is most ugly in the old world and most repulsive of the new. It affects all society, elites down to the poorest. What I dislike most is those who know what they are doing is wrong, yet still do it. Old and modern superstitions – jewellery, social occasions, yet she is a servant to her husband. Many of my friends are frightened into seeking the shelter of this stereotyped illusion of security.

Tagore said, 'The religion we know from books is not my religion. That I have to create inside my heart. This is the only real devotion, and it is created with pain. I have to feel it in my veins. After that, whether I get happiness or not, I do not know'.

Sites of struggle

We went to some historic sites of Chittagong – Jalalabad Hill, where Prithi Lothawadadar and her comrades threw bombs into the European Club in the 1930s. She could not run away with her male colleagues and, to avoid being taken by the authorities, she took a capsule of potassium cyanide and died before they could reach her. Surjya Sen, a teacher, came here with a flotilla of small boats and liberated Chittagong for four days in 1930, urging all Indians to rise up. Gandhi cried 'Chittagong to the fore' in 1930. Subhash Bose collected arms and ammunition here to fight the British in 1942. In 1971 it was over Chittagong Radio that Zia ur-Rahman announced the liberation of Bangladesh in the name of Sheikh Mujib. Zia ur-Rahman was also killed here. The city has a disturbed, violent history.

Memories of the Raj
Vinod Chaudhury lives in central Chittagong; a narrow alley from a busy road leads to a cul-de-sac. A small tree-framed compound behind a stone wall; a crowded room opens on to the street; walls covered with portraits of political leaders, freedom fighters, including Gandhi and Prithi Lothawadadar. Mr Chaudhury, in *khadi* (homespun cloth), vivid watchful eyes over spectacles that repeatedly fall down his nose; a mobile smile, a keen mind; at 90, his energy, intelligence and humanity undiminished.

For him, the valour of Prithi Lothawadadar is living memory.

> In 1929 I was studying. Prithi was a leader of an organisation of anti-colonial revolutionaries, to which I also belonged. It was founded by Surjya Sen, inspired by the memory of the Jalianwala Bagh massacre in 1919, when hundreds of unarmed people were shot by the British in cold blood. Prithi was one of six chosen to bomb the European Club, with the intention of killing Europeans. They fired in retaliation. Prithi told her friends to leave, because she could not run as fast as they. She said, 'The police will arrest me, there may be outrages against me, I will commit suicide.' The British authorities were astonished and shaken to see a girl of 22 sacrifice her life.

The portrait of her on the wall, black and white, shows a young woman, face set in righteous defiance.

> One of the group was caught and charged with conspiracy. The British hanged him in the jail. They did not hand his body to relatives, who were unable to take their leave of him. It was taken out into the Bay of Bengal, weighed down with stones and thrown into the water. They feared any tomb would be a rallying-point for young revolutionaries.

> We had no military training, but we were full of anger against

the British. We saw ourselves as deliverers of India. At that time, the imperialist government was torturing the people. We wanted to start a movement that would make the whole country rise up. Our plan was to die, but we would fight to the last. This would inspire millions to take our place and remove the alien occupiers. We knew we would perish. We thought our sacrifice would serve as an example to all the youth. We had such patriotic feelings, we thought we would destroy imperialism.

The movement began in 1905, after the first British attempt to partition Bengal. Our boys – some had studied in London – were inspired by the Irish revolution, by Japan, Garibaldi and Mazzini, and the uprising in Russia preceding the Revolution. Even in 1914, revolutionary leaders went to Germany, which promised three shiploads of arms. One was to come to Cox's Bazaar, one to Orissa, one to Bombay. Our leader went to take delivery of arms at Cox's Bazaar, but government had been warned. A skirmish took place, and he was killed. People know about Subhash Bose in the Second War, but few remember we also sought help of Britain's enemies in 1914–15.

In the Second War, Gandhi was for the British, but Subhash Bose was with the Axis powers. Gandhi was a lover of peace and non-violence. We hated the British, so we chose what we thought was the lesser evil. If it had not been for the A-bomb, the Japanese army might have overrun India. Of course, it is also more than possible that the Tojo government might not have given us independence.

In April 1930, we briefly defeated the British army and police, and overran the armoury. We took all the arms we could carry, and set fire to everything that remained. As we were celebrating, raising the national flag and declaring Surjya Sen president, we realised a comrade had been badly burned in the fire. Our commander-in-chief took the boy by car and left us. We waited. They didn't come back. The district commissioner went to the jetty to the British ships, and came with machine guns to the police lines where we were waiting. They didn't know exactly what arms we had. We decided to take shelter in the hills until our commander came back.

We took refuge in what was then full jungle. It hadn't been cut as it is now. We waited two nights, then sent someone to town to see what had happened. We hadn't come to the jungle to flee, but to fight. We entered the town, having had no food or water for three days. We came to Jalalabad Hill at dawn, where we hid. There were fewer trees there, a few cowsheds. Some cowherds reported our presence. The military and police came. There was a battle that lasted two and a half hours. I was wounded, but eleven were killed and one died later.

Our leaders decided not to fight face to face. The British had overwhelming force on their side. We discovered the inspector-general of Chittagong would leave on a certain day. When he alighted from the train to take the steamer for Chatpur he would be shot down. We shot his bodyguard by mistake. One of our members was arrested, tried and hanged; one was transported for life to the Andaman Islands. Bengal created many revolutionaries, as did Maharashtra and Punjab.

I left that group in 1939. There were two revolutionary groups. Mine decided to dispense with arms henceforth and to join Gandhiji. We thought our role of arousing the people had been achieved. Now we would support Gandhi in pursuit of freedom, non-violence and truth. By then I had been in prison three times, in 1933, 1939 and in 1941, where I remained for four years. During that period, the authorities were lenient; we were interned under suspicion only. They gave us enough money for food, clothing, and even to support our families.

The best period of my life was spent in jail – the cream of society, the intellectuals, creative people, the best of our generation were together. There I began to love music, literature, even cricket. We had meetings and discussions. I took my BA in Law from jail. Jail was my university, literally. I got higher education there in every way. It was a time of ferment and ideas. The empire was tottering to its close, and in spite of our detention the world never seemed more open or promising.

In 1947 I was in the Bengal Congress committee. They wanted me to go to West Bengal. I could not. Chittagong is my home, I could not leave it. When I become an invalid I may go to Calcutta, where my son is. But my dead body will return. I have told my son – even if I breathe my last in West Bengal, send me back to Chittagong.

Things are not well in our country. After the murder of

Bangabandhu, those who were against the freedom of Bangladesh came to power. They spread communalism. This was their policy and their aim: 85 per cent of people are communal and cannot tolerate Hindus. Democracy cannot be established without communal harmony. We love power, money, cars, houses, not the people. A shadow of democracy exists, but it is a mockery. If the character of the young is not transformed, I see no silver lining. It seems we shall have to fight all over again for the freedoms we thought we had won. That would mean a bloodbath between Muslims.

After winter comes spring, after night, sunrise. I am an optimist. I bear ill-feeling to no one. I coach boys in the morning – my source of livelihood. I maintain myself. One newspaper from Dhaka, *Janakantha*, gave me an award of 25,000 taka in cash, and 5,000 a month. That has helped me, and saved me from scolding my wife. The struggle for life is never finished.

There is no political idealism. Intelligent thoughtful young people go into cultural organisations. Politics is hypocrisy, mendacity. Hasina can do nothing in her own party, because it is conservative, communal and corrupt. I wrote to her a year ago, asking for a ten-minute talk. Her secretary replied, so I know she received it. Till now I had no proper reply.

My father was a civil lawyer. He practised in remote districts near the Tripura border. From him I got my spirit of nationalism. He attended the non-cooperation meetings in 1920–21, when Gandhi urged people to abandon all foreign clothing in favour of homespun, *khadi*. I used to see the *jatra*, the open-air theatre, as a child; the performers delivered stirring speeches, inspired the people on the theme of *svadeshi*, self-reliance. Women would tear off their foreign clothes and ornaments. The songs remain, but the struggle has faded.

Other influences on me – above all, my wife. In 1946, Muslims murdered Hindus in Calcutta, a frightful slaughter. The Hindus united and retaliated. For four or five days it continued. In Noakhali, a place of fanatics, Hindus were slaughtered. My wife was with Gandhiji on his famous visit to Noakhali, trying to halt the killing. He went from village to village; they tried to stop him, throwing stones and nails. She is my inspirer and guide. Without her, Vinod Chaudhury would have achieved nothing.

Bela Chaudhury – pale *khadi* saree with a dark border, grey hair scraped back, thick glasses – a modest, self-effacing woman, teacher, instructor and inspirer of the young. She sits beside her husband, a picture of humanity and wisdom grown out of violent struggle; symbol, too, of a vanishing Bengal of tolerance and the celebration of diversity.

Memories of Liberation V

MR MAHBUBUL KARIM, SENIOR VICE-PRESIDENT OF PROSHIKA:

Soon after the war, I joined BRAC. I was wondering how best to serve my country. My father was upset because I wouldn't take a government job. As a freedom fighter it would have been easy.

BRAC seemed to be in keeping with the progressive politics I was committed to. Not knowing the future I jumped in – I never dreamed the work of NGOs would become a more progressive force than politics. I wanted only to do something for the people. After three years I left to join the Canadian University Service Overseas, a team of about ten. I met the poorest people with BRAC, which in spite of my involvement with politics I had never done.

When I'm asked about the differences between BRAC, Grameen and Proshika, I quote an Indian researcher, who said, 'Grameen is target-oriented, BRAC project-oriented and Proshika process-oriented'. That is the difference, although the goal is more or less the same.

I was in a Leftist group. There were bitter differences on the Left. Some were opposed to the Liberation War, because they feared we would fall under Indian domination. But the real split was the Moscow–Beijing rift. Today it looks foolish and doomed, but then it was deadly serious. The pro-Moscow group supported the war, but the pro-Beijing factions opposed it. Many of us decided to fight anyway. We said no issue takes precedence over this. We must join the liberation process.

After the war there was chaos and confusion. Values had been eroded, everything ruined. The presence of the Indian army was dangerous. The new government asked them to leave. Sheikh Mujib achieved this with his charisma and leadership. But many of those who had disagreed with the war were still armed. They created a law-and-order problem. The outlawed Leftists would not co-operate with government; some looted and plundered.

One reason Sheikh Mujib lost his life was because his party could not control the situation. It was not their fault. There was no administration, the bureaucracy was weak. We had fought partly because Bangalis had had no access to government jobs – army, education, administration. The Pakistanis had taken our resources. It was similar to Partition – when Bengal was divided the industry was all around Calcutta; Dhaka was a provincial town in an agricultural region. We had only fertile land and people. Our exports were jute and tea, but foreign exchange was used to set up industries in West Pakistan.

Expectations could not be fulfilled. Sheikh Mujib's party said if we had autonomy, rice would be cheaper, foodgrains would cost less, life would be easier. Instead, we saw prices rise. At that time, the raw materials for making paper were in Chittagong; it was sent to Karachi and by the time it came back the price had doubled. Travellers from East to West Pakistan could take as much jewellery as they wished, but in the other direction it was not allowed. It was supposed to be the same country but you couldn't bring gold from West to East.

It proved impossible to reduce the cost of basic needs. And that wasn't all. The country failed to produce a true democracy. Then from 1975 military dictatorship lasted till 1991. I do not think military rule a desirable path for any country. The military achieved little in nearly fifty years in Pakistan. And what did it do for poverty in Bangladesh?

Government does not do its job. NGOs have done work which ought to have been carried out by government. When we started going to the villages, there was no provision for the poor. I do not blame the government of that time, you cannot build infrastructure overnight.

We saw then nothing was reaching the poor. Tens of millions of people crossed the border and lived in refugee camps. Politically, the Awami League was the only party with a country-wide base, but it was not organised for getting resources, it was organised for fighting. The administrative and political vacuum was filled by the voluntary sector in Bangladesh, although they were not conscious of it at the time.

When the government saw external aid-flow to NGOs reach

10–12 per cent of total aid, they began to take a keen interest. It still doesn't amount to much. But studies show that 74 per cent of government services reach the non-poor, whereas 66 per cent of NGO resources reach the poor. This gives us credibility. NGOs are smaller but effective.

In the early days, NGOs were criticised from left and right. Rightists said we were agents of Communism, and Leftists said we were agents of imperialism. The Right also said it was the mission of NGOs to make people Christian. This came from those we now call fundamentalists, but at the time they were just seen as religious groups.

The bureaucracy see NGOs as competitors who perform better than they do. It is their job to deliver services, which they fail to do. But today critics include the political parties. Until the 1991 return to democracy the parties didn't know how effective NGOs had been in building awareness among the people. When they went back to their constituencies, they found the people had changed. They were no longer the timid people who listened and didn't ask questions. They had received education and training. The politicians only wanted votes.

NGOs took over some government functions for historical reasons. If there had been good governance it might have been different. NGOs are now trying to negotiate with government to pursue reforms that will make it more responsive to the people's needs. We are actually offering the government a model of how it can be done.

The most recent South Asian Development Report says governments in countries like Bangladesh are elected by a majority of the people, but once elected they serve only the rich. This bias to the rich must be changed. This is why Proshika is involved institutionally. We set up the Institute for Development Policy Analysis and Advocacy. We are asking government to allocate more to poverty alleviation, for more effective interventions, local government reform and so on.

NGOs are necessary political organisations, but non-party political. They have every right to play an effective role in strengthening democratic institutions as well as in world governance.

In the Bay of Bengal

The sea at Cox's Bazaar is dramatic. On the shore, *gamari* trees with scaly grey bark and dark waxy leaves; *jhau* and the pink bells of sand-creepers clinging tenaciously to the shifting earth. An efflorescence of flowers and grasses has taken root in the concrete skeleton of a hotel abandoned half way through construction. Hotels and beach houses are set back from the sea, a precaution against storms. Little shops sell novelties and snacks, delicate shells of sea-creatures, mementoes, ornaments, T-shirts, ice-cream. The road is littered with pink and black plastic bags, disfiguring the natural beauty. It seems that an older tradition of discarding leaves and bamboo is carried over to the indestructible artefacts of industrial society, as though no one notices these do not go back to nourish the environment, but remain, cumulative pollutants.

At sunset, the wide expanse of wet sand is crowded. The beach is grey, but under a vast sky, reflections in the sand are images in glass; the sun sits, a red ball on a shimmering gold plinth of water like some Fascist-designed order of merit. Pink clouds stain the wet earth rose and blue. The breakers, transparent green curls of water, innocent of the potential violence of the Bay of Bengal; their green glass shatters on the beach and melts into the sand. The people stand, silent in the dusk, looking at the horizon, wondering how such beauty can engender destructive cyclones. A boy on a motorbike leaves a long snaking track, effaced by the next wave, which sucks voraciously at the sand.

The main road in Cox's Bazaar is long and congested. It starts as a sandy track at the sea-front, continues past hotels and guest-houses and then narrows into the shops, stores and the Burmese Market. Just behind the shore, workshops sell shells and ornaments made from scavengings of the sea. In shop number seven, at eight o'clock in the evening, Mir Ahmed is reading a newspaper by the light of a single electric bulb. Behind him three or four boys are working. They are making decorative artefacts out of shells. They start with lengths of thin pearly discs braided on plastic thread, work done by women confined to the home; slow laborious work with needle and thread, piercing each delicate little shell without breaking it. The women are paid 7 taka a dozen, and make two dozen a day. Mir Ahmed buys the shells from wholesalers at 7–10 taka a kilo and delivers them to home-workers.

Four boys live and work in the shop. Shabuddin, 10, left home after his father's second marriage: he was ill-treated by the new wife. He is shy and distrustful of strangers. Masud, 8, who has a fashionable layered haircut, and arrived only two weeks ago, couldn't be more different: he travelled alone by bus from Dhaka, where his father is a lock-maker in Gulistan. Why did he leave home? To see the world. At 8 years old? He shrugs. Md Ishak is 15, just arrived from Chittagong, where his father owns one-and-a-half bighas of land. Ali Aklam is the only one from Cox's Bazaar. His father teaches in a *madrasa*. The boys earn 300–500 taka a month. They eat and sleep in the shop.

Mir Ahmed has five children. They do not work, but go to school. The working boys had limited education. They learn to construct elaborate ornaments, incorporating chains of tiny shells into bigger structures with pink scallops, trumpets and whorls of grey-blue, cream and white. These are glued together to create intricate pyramids and chandeliers made entirely of the carapace of dead sea-creatures.

A seaside hustler

At the bus-stand I was stopped by a young man of about 20, wearing tight dirty blue jeans, *chappals* (sandals), a dingy white shirt. He said to me in perfect English, 'I am a poor student, and I need 1000 taka to buy an English dictionary for my studies. I want to become a tourist guide. I enjoy the company of foreigners, because they are more tolerant and their minds are open to the world. Is it true there is free sex in your country? Can you send me some magazines with pictures of men and women making love? I want to be your friend.' The abrupt pseudo-intimacy of this meeting was not my first in Bangladesh. It seems that a whole generation of educated or semi-educated young men have been penetrated by a fantasy of Western life, centred on money, fun and sex, elements absent from their lives. I felt I had been mistaken for the ambassador of a foreign country I do not represent. How could I even begin to dispel this misapprehension? I smiled and said I was only a visitor and could not help. He looked hurt. I gave him 50 taka. Five minutes later, he was talking to another stranger.

The Burmese in Cox's Bazaar

Khinmay works with a Proshika Burmese primary group. She does not know when her family came from Burma. She thinks they are from Arakan: when the Mogul Emperors ruled Greater India, they extended their territory to East Bengal and part of Burma, and Arakan fell under Mogul rule. Khinmay's grandfather was a customs officer in the Pakistani time. Her father is a sign painter.

'Burmese people in Bangladesh cannot observe their religious ceremonies in peace, because fundamentalists object to the Buddhist religion and disturb our worship. We are forbidden to use drums or to perform our rituals openly in public spaces. We are not free.'

Khinmay speaks Rakhain, a dialect of Burmese. Her husband is a high-school teacher. She says there are ten thousand Burmese in Cox's Bazaar, many of them very poor. About 85 per cent of men work on fishing vessels, wages depending on the value of the catch. Most vessel-owners are Bengalis. They work eight months of the year, but not in the monsoon. Women weave at home, traditional Burmese design, but the market is limited. Most own their handlooms, but the cotton thread is costly and they cannot compete with power looms.

I asked Khinmay whether she feels Bangladeshi, or if her heart is elsewhere.

> When I was 16, I went to Burma to see my relatives. My grand-mother is still there. I could not adapt to the life. I was eager to come back to Bangladesh. I doubt I will go there again. The people in Burma did not receive me as I had expected. They said, 'You are not pure Buddhist, you are mixed with Muslims'. I felt I did not belong.
>
> I graduated in 1994. Only 10–12 per cent of Burmese here are literate. You can learn in the pagoda, but school-going is very low. In our community, rural women work in the fields; weaving is an urban occupation. A few have land. In the Burmese market, most women serving in the shops come from villages. The owners are men, who hire two or three women, mostly their relatives.

Refugees from the Burmese junta

There are many Burmese refugees around Cox's Bazar, including, to the South towards Tekhnaf, camps for Rohinyas, minority Burmese Muslims, who fled persecution in their own country. The presence of

Burmese Muslims in Bangladesh is symbolic and controversial. Some see them as bearers of Islamic fundamentalism, others as a drain on the resources of Bangladesh, yet others as people in need of protection. The attitude of the Bangladesh government has become less ambiguous in recent years, and compulsory repatriation has emptied many of the camps.

Joshim, who works with refugees, says fundamentalists use them, recruit them, and exploit their plight to raise money in Islamic countries. 'They have a vested interest in keeping alive the image of poor persecuted Muslims. Even if they could be rehabilitated, many do not wish it to happen. Some escaped from the camps and are said to be "training" in the deep jungle. Others are involved in dacoity, hijacking, criminal activities. Some married local people in order to stay here permanently.'

Such stories resemble all tales about refugees, seekers of asylum, migrants and those fleeing persecution; such myths are traded in every country in the world in which people have sought sanctuary.

We visited Nayapara camp close to Tekhnaf. This is an enclosed extended village, where the most significant buildings are the UNCHR distribution centres and those of NGOs.

The camp official

Md Helal is the Bangladeshi government administrative officer, in post here for three years. His office is a sparsely furnished tin building. His job is tedious; he was reading the newspaper in great detail. He expressed the ennui of life here, his long exile from home in Barisal. The camp was set up in 1992.

> Refugees started coming in 1978, but more than 250,000 came when Burma became Myanmar. They said they were used as forced labour, their Rohinya identity not recognised; many complained of torture. They claim to be supporters of Aung San Suu Kyi, and the biggest exodus came after she won the election that was annulled. Most are illiterate and without leadership.
>
> The programme was co-ordinated by UNHCR. The world forgets. Even in our government, high officers now say there are no refugees in our country. Only 21,000 remain in the camps. Because they are Muslim, many want permanent settlement here; some want to return; others want to go to a third country. We did

205

not accept them permanently. Of those remaining, about 7,000 have been cleared by the Burmese government for return. The other 14,000 have not yet been given permission to go. We receive a letter of confirmation on Monday that certain families are to be repatriated on Wednesday. If any family members have gone out for medical reasons, or are working in the fields, or are in jail, the Myanmar authorities will not take any of them.

People can go out for medical treatment. Some work illegally. This is a rich area. People earn 90–100 taka daily, but refugees work for half that. There are shrimp fields, brick works, salt-making, fishing. Many refugees have become addicted to smoking. Most were farmers, fishing people or forest workers. They are fed by the World Food Programme, distributed by the Red Crescent. All families are entitled to provisions according to numbers. There are eight schools, the teachers are refugees. Few adults are literate. They want to learn Arabic and English, not Bangla. Even what they speak in Burma is akin to Bangla – these frontiers are, as usual, artificial colonial divisions.

Health in the camp is good, the death-rate low. In one week, there will be 15–20 births, only two or three deaths in a month. A new baby gets a full ration of food, so they have an interest in birth cultivation – they sell the baby's ration. UNCHR say that personal life in Burma is now safe. Those who remain are the poorest. They see no advantage in going back. The well-to-do have gone.

It is an open secret that international Islamic agencies are involved. Many leaders of these organisations are in a hotel in Cox's Bazaar. Rich people get money from Muslim countries in the name of these people. They are victims of a conspiracy, not caused by the Burmese government, although of course the government has its own internal repression. It suits the agenda of others to keep them in camps so money can be raised in the Gulf, and they are not beneficiaries.

Local people are not allowed into the camp. It is a bleak, inhospitable place. It is hard to believe that anyone who had an alternative would remain here. A broad treeless street cuts through the camp, buildings of tin and *chetai*. Rocky, arid, empty, a study in sensory deprivation – sun, sky, metal and dust. The metal chimney of a nearby brickworks glints in the light and sends a coil of grey smoke across the blue.

The refugees

A group of men stand in the thin strip of shade of the administrative building. This place has been home to Nur Hossein, Nurul Kobir, Lal Mir and Nur Mohammed for eight years. They seem to have internalised the desolation of their environment, and speak with numb stupefaction; or perhaps they have simply told their story too many times. Nur Hossein's land was taken by the military government for an army camp, confiscated without warning. No compensation was given. 'One day, the soldiers came and destroyed our houses. The government said we had to leave.' Nurul Kobir says the military did not even leave the dead undisturbed, but occupied his family's graveyard as well as their land. There are five in his family – mother, wife, brother and one son. There are eleven in the family of Lal Mir: nine children – five boys and four girls; the youngest born here. Lal Mir says the government picked them up in a truck one day to use as slave labour. They were forced to build an embankment for a dam. 'We were given no food, and ate only through the charity of local people. There had been no trouble between Muslims and Buddhists but only Muslims were forced to work.' Lal Mir knows that people have gone back, but he does not believe it is safe. 'We are not willing to go. So much pain inflicted on us, why return to a homeland that is no longer home?'

'This is the order of Allah. We have no power to change it, but we are sustained by faith.' Lal Mir says they have complained to officials over inadequate food: according to Islamic humanism, the government has a duty to provide basic necessities for refugees. They say the only occupation is 'sleeping, gossiping and enjoying with wives'.

Each person receives 3 kg of rice a week, 110 g of oil, 110 g of sugar, 150–175 g of dal, 300 g of salt; once a month, half a kilo of red peppers. Some have cultivated vegetable gardens in the narrow strip of land near their house. Children go to schools run by Médecins Sans Frontières and UNCHR. There are eight or ten mosques. Lal Mir says repatriations are forced upon them. 'We were tortured there. Who will go willingly?' They came by river, the Naf, dividing Burma from Bangladesh. They have never heard of Aung San Suu Kyi. All but Lal

Mir had a small piece of land. 'I will go back only if they restore my land to me. Now I have nothing.'

The dusty streets of grey mud are studded with a fishbone pattern of red brick paths. The huts are of clay and bamboo, roofs a lattice of bamboo and bags stamped UNCHR. They are in lines, the entrance less than a metre high, so people have to bend double to go inside. Possessions are meagre – a *chetai* mat, bamboo stool, a small stove. The long parallel streets are about three metres apart, criss-cross fencing of bamboo marking a boundary in front; a moneyless community of mendicants, awaiting in limbo a forced repatriation.

Kabir Hossein lives on a corner of one of the diminutive temporary streets. He has worked as day labourer in melon fields and salt beds. He and his wife, Fatima Tujuhara, have five children. They are courteous, extinguished people, expecting little, receiving less. Here, many own nothing – a bare interior of pale beaten earth, ragged matting, a *gamcha*, a *lunghi*; a string of rags across the room, a blackened pot, a few tin vessels. They say, 'You see how it is. Who would not go if they did not fear for their safety?'

Along the Naf river, extensive melon-beds, swollen striped fruits pale against darker leaves. This is a salt-making area: rectangles of brackish water evaporating in the sunlight form a crust of crystal, scattered brilliantines on grey earth. Here and there pontoons and half-bridges end in mid-river, with ladders down to boats, to deter forbidden border crossings.

Next morning, we learned that forty people had been deported from Nayapara soon after we left. The repatriation took place according to bureaucratic formalities. The families were not informed of their departure until the time came to pick up their scanty bundles and go.

Towards the Hill Tracts

On the way to Rangamati, we left the main Chittagong Road to visit Banderban in the southern part of the Hill Tracts. The road twists through the hills in capricious bends that overlook fallen scree on denuded hills, while on the other side the aerial roots of an ancient banyan tree hang above us like a hungry polyp. In places, the ashy ghosts of shrubs from slash-and-burn cultivation. The stark red candelabra of a *shimul* tree in lone festive splendour. Thickets in the valleys give a hint of untouched forest – dense clumps of vegetation of variegated greens. Everywhere, cut into the earth, the rain-smoothed steps, as many as fifty or sixty, leading to indigenous people's settlements of bamboo and straw, perched on poor platforms of earth.

The houses cling to the flanks of the valley, as though scattered at random. As the road rises towards Banderban, it passes an invisible frontier, after which there is a dramatic increase in the number of Adivasi faces, although Bengali migration has transformed the area.

The tribal people are now a minority in many areas. Government 'gave' land to settlers; the army evicted the indigenous people. When the Shantibahini – the guerrilla army of the Adivasis – retaliated, there was a twenty-year war. The Peace Accord negotiated between the Awami League government and the Shantibahini and signed in 1997 awaits implementation. Bands of dissenters, unreconciled to the agreement, remain in the deep jungle. They sometimes kidnap local leaders, traders or settlers, raiding buses or other vehicles at night; but the hills are more peaceful now than for two decades.

The area was highly militarised during the conflict, and more than 9,000 people were killed. Some 500 army camps were set up in the hills. Women and girls were raped and tortured. Both settlers and Adivasis were murdered. The Bangladeshi nationalists of the BNP are intolerant of the hill people, because they are Buddhist or animist. The Awami League Bangali nationalists refused to concede autonomy at the time of Independence. Their greater generosity now has come too late.

A living example of cultural pluralism

A meeting of women's leaders provided one of the most diverse groups I met in Bangladesh – Chakma, Marma, Thachungya, Tripura, Hindu, Muslim and Christian. They performed songs celebrating the diversity of Bengal – mainly patriotic, although it seemed to me that the tribal people have little enough to celebrate under pressure of Bengali occupation of the hills. One woman, a Hindu in her 50s, with a careworn face and pale thin hands, sings a devotional melody; an intense song saturated with Sufi spirituality – a passionate, poignant moment. The room is silent. Her voice is not beautiful, but haunting, sad, threnodic. Its subject is the simple offering of a flower to a god; but it becomes something more – a lament for a Bengal where cultures nourished each other, Islam and Hinduism took and gave freely, had not yet been defined as antagonistic, exclusive. She covers her face with her white saree, and as she exhales, the material flutters. When she has finished, she wipes the tears from her eyes. Here is the best of Bengal, the celebration of its mingled traditions, its openness, a delight shared even by the poorest in a rich co-existence of mutually complementary religious traditions. More than any explanation, in this touching moment I gained a glimpse of what my guides were trying to tell me about their Bengal.

After Independence

DR FARUQUE:

Our work began in the wake of the assassination of Sheikh Mujib and his family, and three months later the military takeover. This was very painful, utterly destructive. There was little public protest at the usurpation of governance by the military. Political protest was not possible. At first, because close associates of Sheikh Mujib appeared to have taken power, it looked like an internal struggle, because Mushtaq and his colleagues were from the Awami League. The non-corrupt part of the Awami League could not marshal public support. There was anger at the heinous crime, but that did not lead to protest, because there was no focus for our feelings.

Army rule could not be resisted because it was army rule. It also had implications for NGOs. The Foreign Donations Act of 1978 was aimed at curbing NGO activity, although NGOs didn't pose a threat then – they were still developing. By today's standards, they were still small. But it unnerved the fundamentalists, who were being rehabilitated. The military approved of the assassination of Sheikh Mujib, because it was backed by the pro-Pakistanis. After liberation, religious-based political parties were outlawed. They were rehabilitated in the late 1970s; some communal parties came into the government of Zia.

The bureaucrats who monopolised foreign credit also recognised that significant donor resources were going to NGOs. We can see how an alliance between the two interests, bureaucrats and fundamentalists, led to that Ordinance in 1978. We fought it collectively, but delays in getting approval for projects, sometimes for years, began to cripple our activity. Soon after that, the student movement arose, the social and political pressure for ousting Ershad. Many NGOS – not all of them – supported the movement, because they knew army rule was not going to benefit the poor. Democracy had to be restored for the sake of the poor. Some NGOs said they should stay out of politics – we'll do our work, serve the people, we have no business with this. But many of us said the interests and rights of the poor had been violated. We should think in terms of human rights. Fifty-six NGOs supported the movement against Ershad.

Three days later Ershad fell. Our critics thought we had timed it well, but we had no way of knowing. It took great efforts to reach that point – NGOs had never before taken political action. We should be given credit for that, if not for the timing. I said, 'Next time, we'll be ahead for that one'. And in the 1996 movement we were leading the pack.

NGOs set up the Election Watch for the transition of power after Ershad. In 1991 Khaleda Zia was elected with the help of 14 seats from the Jama'at. In 1992 Jehanara Imam started a civil society movement, which sought to put war criminals on public trial. NGOs publicly supported it. We got a tough letter from the NGO Affairs Bureau. The Prime Minister's Secretary, who had also been a freedom fighter, called us to a meeting. He said, 'the PM is mad with you for doing this. This is politics.' I told him, 'Mr Secretary, we are NGO people, but we are also citizens of this country. Working for an NGO has removed us from citizenship? Asking for a trial of war criminals is making politics? Is it not a human rights concern? Is it not the duty of every citizen under our Constitution to call for justice?' He said, 'No no, NGOs cannot do politics. There may be a historical conjuncture, as when you supported the democratic movement against Ershad. That was good.' I said, 'That allowed you to come into power. But this is not good because it embarrasses your partner, Jama'at-e-Islami. I tell you, any citizen of Bangladesh who supports war criminals forfeits the right to call himself Bangladeshi.' He had been a valiant freedom fighter. I said, 'You should be the first one to congratulate us for what we have done.' He said, 'No, no, then it was different, the founding of the state – this is not the same.'

NGOs came under pressure. They said we were converting people to Christianity. At the time of Taslima Nasreen, the fundamentalists were very aggressive. They had *hartals* and processions, they burned clinics, hospitals and schools under pretext that these were proselytising Christian organisations. BRAC lost a hundred schools. Against Proshika they could not do much, maybe because of our work with the people. We organised NGOs to resist, knowing government would never do so. Having failed to punish us, they encouraged the fundamentalists. We told the PM's Secretary, 'Replant the trees they destroyed. Give compensation for the burned schools.' Of course they would not. We had to defend ourselves.

We organised a campaign of social disaster management. We had shown we could manage natural disasters: now we faced social disaster. The question was: were fundamentalists harming poor women and men, or were NGOs harming them? We asked: who are the fundamentalists? What was their role in the liberation of our country? We trained NGOs, who went to their village groups and gave workshops along the same lines. It was a resounding success. The attacks stopped. In 1994–95, fundamentalists issued *fatwas* against many others than Taslima. It suited the West to have a female counterpart to Salman Rushdie. She played a role in the agendas of others, including, of course, Western sentiment against Islam.

On the twenty-fifth anniversary of Independence, we planned a big rally. We wanted to bring 250,000 people to Dhaka at their own expense for the Grass-Roots People's Organisation Rally. The meeting was banned by the government. We decided to go ahead anyway, and got a High Court ruling against the illegal ban. We set up a stage in front of Parliament. The police left and we worked through the night. Thousands came from all over the country. It was headlines in every paper – three lakhs of people. A demonstration of people's power.

The BNP called an election on 15 February 1996 without the participation of the Opposition. The turnout was 10 per cent. It totally lacked credibility. They could have brazened it out, saying the Opposition chose not to take part; but instead, they claimed a high turnout. This was unacceptable. The atmosphere was close to civil war, a military takeover, a famine – it was like all three.

We organised. This time, civil society was our mass base. There was a rally in Motijheel, with business groups, professional organisations. It was a citizens' rally, not a political demonstration. A week later we made a human chain, one thousand kilometres, a million people. A caretaker government was installed. We began a voter education programme, to increase the turnout of women especially, and to encourage people not to vote for fundamentalists. Turnout was 73 per cent. The previous record had been in 1970 – 53 per cent. Many more women voted. Jama'at's seats dwindled from nineteen to two. We reached ten million people. It was a joint NGO effort, but Proshika was the leading player.

This phase of our work connects grass-roots organisation to the democratic rights movement, preventing mischief by political parties. It was a milestone in NGO activity. Non-party political education action is also development. Before 1996, student fronts were the main players in politics. But civil society is now the main participant, especially NGOs. This corresponds to a degradation of the student role, through the control of students by the parties.

Here is an extraordinary turn of the wheel. The work of NGOs took place in the vacuum left by the destruction of idealism, the corruption of the political process, and later by the elimination of any political group that claimed to speak for the poor. Through organisation, education, economic participation and social advance, people are being prepared to re-enter politics. But where are the parties they can vote for? How can popular movements retain their structure, their idealism and their commitment without being poisoned by the corruption, violence and cynicism which mark the mainstream political parties that have become the personal fiefs of factions of the possessing elites? The hardest work remains to be done.

Can education replace direct experience of social injustice? Can training be a substitute for knowledge that comes from the lived daily witness of poverty and insufficiency? Can culture replace ideology? Can 'motivation' become a surrogate for action that comes from a sense of outrage at the gross inequalities in daily life? Where are the informing myths to come from that maintained faith in Socialism?

This flaw in Proshika is not of its making, but comes from the decay of the Left, the abandonment of struggle, a retreat from the belief that history was on their side. The reclamation of idealism is inseparable from the work of the regeneration of the environment, liberation of the occupied territories of development, of democracy, of human rights.

Rangamati: a drowned town

On the way to Rangamati, we stopped at a checkpost; a notice in English said 'All foreigners to report here'. The amiable military officer asked my nationality, and then, with distinctly unmilitary imprecision, wrote it in biro, with the number of the jeep, on the palm of his hand.

Rangamati is a drowned town. The creation of Kaptai lake for a hydroelectric scheme in 1962 submerged thousands of acres of Chakma land, and with it the capital of the Hill Tracts. A new city has grown up around the lake, a circular town, with roads along the waterfront. What were peaks of hills are now islands and embankments surrounded by water, and reached only by country boats. Bengali settlers have occupied much of the lower land, while the indigenous people live in flimsy huts on platforms carved into the steep slopes, reached by long flights of shallow, dusty steps. We visited one island, which had been taken over by a well-to-do Bengali. He came to meet us by boat when we hailed him from the causeway. He has a substantial house, a good plot of land, fruit-trees and bamboo-groves – a whole island has become his private domain.

Proshika's office is on the first floor of a stone building, with a wide verandah overlooking the lake and its islands, the thin vegetation of what were summits of ancient hills. Here and there patches of grey on the slopes show where some families have continued *jhum* cultivation.

Most of the jungle has been felled. In the devastated environment may be read the fate of the indigenous peoples. They face the tragedy of an ethnicity without culture, the customs and traditions of the hills embalmed only in folk-museums and ornaments for tourists. The social and cultural organisations want to reverse this; but for most indigenous people the culture has dwindled to the distinctive language which, banished from public spaces, has retreated to the home.

The Jhum Aesthetics Council

We went to the office, close to the market-place, of the Jhum Aesthetics Council. This is a vibrant cultural organisation of the hill people. There was a power-cut. The market traders had set candles where they sat, cross-legged, beside their potatoes, tomatoes, spinach, garlic or onions, flames flickering on produce sprinkled with water to keep it fresh. The scene has the appearance of a religious ceremony, the mounds of vegetables votive offerings.

In the room people come and go. Without the fan, it soon becomes oppressively hot. Jimit Chakma, who wrote a play we had seen in Dhaka, evoked the richness of the tradition of *jhum* cultivators within living memory. He has a collection of photographs of Chakma artefacts, made from local materials, the cultural apparatus of daily living. Most are no longer made, because the bamboos and grasses, shrubs and trees from which they were made no longer exist. 'No more than 10 per cent of the vegetation of the hills survives. People blame *jhum* for damaging the environment; but everything we burned regenerated. What we have seen now is an uprooting of everything, driving plants, trees, flowers, birds, animals, and people to extinction.'

He shows photographs of fish-traps, bird-traps, baskets for storing food and collecting fodder, for fruits, yams or leaves; implements for cutting that did not damage the trees, tools for digging, planting, harvesting; bamboo needles for the intricate weave of delicate objects, the latticing of dainty cylindrical boxes – the spare, elegant accompaniments of a broken self-reliance, the ancient contrivances of a way of life that was itself an expression of the demolished jungles.

The people's anger at the destructiveness imposed by alien rule is tangible. The incomprehension of 'progressives' of all political ideologies has brought to ruin a sustainability which they now earnestly praise and pay homage to, not to preserve it, much less to learn from it, but in order to ensure that even the memory is obliterated. 'Here', says Jimit, 'is the real hypocrisy of the millennial rhetoric: while the Western world speaks of environment and sustainability, its actions show no commitment to the fate of those whose cultures embody what is acknowledged to be essential for planetary survival.'

A sense of melancholy descends. A bottle of what looks like mineral water appears; only it is *garam pani*, liquor from fermented rice, which is also part of Adivasi culture and, naturally, repellent to Islam. It is made from a traditional variety of rice. This bottle has been fermented only once, and is less potent than the twice-fermented. The varieties of

215

rice grown by *jhum* have not yet become extinct like the those of the plains, because rice-strains adapted to the steep hills were not replaced by hybrid high-yielding varieties.

The liquor is slightly clouded with a faintly bitter taste. Some drink it diluted with water, others take it neat. They serve chicken and dried fish. For me, an emissary of the West, they have bought a large silver-foil packet of potato crisps.

That many indigenous people use alcohol is often quoted as evidence by the settlers that this is an inferior or immoral culture; the greater freedom of women only confirms this view. Jimit says, 'Settlers came as colonists, to extract, to take away our carefully harvested wealth. Zia ur-Rahman told them that if they settled in the hills, they would get land and money. What they were not told was that everything they would enjoy belonged to other people.'

Tourism, Bangladeshi-style

We stayed at the Parjatan Hotel above Rangamati. Parjatan is a government-owned corporation devoted to tourism. On the wall of the hotel, painted in bright blue: Tourism is Joy and Friendship. There was little sign of either. The hotel comprised a central building, and some satellite 'cottages'. Unwilling to supplement the (no doubt meagre) salary of the manager, who pored over scratchy schedules for 20 minutes, we were directed to one of the cottages where there was no water. I washed in the remains of a bottle of mineral water, and shared my room with a giant spider and a host of mosquitoes. Next day, in the lugubrious dining-hall, we asked why there was no background music, perhaps some Chakma songs to spread the pro-claimed joy of tourism. The manager said, 'See, I am only a humble employee. I cannot influence policy at such a high level.' Next day we slept in a Buddhist temple.

The experience of the Chakmas

Shopon Datta Chakma is a member of the cultural group. His view of the hills is typical of those battered by twenty years of low-intensity warfare that have scarred the social landscape, just as exploitation and avarice have ruined the material environment. A quiet man, about 40, he lives fifteen kilometres from Rangamati. His family has five acres of land, for 'primary use', which means de facto possession, because no record exists of land ownership among the Chakmas, although three acres are waterlogged and cannot be farmed.

I heard from my parents and grandparents that the Chakmas used to live near Chittagong, and slowly retreated to the hills. As *jhum* cultivators, there was no crisis, no poverty. We left the places we cultivated to regenerate, so as not to disturb the ecology of the hills.

When British India divided, Chakmas were divided: one group supported Pakistan, but the Chakma king and others supported India. In the 1960s, the Pakistani government constructed a dam in the hills to produce electricity, and the land of thousands of Chakmas was submerged. Small compensation was given, but not all those displaced received it. From that time, this became an area both oppressed and depressed. In 1971, we Chakma people fought against the Pakistanis, gave sanctuary and shelter to freedom fighters. We offered food and safe places in deep jungle where the Pakistani army could not reach.

After liberation, our representatives asked for autonomy for the Chakmas and other Adivasis, with their own representatives. This would recognise an identity different from that of the Bangalis. Not independence, autonomy. Sheikh Mujib regretted he could not do it. After 1975, when Zia came to power, the army was sent here to protect Bangalis whom the government encouraged to come.

When Sheikh Mujib adopted a strategy of delay, Left-oriented groups advised the Chakmas to organise people to fight for autonomy. Even before 1975, Maulan Bashani had set up the Shantibahini. They were not armed, but were a popular democratic organisation. Only when the army came after 1975 and Bangalis migrated here, the Shantibahini started armed reaction. Thousands of Chakmas fled to India, and there came under the leadership of those advocating armed struggle.

Many settlers saw an opportunity to take advantage of the Chakmas. We had always traded with Bangalis at Chittagong, so they were not like foreigners. But when they settled, our relations with them changed. We became victims. The loss of our resources, our trees, our jungles, accelerated. The army disturbed Chakma villages, Bangalis took them. I didn't go to India: my

217

land was not fertile and of no use to settlers. Bangalis cut and sold the remaining trees. Many had already gone, partly through corruption of the Forest Department in British and Pakistani times. The hills have a long history of loss.

We practised *jhum*. In this dry season, we cut back bushes and set fire to the undergrowth. In June and July, with the rain, we planted paddy, local strains suited to the slopes. We stored some paddy from each year's harvest for seed the following year. We use pesticides now, but then it was unknown to us. Our rice varieties were *Range*, *Galam*, *Koborok*. *Koborok* was scented, so fragrant you could smell it in the fields. It was kept for festivals. *Jhum* is now declining because it has no time to regenerate. It is now a losing concern. As the old trees were felled, natural fertilisers – the animals and birds which gave the natural fertiliser – went also, so the soil is impoverished.

Our culture was the breath of the forest, the expression of our environment. Some literate people are now trying to learn and collect; but culture is a living thing. We can make people aware of the old plantations, recreate the forest and not sabotage it all again. Slowly we can recover some part of our heritage.

I have two children. I want them to learn Chakma culture. We speak Chakma at home. I am committed to it, it gives me life. I cannot express myself as fully in Bangali as in Chakma, and that is something I feel passionately. I remember the old houses on stilts, so animals could not enter – tigers, bears, monkeys, elephants. The animals have gone, like the trees, scores of bamboos, medicinal herbs and shrubs our herbalists knew. Our people suffer from a sickness of the heart.

The historian of the indigenous people
We visited Dr Khisa in his concrete house on the road out of Ranga-mati, behind a walled garden. It was completely dark; scratched by bougainvillea in the fragrant lightless garden, we followed a cement staircase to an upper-floor study, full of maps, documents and ancient mildewy volumes of colonial history. Dr Khisa is a physician, a Chakma and historian of the Chakma people. He speaks as chronicler of the decline of a way of life that remained – partly because of the British presence – virtually intact even into his childhood in the 1930s.

There are many theories of the origin of the Chakmas. Our place of origin is not known. The view that we came from South Assam is most plausible. We belong ethnically to the Tibetan-Burma family, but our language is related to Bangali. The Chakmas moved southward, invaded Chittagong, crossed the Arakan border into Burma. The ballad-singers tell of conquests, battles, settlements and marriages in Chittagong and Arakan, from where our kings came. About five hundred years ago, the Chakma kingdom was annexed by Arunjug, king of Arakan, and they became his subjects. Some were taken as slaves. With followers, the king fled to the present Chittagong. Folk-singers, accompanied by *dothara*, used to sing these stories all night long.

The capital of the Chakma kingdom moved with time. In the British period it settled at Rangamati. After Plassey in 1757, the Chakma kingdom was not disturbed by the East India company. In 1798, Francis Buchanan, an official of the Company, came to these tracts and wrote a book, which gave a very authentic description of the area. Only after 1857, the British Queen took over the whole Indian empire, and in 1860 the Hill Tracts came under British administration.

The immense extraction of wealth from Bengal during the British period did not apply to the Chittagong Hill Tracts. The territory was broken into local units answerable to the Chakma king. The headman of each area was responsible for taxation. The kings collected the tribute paid to the British. The Chakma king is not king of a *place*, but of his subjects. Wherever they go, he is their king. He collects a capitation tax from the produce of *jhum*; whether small, big or medium cultivation, the rate of tax is according to the number in the family.

There was no cash money in Chakma society. Everything was paid in cotton. The Chakmas paid tribute to the Mogul kings, five hundred maunds a year. The Chittagong Hill Tracts, for that reason, became known as the Kingdom of Cotton in the Mogul period.

In the hills, *jhum* involved paddy, *til* (sesame seed), inter-cropped with vegetables. Food was grown for consumption, cotton for clothing, and sesame for trade. All the Chakmas required from outside were salt, dry fish and earthenware for cooking and storing water. They were expert weavers, as may still be seen. Unless she was able to weave, no girl could be married. They had rich supplements of food from the jungles – the edible parts of bamboo shoots, many varieties of yam. There were scores of species of fish, crabs, snails, lizards. They had special traps for catching birds. They used bamboo fish-traps, and powdered tree-bark sprinkled in the water made the fish drowsy, so they swam into the traps. They had a comprehensive knowledge of herbal medicines. Some have been synthesised by transnational companies and even patented. *Rauwolfia serpentina* was used by Ciba-Geigy for blood pressure. I do not know all the botanical names.

The tribute to the Moguls was small – five hundred maunds of cotton was not a great burden. The East India Company also received some small tribute of cotton, but after 1860 it was converted into money. The demand the British made of the Chakma kings was 2,200 rupees annually, and the amount increased steadily throughout British rule. The District Commissioner was established at Rangamati, and direct administration was created for the first time. In every rupee were sixteen annas: six annas went to the headman, six to the British Government of India and four to the king. In fact, the king became a zamindar.

You cannot exaggerate the violence of the imposition of monetary tribute on a non-cash economy. Money was unknown. There were, of course, other means of exchange – food, animals, fish, pigs, produce from the jungles; and the jungles supplied people with many items of subsistence – animals, birds, medicines – for which cash was not needed.

I was born in 1933, and as a child I never saw a shop that sold rice. No one bought or sold rice. Salt, earthenware and dried fish were the only marketed items. Clothing, too, was never bought or sold. People's demands were very small. They had no property. Everything they owned – iron, tools, clothing – could be held in a small bamboo basket, the traditional design you can still see, braided grass around the forehead, and the woven basket carried on the back.

During *jhum* cultivation, people used temporary shelters. They stayed six or seven years and moved on when soil fertility was reduced. They could do so, because, few in number, there was no threat to the ecology of the hills, which were left to regenerate. The population of the Chittagong Hill Tracts was less than three hundred thousand. Now it is twice as many.

At the time of Partition in 1947, 97 per cent of the people were Adivasis, and only 3 per cent were outsiders. The British discouraged outside settlers. The police commissioner had the power to expel any outsider within twenty-four hours under terms drawn up by the colonial power in 1900. At Partition, with the making of the predominantly Hindu and Muslim states, it was assumed the Adivasis of the Hill Tracts, 97 per cent non-Muslim, would come under Indian control, like Assam. But economically, the Hill Tracts are connected with Chittagong district; it was said they could not survive without Chittagong. So they were placed with Pakistan.

The Pakistan government established the Kaptai dam in 1960 – the biggest enterprise ever undertaken in the hills by the Pakistanis. Fifty-four thousand acres of the most fertile land was submerged overnight. The ecosystem was totally destroyed – plants, animals, vegetables, trees were all drowned. Over twenty-thousand Chakmas and others were displaced. Some migrated to India, others found shelter where they could. This blow to the Chakmas is comparable only to the disaster of the British tax-system or the Partition of India. After 1960, our culture was virtually wiped out. Where could we go? The educated went to offices as clerks, teachers or administrators.

Formerly, people had no need of education: they learned everything from their family and their environment. Nobody went to serve in an office – it was unheard-of. The Kaptai dam was a great assault on our culture. The present government is planning another – they are proposing a dam in Banderban for electricity; as well as that, fifty-five thousand acres are being set aside for the army and for international companies to come and plant commerical monocultures.

In the Hill Tracts permanent homesteads were never established. Villages were not registered with government. We were semi-nomadic, so when survey maps are consulted, our living places are shown as vacant lands, blank spaces. It is on these they want to plant their monocultures, funded by the Asian Development Bank or World Bank.

221

Our future lies in three ways. The poor will migrate, maybe to cities; a section will be converted to Christianity or Islam. The elite – engineers, doctors – will stay in towns. When we were *jhum* cultivators, we had a small hut erected on a bamboo platform. In the plains, we had houses with earthen walls and tin roofs. Now that our educated serve in offices, our aim is to make a building. Do you see anything tribal in my home? We are fighting a lost cause. The cry of the indigenous people is that the British turned abundance into scarcity by imposing tax on a non-monetary society. They took the trees and forest produce. The Pakistanis took what was left. Then Bangalis came and took the land. Now foreigners come and say, 'Why have you destroyed your forests? We must preserve them.' But they plant mono-cultures, not jungles.

The tribal people moved, as they were threatened by invaders, into deeper and deeper forest. Now there is no forest to retreat to, and we are lost in the deep forests of the mind.

The Peace Accord

In 1997, the Awami League government signed an Accord with the leaders of the people of the Chittagong Hill Tracts; but not before an estimated 8,500 people had been killed and 70,000 had fled to India, where thousands remained for years in refugee camps.

The war between the hill people's army and the Bangladeshi army was a consequence of government policy, which was to settle Bengalis in the relatively thinly populated hill regions. In part, this was an answer to landlessness, but its ulterior purpose was the Bengalisation, indeed, Islamisation of Buddhist and animist hill people, with their exuberant culture, where men and women mixed freely. Among those who came were land-grabbers and opportunists who saw a chance of cheating the indigenous people of land and resources.

The Adivasis experienced this as another colonial invasion – this time by the very people whose own experience of colonisation had been so long and bitter. Was it because they had for so long been on the receiving end of it that the Bengalis knew well how to conquer, and how to intimidate and oppress those weaker than themselves?

The guerrilla war was bloody and bitter. It continued for twenty years. When the Awami League government was elected in 1996, negotiations began between the Shantibahini and government. The

Accord was signed at the end of 1997, and most of the Shantibahini surrendered their arms at the sports stadium of Khagrachari.

The people's negotiator

Santu Larma was the Chakma negotiator as leader of the Jana Samhata Samiti, a position he assumed after his brother was killed in the conflict. Factions opposed to the agreement continue sporadic attacks, not only against the military, whose presence remains conspicuous, but also against those whom they see as having betrayed the indigenous people by their 'compromise' with the government.

I met Santu Larma in his highly guarded house on a hilltop in Rangamati. He wants to make the best of the situation, but since three years had elapsed since the Accord, he set out clearly the elements which had not been implemented. He spoke quietly, with a strong undertow of sadness: the smile conceals doubts over the good faith of the government and its intentions towards the agreement. After all, the Chakmas have effectively laid down their arms.

We signed on behalf of the indigenous people. Our struggle began with the creation of Bangladesh itself. The problem has always been how to preserve the identity of the people of the hills, their land rights, their rights of culture, language and religion. The people only want democratic rule. Ever since Partition, this area has been seriously oppressed. There was no change between the rulers of Pakistan and those of Bangladesh: the policy of Islamisation has been the main point ever since 1947. Pakistan tried to extinguish the Adivasis, and began by destroying the special administrative status established by the British in 1900. In the first Constitution of Pakistan, the 1900 arrangements were incorporated, but by 1960 they were abandoned. This coincided with the Kaptai hydroelectric project. Constitutional protection was abandoned and the economic life of indigenous people was shattered. Crippled socially, politically, economically, they had to find other means of surviving.

The spirit of that agreement is to preserve the characteristics of the Hill Tracts people, their rights to land, culture, religion and democratic administration. There is to be an elected body representing the local people, which will hold power of administration in the three districts.

Since the Accord was signed, crucial issues have yet to be implemented. The violence drove more than seventy thousand to take shelter in India. There is provision in the agreement for their rehabilitation; not only returnees, but also the internally displaced. The government has no mechanism for restoring their homes. Bangali settlers have occupied or taken illegal possession of Adivasi land. one hundred thousand families were internally displaced. Many are still in deep forest, and cannot come back to their homes because of Muslim settlers and the army camps, many of which are also on land that belongs to the Adivasis. Those people are without resources; the rehabilitation of both groups remains unimplemented. The government also gave an informal commitment that the four hundred thousand settlers would be given land outside the Chittagong Hill Tracts when the Treaty is implemented. It seems the government wants to rehabilitate them *within* the CHT, which violates the agreement. Government will no longer even talk about it.

More than five hundred camps of various branches of the security forces were set up. Of these 'temporary' camps, so far only a handful have been withdrawn. The military administration has not been discontinued. This should be withdrawn at the same time as the camps are closed. Again, no steps are being taken by government. Special administration foreseen for the CHT has not been properly established, and until this happens, no proper development of the area can be expected. The resolution of land disputes is outstanding. A Land Commission is to be set up, but so far, nothing is in place. The Chairman of the Land Commission was appointed, but he died of a heart attack. We await the appointment of another retired Justice as chairman. Preparation of a voting list of permanent residents is also awaited. On the current lists, there are many outsiders: registered voters are not permanent residents, but businessmen, service-holders, settlers. A reliable voters' roll is urgently needed for elections. If a new list is not prepared, we will be unable to control the new administration.

Opposition to the Accord comes from elements in the governing party, the opposition parties, business circles, outside settlers. There is also a group of young educated boys from the CHT who oppose it, either in collaboration with the ruling party or with the fundamentalists, who are using terrorism and guns. Some claim to represent the United People's Democratic Front, which has not accepted the Accord.

It seems the government is trying to destroy the agreement by failing to implement the Accord. If we can lead a forceful movement for implementing it, government may be encouraged to do its part. Pressure must be placed on them by democratic popular movement. But that is not enough. Other social and political organisations should also make their voices heard. And the international community should bring pressure to bear to help them overcome their hesitation.

If it is implemented, we can campaign for more autonomy and our people will recover some of our customs and traditions. We have the resources. We can restore our heritage. We are in contact with Survival International and Amnesty International. We need all the outside help we can get.

The fractured culture

Early morning in the Parjatan Hotel. Outside, in the garden, the creamy *bonerfol* or jungle-flower spreads its sweetness over the lake. Sulphur-coloured butterflies drift as languidly as waste paper on the breeze. Inside the drawing-room of the bungalow, I met Sukheswar Chakma, a college lecturer in Rangamati. An active member of the Jhum Aesthetics Council, he has a wide knowledge of Chakma culture, a combination of oral tradition and research. He recognises the beauty and poignancy of a culture from which he has been partially estranged, and from which many Chakmas are becoming more alienated.

Ours is a rich culture. Our houses were made in keeping with our surroundings; on the hill slopes we build with wood and bamboo. We do not cut the hills, fell the trees or harm them in any way. So it is with our values. We do not catch fish for sale, nor hunt animals for the market. We hunt and fish only for our sustenance, without surplus or excess. We take from the environment only for immediate use. Chakma society contradicts the assertion that the market economy is an expression of 'universal' values or, what is worse, human nature. Our culture saw resources as part of our lives. These are now being transferred to the market economy, because to the market they represent accumulated natural capital to be turned into cash.

This culture has preservation of the environment at the centre of its values. We have lived in this way for centuries without destroying our resources. Why is it now that the forests die? Because people can no longer get water, the earth is dry, the trees used up for alien purposes. In the Hill Tracts area, the topsoil is very limited – if trees are removed, the soil is eroded and all that remains is rock. I went once to an area colonised by settlers. I saw fishermen catching fish and laying them out to dry in the sun. I was astonished, because this is not an idea of indigenous people. This is a culture of aggression, against us and the means of our survival. This is the cause of the conflict, which goverment and settlers appear not even to understand.

The backbone of our culture has been broken. The patterns and fabrics of our dresses are sold to tourists, not local people. The main defining instrument of our culture now is the language. But they teach Bangla in the schools and our language is used only at home. The government does not value our religion, although the religion is not the same thing as our culture. There are many elements in Chakma culture at odds with Buddhism. We slaughter cows and goats as well as pigs, but in Buddhism this is not allowed.

An undertow of animism remains. Many practices and customs survive from our ancient forest religion. We sacrifice birds or animals in marriage ceremonies to named gods – Gozen, or Bietra, his son. Buddhism does not allow pluralism of gods. Our animal sacrifices make us closer to Islam. Our Buddhism is also mixed with Hinduism.

The Chakma people came from the East over many generations. Their religious writings were preserved on the leaves of trees. Our ancient religious forebears used to wear half-dress, a small cloth, but Buddhist monks wear long coloured dress. They lived in temples, whereas the old Chakma *luri* or priest lived in common houses with the people. Originally, our Buddhism was a fusion of animism and Buddhism. In the late eighteenth century, a monk came from Burma to the Hill Tracts and re-converted our people to real Buddhism.

There are many contradictions between Buddhism and Chakma

religion, and older traditions persist. In Buddhism, you cannot avoid your sin – the principle of cause and effect operates. In Chakma belief, you can. Bonobhante is a jungle priest who meditated in the forests – perhaps an influence of Sufism. People still believe in him, and do puja to a stream or river. If someone is lost, they do *puja* to a goddess, Buddema. At times of drought, they make sacrifice to Debaraj, a sky goddess. In tradition, at time of death, people tied a thread to the body of the deceased person, and then to all the relatives – son, daughter, wife, husband and so on. The priest cuts the thread, so the spirit of the dead person can depart. At childbirth, the local midwife uses a herbal infusion called *gila* (seeds of the *khaje* tree), in water to which gold and bronze objects are added; the water is used to clean the baby and mother, and is sprinkled in the house. At marriage, when the bride comes to the groom's house, the same water is spread.

When our people go to the forest, they never utter the name of the tiger. If they name it, the tiger will come; the tiger was a very ferocious animal, both feared and venerated. They also believed when you boil rice, the stick you use to stir it must never be used to take food, because if you do so, a member of the family will be eaten by a tiger.

Our ballad singers, *ganguli,* used to sing the myths and stories of the Chakma people. We can preserve formal cultural expressions, but not the living, organic, everyday, which is the fabric of culture. Our history is remembered through oral tradition. The British could not occupy the Chakma jungles. They closed our areas, so some of the elements we depended on could not reach us, especially salt, earthenware vessels and dried fish. The present Chakma king is a lawyer – the first one from the Hill Tracts, but he stays in Dhaka.

The experience of Sukheswar is that of many young Chakma intellectuals. Arrested and detained in 1989, aged 19, when the conflict was at its height, he was held for three months as a member of the banned Communist Party. He left the party to work in the social and cultural fields, that symbolic refuge for many former Leftists in Bangladesh, from where they hope – in some not very clearly articulated way – to reclaim the occupied territory of politics.

An alien regeneration

Most hill people are committed to their language and culture, but they do not defend it with the same protective zeal as the Jhum Aesthetics Council. The Bengalisation of the people is as visible as the foreign species with which the rocky nakedness of the hills has been reclothed. The teak, shedding their broad dry leaves in March, are harmful to the hills: they damage the soil fertility and permit no intercropping. The British brought teak from Burma, which was used for railway sleepers. Other exotic species include *ipil-ipil* from the Philippines, which absorb too much water, especially on the slopes. It is the same with the eucalyptus from Australia. Even the efforts to regenerate have come from outside, do not reflect the knowledge of the jungle people. They know their trees – *karai* which provides fodder and firewood, *garjon* which gives hard wood for house-building and furniture, *hattul*, of which some varieties are used for house frames, others for traditional artisanal objects, baskets and containers. There were scores of bamboos, many of which have now become extinct. Medicinal uses of plants and leaves were widely known, but even the names of them have been forgotten by the people, and are known now only to specialists and ethnobotanists.

The Chakma people

I wanted to meet people who were not activists. It was arranged we should visit some households on an island created by Kaptai lake.

We went to the lakeside. Between houses that skirt the water we reached the edge of the lake; an expanse of coarse sandy grass and lilac flowers of *dholkulmi*. There was no one to take us to the island. We went to the village of Nutonbustee, where Sanjay Tanchungya was working in his father's small dry-goods store. Sanjay took us to where some country boats were moored; shallow unstable craft, many half full of water. He scooped out the water from one of these, and four of us clambered into the oscillating boat. Pushing away from the edge, the boat threatened to capsize. My companions decided they would not risk throwing me into the deep water, even though the journey was only about 350 metres. We would stay in Nutonbustee instead.

I watched Sanjay bale out the water from the country boat, with one hand, at great speed. He seized the water so that it seemed to become solid in his grasp for a moment, before cascading in fragments over the edge of the boat. In Bangladesh, water is a different element: it was the same with the man cleaning the wheels of a truck immersed in a pond, the woman washing the child in the slum, the boy sprinkling water to lay the dust outside a shop. The water becomes a ball of glass in the hand. The woman scoops up the liquid from a plastic bucket or tin can, and applies it like a transparent garment to the child's skin. Water becomes another substance in Bangladesh: as water and land change places all the time, water itself changes its nature beneath the dextrous fingers that know how to manipulate it.

Sanjay took us back to his father's shop, where he sat among the biscuits, candles and soap in a baseball cap, with a gold ring in his right ear. He is in Class X. After school, he will work in the store. His father is Tanchungya, his mother Chakma. If he had the chance, he would leave. His earring is not for decoration. If a child dies in the family when a new one is born, the parents put a gold ring in his or her ear. Sanjay is the only boy, and the earring is to protect him. It will ensure long life and prosperity, and no one will be able to harm him; a gesture, perhaps, to some forgotten animist deity. Sanjay speaks Tanchungya at home. On his cassette player he plays a modern Chakma love-song, much influenced by Bengali. Sanjay has forgotten the old songs and poems. He is fifteen.

We went to a solid earth-walled house off the main road and met some women of a Proshika primary group. Rumki took a loan of 3,000 taka for handloom-weaving. She works at home, following Adivasi custom, and sells in the local market. The irony of an NGO giving credit for what was once an indispensable skill for life but is now an employment opportunity is not lost on the women. Rumki lives on the island we wanted to visit – we should have crossed with her, she says; her family makes the journey daily, and none has fallen in the water. Rumki weaves traditional Tanchungya cloth – the *haddi* covering the upper part of the body, and the *pinon*, a long, tight, skirt-like garment. It takes her a week to make a *pinon* for a profit of 100–150 taka. Her husband farms five bighas of paddy in the plains; sometimes they do *jhum* on the higher slopes of the island. Rumki had one year of education and had to work as a child. Her children will go to school.

Rumki says that the old Tanchungya songs 'have been forgotten'.

229

The decay of culture is referred to in a strangely impersonal way, as though it had occurred without agency. The young imbibe the ubiquitous Bengali culture. They speak Bangla in town, in the streets, at school. They are losing interest in the traditional songs. The joint family is also breaking down, as young people live separately with their children. Rumki learned to weave from her mother and grandmother. 'The old patterns are still in our fingers. We are not very poor, but naturally Bangalis are richer than we are. It is their country, their language.' She speaks without bitterness – a matter of fact.

Silpi Marma is in a newly formed Proshika group. She and her husband own no land but the homestead: they never practised *jhum*. She remembers a little of the old songs that they learned as children; she sings a few lines of a *paw khela*, a water-game they played. Like all people recollecting cultural fragments on the edge of extinction, shame overcomes her; and she dissolves in a laughter that has nothing to do with a sense of the comic. The biggest festival of the Adivasi year is the Biju festival. They wear traditional dress, visit relatives' houses, go to the temple, take rich food and local liquor. Silpi is 25. She heard of a time called 'the Pakistani time', but cannot recall what happened. The women remain tantalisingly close to the culture, but it is archaic and has no relevance to the hoped-for life of the next generation.

Dipa Dewan is a Chakma studying in Class X. Her ambition, she says, is 'to get a good job, *chakri*, in government as first choice, in a big private company as second, and any other private business as third'. It seems she has been influenced by the priorities of Bengali youth; but as we speak it is plain that it is more complicated. She is sad that Chakma language is now used only at home. It isn't forbidden at school, but the school context is wrong. It is the mother-tongue; school is the wider world, and the wider world is not a Chakma one.

Dipa sings a traditional folk song of the love of the Chakmas for Rangamati, the hills and trees, birds and flowers, this Eastern land where the sun rises, land of morning and festivals. As she performs the older song, her voice is transformed, her face and gestures reanimated by an older sensibility. She doesn't want to leave Rangamati, but if a job outside comes, she will go; visiting her relatives and friends at the time of festivals. 'Wherever I go, Rangamati will be with me, because it is within me.'

Proshika has an ambiguous attitude to 'culture'. Culture means folk song, cultural performance, drama, recitation, dance, music; and the forms are often adapted to give contemporary messages of a liberal humanism. Where the culture celebrated backward-looking or socially regressive values, it is adapted to offer more palatable ideas. Culture does not, it seems, represent daily life – the folk beliefs, sayings, proverbs, superstitions, assumptions built into received linguistic formulae. It is a very delicate process to unpick a culture, to use it eclectically, to create a new and more generous social fabric out of that which clad women in the *burkha*, surrounded childbirth with superstition, made the poor acquiesce in their oppression. Whether such a subtle and unpredictable strategy is a credible weapon against the solid certainties of fundamentalism remains to be seen.

7 ❧ Two Festivals

The split cultural personality of Bangladesh
That the division in Bangladesh should now appear as polarisation between a Bengali and an Islamic identity is a result of developments that have little to do with Bangladesh. The reaction of Islam to Western global dominance, cultural and economic, is reflected in all Islamic societies. This is potentially disastrous for Bangladesh, since *dhormo* – whether Muslim, Hindu, Buddhist, Christian or animist – and Bangali culture have coexisted for centuries. The work of Proshika is devoted to the retrieval of a living and tolerant interaction of diverse religious traditions. Fundamentalism is against the spirit of Bengal, although, alas, not against the spirit of the age, which has seen a hardening of dogmas of religion and race. These have been quick to invade the ideological vacuum left by the death of socialism.

These elements of identity are still not a problem for most people in Bangladesh. This became clear during two of the great festivals, which in 2000 fell within a month of each other. Both express and celebrate a different aspect of popular feeling. They enrich and blend a complex of values which, despite all its problems, embody the best traditions of a uniquely humane and tolerant culture.

21 February – Language Day
The twenty-first of February is one of the most significant days in the national calendar of Bangladesh. It commemorates the culmination of the language struggle in what was then East Pakistan. The Pakistani government had tried to impose Urdu as the national language upon

East as well as West Pakistan. The resistance by Bengali speakers was spontaneous and widespread: five students were shot dead by the Pakistani army in 1952; the site is now the Shaheed Minar, the martyrs' memorial, in the university area of Dhaka.

The festival took on new vibrancy in 2000, because UNESCO, in recognition of this, declared 21 February Mother Tongue Day. This enhanced the occasion all over Bangladesh, where every small town has its version of the Shaheed Minar. The language movement was the first serious revolt in the East against Pakistani rule, barely half a decade after the creation of Pakistan. It prefigured, eighteen years later, the emergence of Bangladesh. For many, this defined the colonial nature of the state that they had elected to join after Partition.

A daily programme of Bengali song, dance and poetry was held throughout February at the Shaheed Minar, folk and traditional songs, the works of Rabindranath Tagore, Nazrul Islam and contemporary poets and writers. The Awami League government, which claims to represent the secular forces against the rise of Islamic fundamentalism, made much of the international recognition of 'Ekushey February'. It is symbolic of the political conflict in Bangladesh, which shows itself as a clash of cultures between Bangali tradition and a fundamentalist version of Islam which has declared war upon it.

Ekushey February coincided with the month-long Dhaka Book Fair. Thousands of people, most of them young, besiege the stalls, where the country's writers, poets, dramatists are on hand to discuss their work and sign books. Popular regard – even reverence – for writers is extraordinary in a country where even the official level of literacy is only about one-third. The book fair generated enormous energy and excitement. Students and professionals, business people, garment workers and hotel personnel, military and businesspeople, government employees and industrial workers were caught up in the crowds that throng the ground, churning the mud beneath their feet, pulling shawls around them in the chill February night, stumbling beneath the pale light of kerosene lamps whenever the customary 'load-shedding' blacks out the site. There is something characteristically Bengali in this humane interest in literature, this intelligence of the heart: a liberal, secular gathering; an inspiring, but partial, vision of Bangladesh. It was certainly the most joyful gathering I have ever seen, full of good humour and passion, a mixture of innocent exaltation and spontaneous sociability – quite unlike any I have seen in the West, as remote from the tribal chants and aggression of football crowds as from the lachrymose heroics of charity pop concerts. Different, too, from the book fairs of the West, those market-driven events which suggest a love of commerce before a love of literature. Even so, almost one thousand new titles were published in Bangladesh in February 2000.

The twenty-first of February is a time of high emotion. At midnight, the President, Prime Minister and Leader of the Opposition, in a rare exhibition of unity, lay wreaths at the Shaheed Minar, their breath condensing in the cool air. Tireless crowds of young people walk the closed streets of the university area through the night, beneath the canopies of *korai* trees, trampling the red cups of *shimul* flowers on the road. From the very early hours, a procession of people, carrying magenta bougainvillea, garlands of marigolds, bouquets of gladioli, sometimes a single red rose, shuffles towards the memorial to deposit its tributes to the martyrs. The dawn is chill and misty: formal cultural and political groups carry black banners, stiff wreaths of dark green, while many individuals wear black-ribboned rosettes in remembrance of the dead.

The occasion becomes a vast *mela* (festival): tens of thousands of people, dressed in their best – white *kurtas* embroidered in blue and dark red; women in violet, orange and green sarees, with flowers in their hair; a sound only of feet and voices on the traffic-free streets, where traditional motifs have been painted by students from the Institute of Fine Arts; these are quickly strewn with crimson and gold petals.

The occasion also attracts vendors and hawkers of all kinds: paper hats stamped with the emblem of the Minar, zinc pails of dark roses and pink gladioli, ribbons and rosettes, idealised portraits of the dead; but most have nothing to do with the celebration – plastic windmills, dolls and toys, bangles, balloons; sour boroi-fruits, apple-green ice cream, chocolate, *poori*, luridly coloured snacks, second-hand books, strips of pale cucumber and red carrot, yoghurt in a plastic bucket, oranges, bananas, molasses-based sweets, biscuits, Fishermen's Friend and chewing gum in plastic jars, *channa*, peanuts, hair-slides, buttons, velvet wrist-bands, earrings, watches made in India under licence from Sekonda. The beggars have also been brought out by the festive multitude; men with distended limbs writhe on the ground beseeching help in the name of Allah; a child lies on his back, waving a withered leg; a child pushes her mother, features effaced by leprosy, in a crude wooden cart; an old woman lies inert, her tangle of iron-grey hair a trampled flower on the ground, a metal container by her side, in which people have placed coins and notes.

Part kermis, part festival of remembrance, both political statement and cultural celebration. Groups of schoolchildren walk demurely hand in hand; a little girl with solemn black eyes clutches her outsize dahlia so hard it has wilted on its stalk; a very old man, frail and skeletal, who can scarcely walk, is assisted by his daughter at what will be his last Ekushey February. Two young men, fingers intertwined, each carry a red rose in their disengaged hand, sedately epicene, immensely touching. Another young man has decorated his bicycle with rosebuds tied with tinsel like a wedding vehicle. A mother pauses to pin a black rosette to the festive pink frock of a five-year-old; in her haste, the pin pricks the child and she starts to howl. Three youths have painted their noses and faces red and black, the first and last letters of the Bangla alphabet in gold on their cheeks. This is not self-indulgent nor romantic: all are doing computer studies, and like many of their contemporaries they want to go abroad. 'We love our language', they say. 'We are Bangali before Mussulman. The true story of our culture was suppressed during the years of military dictatorship. Wherever we go, we shall always be Bangali.'

The streets are blocked to traffic by metal barriers covered with barbed wire. Even the police relax and smile, although there are no bribes to be had today; they, too, are holding flowers. All Dhaka seems to be present. But this is an illusion. There are significant exceptions. The Islamic fundamentalists are absent; they regard the placing of flowers as a 'Hindu' form of idolatry, and they see Arabic as of greater relevance to their culture than Bengali. Secondly, the very poor – apart from hawkers and vendors – are not there; the urgency of making a daily living cannot be suspended. Yet these absences are eloquent: the more so since it is the objective of the fundamentalists to win over the poor in their crusade against secularism, which means against the eclectic humanism of Bengali culture.

In Ramna Park, where *dumor* and *gulabjal* trees have already begun to shed their incontinent fragrance, groups of young people perform apparently improvised offerings of Bengali folk songs, devotional songs, love songs, rural work songs. People cluster around these makeshift concerts, performed with the subdued passion of subaltern cultures, which have never been dominant in the world, but have always been victims of the more powerful Urdu, English, Hindi.

Such a powerful release of feeling. But curiously, this celebration of humanity and culture does not seem to extend to suffering flesh and blood of the present. Is it because institutionalised nostalgia is safe, because there is security in finished struggles? It seems to leave little room for the unliberated of present-day Bangladesh, the majority, whose lives unfold and perish in secrecy and silence; the emblematic poor, invoked ritually by politicians the better to ignore them. These effusions are not expressed in the language of the poor, even though that is also Bangla, but are shed at the shrines to dead heroes, of which Dhaka contains many: the heroic representation of the forces of liberation, metal and cement celebrations of victory, idealised emblems of men and women with clenched concrete fists blanched by birdshit, the abstract spindles of the language memorial.

The crowds move on – street-theatre, presentations of the triumph of Bengali over Urdu, banners carrying multilingual slogans to the sweetness of the mother tongue. Some actors, covered in white paint like statues, stand in front of a large black canvas, chalking white fragments of Bengali poetry. A lone protester, wearing a mask and dressed from head to toe in black polythene, is calling the people to reject the plastic bags which fill the ponds and streams with their bubbles of non-biodegradable plastic; but he seems an intrusion into this curiously complacent grief at old wrongs.

A poignant, beautiful day, as much for what was excluded as for what was commemorated. If Ekushey February is one of the great days of the Bengali year, certainly the greatest festival of Islam is Eid-ul-Azah, which, in 2000, took place less than a month later.

Eid-ul-Azah

This three-day celebration commemorates the sacrifice by Ibrahim of Ismail, his son, of proof of his devotion to the Almighty, who, satisfied with such total obedience, intervenes and substitutes a cow, goat or camel for the beloved son. Like the Biblical story of Abraham and Isaac, it marks a moral evolution in the replacement of human sacrifice with the killing of an animal.

236

In the week preceding Eid-ul-Azah, I was in Rangamati, in the Chittagong Hill Tracts. The road from the hills to Chittagong was crowded with men, women and children, some leading a single animal, others herding half a dozen or more, controlling them with a bunch of twigs plucked from a wayside tree. Children constantly fed the travelling animals – fodder, leaves, dry grass – for the worst thing that could happen on their long path to market would be a loss of weight, and hence of value. The children were at greater pains to feed the animals than to take food themselves.

There were cattle-markets in every town and village; animated groups of men walking around each tethered cow and goat, assessing the quality and the likely standard of the meat. Chittagong itself had become one big street-market. The main thoroughfares were blocked. Buses, taxis, trucks stagnated in their own fumes for many hours, while bargains were struck, business concluded, and the creatures led away by their purchasers.

In Dhaka, too, informal animal-markets were set up all over the city in the days leading up to the festival: goats with shiny black pelts, their horns painted a celebratory blue or green, changed hands at between 2,000 and 3,000 taka (about US$50). Cows – some lean with the corrugation of the rib-cage clearly visible under brown and white fur, others sturdy humped creatures – for sale at between 6,000 and 20,000 taka (US$100–400). Some of the biggest beasts fetch 100,000. The cows are garlanded with marigolds, purple and silver tinsel decorations. They wear hats of silver or gold paper; horns have been painted, a yellow wreath draped on the hump on the animal's back.

On the night before Eid, the streets are crowded with people leading the creatures to their homes in dust set up by hooves and feet. Tied up in courtyards and gardens, attached by chains to doorposts, and fed on leaves, grass and flowers – a taste of paradise before slaughter. I was invited to make the acquaintance of the cow bought by the family with whom I was to spend the day. It was two o'clock in the morning before they reached home from the market.

On the day itself, people rise early, take a bath before saying *namaz*, but no breakfast. Then it is time for the ritual slaughter. There is no space in Dhaka for this to be done privately. As a result, the streets become scenes of a vast and distressing carnage. The Imam, dressed in white muslin, says the blessing – *Bismillah, Allah-u-Akbar*

237

– and the *hujur* plunges the knife into the animal's throat. The windpipe is severed, blood gushes on to the pavement, seeps into the dust at the margin of the road. The eyes are bluish with a film of terror. There is no sound but the rasp of knife on skin.

Some animals are bound before they are killed; hind legs tied together, then front legs; then front and back together, so that it can be easily felled to the ground. Two or three men sit on the struggling beast, and the *hujur* probes the neck with his fingers so that the end will be swift and noiseless. Many people believe that the animals are aware of their sacrificial status; on the night before they are to be killed, they weep: thick glassy tears fall down their sad faces.

At the edge of every street, the same spectacle, continuous, because not everyone performs *karbani* (sacrifice) at the same time. A man, barefoot, in a blue check *lunghi*, takes a bucket of water to swill away the blood; he kicks the sluggish mixture into the drain, feet bathed in crimson. The white clothes of the Imams who go from house to house pronouncing the blessing become more and more blood-stained, especially at the lower hem; they look as if they are wearing a novel design of tie-dyed material.

The compound of the house where I spent the day is shaded by fruit-trees – palms, flaking red bark of jackfruit, mango flowers in bloom, a lemon tree with two ripe fruits, a guava tree with dark shiny leaves. The family have hired some butchers to help dismantle the carcass of the cow. The two men work side by side with the elder son and his cousin, while the father looks on. They have bought new bamboo mats, on which the work of demolition is carried out; the soft yellow *chetai* becomes a fresh vermilion that dries to congealed maroon.

The skin is inflated with air, so that it may be more dextrously separated from the body. The pelts are given to the mosque, which sells them to the foul-smelling tanneries of Islambagh – each skin is sold for 500–800 taka, according to quality. As the work proceeds, the spectacle of the slaughterhouse takes on the more reassuring aspect of the butcher's shop. The cavernous vault of the creature from which the entrails have been removed is cut with an axe that cleaves the bones cleanly. Only the red stains in the road give a clue to the massacre that has occurred – at least one hundred thousand cattle will have been killed in Dhaka today.

Of course, it is only the rich and middle class who can afford such an offering. Many families pool their resources, so that they are entitled to one-quarter of a cow or half a goat. Scales are hired from a local grocer – 100 taka for the day – to ensure that the portions are equal. As the meat is cut into smaller portions, it is carried indoors in aluminium vessels, where the women chop it further and sort it by quality, so that each gets a share of the best and poorest.

After this begins the task of dividing the meat, according to Islamic custom, into three parts: one-third for the consumption of the household, one-third for neighbours, and, in the tradition of *jakat*, one-third for the poor. Stomach and intestines are set apart, a pale swollen ball of half digested food and the *gobar* that will be extruded, some of which will find its way on to the rubbish-dumps of the city to add their stench to the other roadside pollutants.

Meanwhile, at the black metal gate, the poor gather, claiming their share. Women and children carry black plastic bags, some holding the charitable offerings of other houses in the neighbourhood. Children peer beneath the gate to see if the meat is ready for distribution. At one point, they opened the door and poured into the courtyard, eager, excited, hands outstretched, so that they looked like a hungry revolutionary crowd, although revolution is far from their mind.

They advanced to the verandah of the two-storey building, which is protected by a grille. Noorani, from Barisal, land eroded by the river, mother of seven young children, works as a maidservant in a nearby house; Seema, pregnant wife of a rickshaw driver, with one baby on her arm and a toddler by her side; Shilpi, abandoned by her husband in Comilla with two young children. 'Go away', they are told, and they have to be driven out physically, a tableau of retreating supplication. The gate is then closed against them. 'They go from house to house', my friends say, 'and many finish up with more meat than we do.'

When the chopping and sawing is complete, the waiters at the gate are admitted. They run across the trodden grass, leaving bare footprints of blood. My friend's mother takes a big aluminium vessel, which rests on her hip, and plucks random handfuls of meat, which she places in the skinny hands stretched through the verandah grille. Some are luckier than others. Then the bowl is empty. The people do not disperse. More meat appears. Then, when that has gone, she shows the empty bowl, indicating there is no more. The people are

239

then told to go, in the unceremonious way in which the middle class are accustomed to dismiss the poor. They will return till late in the night. And indeed, when Noorani comes back, having gone to another house at the crucial moment, she is not disappointed. Nor were the poor given only the inferior parts of the animal. Here the idea of charitable giving is taken seriously – this is also part of the sacrifice.

The gang-leader of the *keshai,* the butcher's labourers, comes to collect his money. There is an altercation. He had promised three workers, and only two turned up. He expects to be paid for three. A compromise is reached, and he goes away, angry, bloodstained, a murderer's hireling.

By now it is late afternoon. The women of the house have been working for days to prepare the Eid meal. But first come the sweets – *shemai*, vermicelli in milk with sultanas and nuts, *payesh*, which is similar but richer, made with ghee, custard, caramel (what they call 'pudding'), fruits, coconut water, Fanta and Coca Cola. Then the meal itself. I feel guilty, a spectre at the feast, since to add to the list of my exotic characteristics (the principal one being that I am without family, and therefore not a full human being), they accept that I don't eat meat, and have forbearingly, if uncomprehendingly, provided a separate vegetarian meal.

As it grows dark, the people who live in the slums and on the streets take their bulging, dripping plastic bags to where they live. On the sidewalk, blackened aluminium pots are simmering on improvised stoves of brick, the dead leaves, wood or plastic used as fuel creating eddies of smoke and scarlet flame in the dusk; an unusually savoury smell of meat arises from these little triumphal bonfires of celebration. Children stir the fire, urging it to burn faster. Jehanara, one of six children of a migrant family from Mymensingh, 6 years old and run over by a baby-taxi, lies on a piece of blue polythene, up to her hips in plaster, patiently waiting for her share, after the men and boys have eaten. Her mother is a maidservant, earning 200 taka a month; her father, a construction worker. They live on the pavement outside the twelve-storey block of flats where he works. While he builds apartments for privilege, his family remains on the street, where they eat, wash, sleep and shit without privacy, without shelter.

Next day, there is a smell of blood in the air, decaying scraps of meat. Blue-black crows pick at a bare jawbone; dogs snarl over some remains. Teeth grin out of a drain; some furry ears have been abandoned on the pavement; hairy hooves, the contents of a stomach. The children of the poorest dive in and out of the yellow metal skips, which still bear the announcement that these were part of some distant World Bank project to clean up the city, scavenging for some last vestiges of the feast.

8 ❄ Inconclusion

Proshika took up hopes that pre-dated the War of Liberation, and were enshrined briefly in the post-Independence Constitution, hopes swiftly trampled by the post-war ruin and famine, and more comprehensively dismantled by sixteen years of military rule. Proshika re-dedicated itself at that time to ideals crushed even before they had had time to flower. Out of the humanitarian impulse to remedy the worst of the post-Independence suffering, Proshika organised the people with the aim of securing a more enduring improvement in their lives. In the mid-1970s, this was an audacious initiative, since it always involved an implicit challenge to the rulers of the country, even though at the time a commitment to 'development' was not seen as contentious.

Over time, the forces of conservatism became stronger, the dominance of the rich more entrenched. Poverty and injustice were not addressed. The forces opposed to the freedom of Bangladesh, and their alliance with fundamentalists and sections of the ruling elite confronted popular resistance from Bengali nationalists and their allies among the poor, women, NGOs. This polarised the work of Proshika in a way that could not have been foreseen.

The degradation of politics has driven many NGOs to work in the cultural movement, with a growing 'civil society' – paradoxically, in order to rescue and rehabilitate political struggle. This involves education, participation, the dispelling of ignorance, an enabling of people in ways that will permit them to become full actors in the governance of their country, and not mercenaries in conflicts between factions of the ruling class. It seeks to rescue a vibrant and participating democracy from a sterile electoralism in which voters remain passive spectators of their own fate.

It goes without saying that this strikes against vested interests – a religion become fundamentalist, an intolerance of minorities, the beneficiaries of growing inequality and exacerbation of social injustice, the criminalising of politics and the politicising of crime.

That this struggle is still partly covert – embodied in cultural conflicts between Bengali culture and Islamic culture, in which women become central – does not make it any the less violent or immediate. It is emerging now from the twilight into which it was plunged by the years of oppression, and the people of Bangladesh are called to choose between a secular, tolerant mixture of tradition and the modern world or the imposition of the orthodoxies of a religious monoculture which suppresses the Bengali element in the popular consciousness. Fundamentalism is incompatible with social justice, education and the elimination of poverty. It would insulate the poor of Bangladesh from the modern world, even while its leaders continue to enjoy the luxuries of foreign travel, Western education and health-care for their families.

In the definition of this coming struggle – which is also, tragically, a replay of an older struggle against colonialism and alien rule – Proshika will have been a major agent of instruction and commitment. It cannot be said with certainty which will prevail, but to have been on the side of social justice, tolerance and humanity can never be wrong.

Dhaka and London, October 1999–January 2001